THE PENDULUM OF BATTLE

THE PENDULUM OF BATTLE

Operation GOODWOOD, July 1944

Christopher Dunphie

Leo Cooper

First published in Great Britain in 2004 by
LEO COOPER
an imprint of
Pen & Sword Books Ltd,
47 Church Street, Barnsley,
South Yorkshire.
S70 2AS

A CIP record for this book is available from the British Library

ISBN: 1-84415-010-0
A catalogue record for this book is available from the British Library

Printed in Great Britain by
C P I UK

CONTENTS

INTRODUCTION AND DEDICATION

From the end of the Second World War until 1979 the British Army Command and Staff College took its students annually for a week in June to visit the Normandy battlefields of 1944. This was a welcome respite in the middle of a fairly intensive year-long course. There they listened, enthralled, to accounts of several actions, from some of those who had fought in them. One of the battles studied was Operation GOODWOOD, the large tank battle east of Caen, 18/21 July 1944, six weeks after D-Day. Indeed GOODWOOD has been studied and argued about by generations of soldiers and historians since 1945. And yet the judgements of many have frequently conflicted. Was it an attempted breakout which failed? Was it a success or failure? It seems extraordinary that different authors, given the same facts and statistics, can reach such diverse conclusions about just five days of war in a very small area. The reason for this is, perhaps, that the name and reputation of GOODWOOD have become almost inextricably entwined with the name and reputation of General Montgomery. Many writers have used GOODWOOD to tilt at his image. This is not really surprising. Montgomery clearly considered himself to be the most able of all Allied generals, with the possible exception of Field Marshal Brooke, the Chief of the Imperial General Staff. He was not one to hide this view. GOODWOOD did not go entirely as planned - but then no battle ever does. And it was followed by a genuine crisis of confidence in Montgomery's conduct of the Normandy campaign. So it is relatively easy to use GOODWOOD as a vehicle for criticism of a man who seemed to set himself so high.

I have tried to unearth the true hopes and plans for GOODWOOD, as seen by its authors, and to outline its achievements and significance in the wider context of the Normandy campaign. I have also discussed some aspects of the command riddles which surround the battle. But of more importance has been trying to bring the story of the battle to life through the memories of a few of those who fought in it.

Perhaps the most beneficial aspect of the Staff College Battlefield Tour was the opportunity to study the speakers and learn how men responded to the most unnatural business of fighting. Inevitably they had all performed well. It would be easy to label them, and indeed all of those who have been kind enough to tell me their stories, as 'heroes', a name the press seems to attach nowadays to anyone who has ever worn uniform. I suspect that all would fiercely resist such a label. Of course some people, probably very few, genuinely did not experience or understand fear. They could be pretty uncomfortable bedfellows for those around them. At the other end of the spectrum were others, probably far fewer than one might expect, who simply could not stand up to war and had to be quickly weeded out. But the vast majority in between found it possible to 'do their duty'. That duty may have required them to undertake the most unnatural activities, such as capturing a hill which was held by someone whose main aim was to kill them. What made men able to respond in this way? I doubt whether it was national pride or the honour of the cause. The reputation of the regiment, pride in the cap-badge, certainly played its part, but the strongest bond was the fact that they were serving amongst friends who they could trust with their lives. They were probably more frightened of letting those friends down, of being seen to be the one who failed, than they were of the enemy. To lose, publicly and dramatically, the respect of one's peers, and doubtless with it one's self-respect, would have been too awful to contemplate. And the shame would be even more obvious for someone whose rank and position required him to show leadership. One of the accounts in this book concerns Captain Peter Walter of 23rd Hussars. Once, having told his story to a battlefield tour audience, he was horrified to hear it described as 'truly heroic'. Normally the mildest, gentlest and least military of men, he fiercely interrupted the speaker: 'No, no. You don't understand. There was nothing heroic in what I did. These were my friends being blown to bits in this cornfield. It was my duty to try to look after them. I only did what any normal man will do for his friends.' In those few sentences Peter summed it all up – the strength of the team; the duty of the leader.

I suppose that everyone joining the Army asks themselves one crucial question: 'How will I respond when the bullets start to fly?' It is a remarkable, but I believe true, fact that there has only been one year since 1945 in which a British soldier has not been killed in action somewhere in the world – 1968. But since Korea, in the early 1950s, almost all operations in which the British Army has been involved have been of very low intensity. Even those who assaulted Mount Tumbledown and others in the Falklands in 1982, or, as I write, have just confronted ancient, worn-out Iraqi tanks in their Challenger Mk 2s, would probably admit that their experience falls some way short of facing a German panzer division, equipped with Tiger tanks and 88mm guns. In my view the most important lesson gained from battlefield tours, and it is as relevant today as it ever has been, is that ordinary men, finding themselves in extraordinary and terrifying situations, managed to overcome their fears and do their duty. Some excelled and, by seizing the pendulum of battle at a critical moment, managed to impose their personalities on the battlefield with significant results. I hope that several examples of this will be obvious to the reader.

I hope, too, that the mutual respect and trust that was such a feature within the regiments which went to war in 1939-45 would recur if a general call-to-arms ever came again. I know that it is as strong as ever in the regular armed forces today, as the many demands placed upon them in recent years, not least the recent Iraq war, have made quite clear. But I am by no means so certain about the civilian world, where litigation, blame, compensation and self-interest stand out in almost every page of the daily newspapers. I wonder whether the flag of 'duty' would again fly at the top of the mast. I hope that the call does not come - and if it does I hope that I am wrong to be worried!

I am most grateful to those who have encouraged this book, dating back to my time as an instructor at the Staff College in the mid 1970s. General Sir Hugh Beach, then the Commandant, gave me much support and allowed access to the Staff College Battlefield Tour records. I have also drawn from the regimental histories and war diaries of units involved. But above all I am grateful to those who have told me their stories, whether personally, by letter, or indirectly through Staff College records. There is, however, a danger in this sort of research. For example, two officers from different regiments told me stories which seemed to happen at the same time and place. Neither was aware of the presence of the other with a number of tanks, and both were amazed when, during my research, it emerged that a battery of German assault guns claimed to have moved through the same area at the same time, unnoticed and unmolested. But perhaps this clash of memories is not really surprising. Two of us recounting to the police details of a bank robbery which had just taken place on the other side of the road would doubtless give descriptions which conflicted to some considerable degree - and that would be without the bonus of someone trying to kill us at the same time. Not only are memories likely to wander a bit after so long, but the fog of war is real and the front-line soldier in a dangerous situation such as GOODWOOD has enough to occupy his attention looking out for the enemy and keeping touch with the rest of his troop, squadron and regiment. What other regiments may be doing nearby is probably of little concern to him at the time. All that the chronicler can do, confronted by such a clash of memories, is to try to deduce the most likely run of events, in the clear knowledge that he may well be wrong. I must therefore apologize to those whose memories conflict with my deductions. I have faced one other difficulty – I have never, I am glad to say, been to war. The odd sniper's bullet, from time to time, is of no significance beside the experiences of those who have come under fire from hidden anti-tank guns and have seen their regiment and their friends blown to bits around them, or those who have been subjected to heavy bombing or artillery fire. Painting a picture of a subject that you do not know at first hand is a dangerous business. I ask the reader to bear this in mind.

I must also apologize to those who feel that I have given insufficient weight to their regiment's achievements. GOODWOOD has always been seen predominantly as a big tank battle and studies of it have concentrated on this, almost to the exclusion of the flanking attacks by the Canadians and 3rd Infantry Division. I have tried briefly to outline all sides of the battle, but to use the armoured advance of VIII Corps, and in particular 11th Armoured Division, as the frame within which to paint a picture of men in action. It has therefore been from 11th Armoured Division that I have drawn most of the personal accounts.

And this leads to my dedication. The Staff College GOODWOOD team was led by Major General Pip Roberts, generally accepted as the outstanding British armoured commander of the Second World War. At GOODWOOD he commanded 11th Armoured Division, which led the tank charge towards the Bourguébus ridge. His quite exceptional team of speakers were Major Bill Close, the leading squadron commander from start to finish; Captain Peter Walter, whose actions nearly won him the Victoria Cross; Brigadier David Stileman, in 1944 a twenty year-old rifle platoon commander; and the redoubtable Colonel Hans von Luck. For Peter and David the war lasted only a few weeks before both were seriously wounded. All the other three were almost continually in action for five full years, from May 1940 till May 1945. Fortunately no-one suggested that any of them should receive counselling - the counsellor would undoubtedly have lost! In addition to hearing their formal presentations during the three years that I was an instructor at the Staff College and on many subsequent battlefield tours, it was especially fascinating to listen to their 'off-duty' conversations. Pip Roberts and Hans von Luck, having fought one another across the North African desert as well as at GOODWOOD, had become close friends. To hear them reminiscing over excellent Normandy food and drink was akin to watching a top-class singles at Wimbledon, as each remark by one sparked off another fascinating memory from the other. The message which came so clearly through was that although men will do their duty in war, however horrific, the real prize is the harmony between nations. To have enjoyed the friendship and recollections of all five members of the GOODWOOD team, was a huge privilege. Countless British Army officers, over many years, have learned unforgettable and invaluable lessons from them. It is to them that this book must be dedicated.

Major General GPB Roberts, CB, DSO (& 2 bars), MC, Legion d'Honneur, Croix de Guerre.
Colonel H von Luck, Knight's Cross, Iron Cross 1st and 2nd Class.
Major WH Close, MC (& bar).
Captain PC Walter, DSO.
Brigadier DM Stileman, OBE, Polish Cross of Merit.

I am particularly grateful to David Stileman for all his support, advice and constructive criticism throughout this project. The gestation period would have put an elephant to shame! David has played no small part in ensuring that the birth actually happened! I am also hugely grateful to my wife, Sonia, and son, Charles, for their encouragement, patience, proof-reading and helpful comments. And my thanks to Graham Taylor, of the Photo Studio, Blairgowrie, whose computer wizardry produced the maps. Finally, I must thank all at Pen and Sword Books for their limitless support – Henry Wilson, Barbara Bramall, Paul Wilkinson, Jenny Shaw and others.

Bridge of Cally,
Perthshire.
February 2004

Chapter 1

BACKGROUND, PERSONALITIES AND RELATIONSHIPS

With the passage of time and the annual pilgrimage of veterans to the Normandy beaches, D-Day has almost become accepted as a great victory. This is somewhat misleading. In fact the events of 6 June 1944 were just the start of a prolonged and bitter campaign in Normandy as the Allies wore down the German forces until, at the end of July, they launched the breakout which would ultimately lead to the unconditional surrender of Germany some nine months later.

The Supreme Allied Commander for the entire operation was the American General Dwight Eisenhower. Under him, the three single service commanders were all British – Admiral Sir Bertram Ramsay, General Sir Bernard Montgomery and Air Chief Marshal Sir Trafford Leigh-Mallory. As Commander-in-Chief of Twenty-first Army Group, with Lieutenant General Omar Bradley's First US Army in the west and Lieutenant General Miles Dempsey's Second British Army in the east under his command, Montgomery was responsible for the planning and conduct of the land battle. On 7 April he addressed all general officers and their staffs. At this, and at a later briefing on 15 May attended by King George VI, the Prime Minister

Map 1. The phase-line map – a staff planning tool, not an opertional plan.

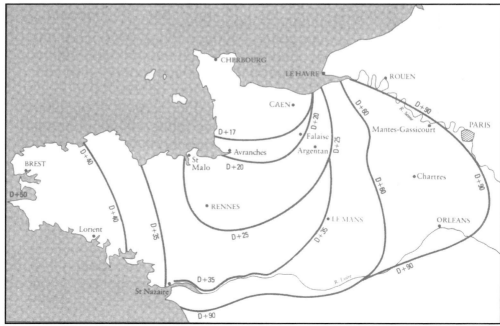

Winston Churchill, Eisenhower and the Chiefs of Staff, he outlined his plan. As the Map 1 shows, he indicated a series of lines which he hoped that Twenty-first Army Group would achieve by the dates given. Although the River Seine was crossed a few days short of the D+90 estimate, many of the interim dates were not achieved, and this fact has been used by some historians to criticize Montgomery's generalship. This criticism is both unfair and misleading.

There are certainly grounds for criticising Montgomery during the North-West Europe campaign, but these criticisms, some of which will be addressed later, should apply, for the most part, to his relations with others rather than to his conduct of the campaign.

At Salerno in southern Italy in September 1943, and at Anzio just south of Rome in January 1944, landings had been launched with no outline plan for subsequent operations. The landings were almost seen as operations in their own right. Montgomery did not fall into this trap in Normandy. Indeed, it seems inconceivable that a commander of his dedication, experience and professionalism would have launched his armies into Europe without a clear idea of how he intended the battle to develop. D-Day was just the means of entry into a new theatre of operations. What mattered next was the campaign that must follow the landings. Throughout the early months of 1944 Montgomery and his staff addressed this problem. There was a clear requirement for a definite battle plan and an estimate of progress so that the vast logistic organization which must support the campaign would have sufficient data úpon which to base its plans to feed in all the reinforcement units, weapons, vehicles, stores, fuel, food and ammunition essential to support the advancing armies. Those who criticize Montgomery for failing to achieve the stated phase lines of this map miss the real point – it was a staff planning tool, not a detailed operational plan.

To paraphrase the Prussian Field Marshal von Moltke: 'No plan survives intact the first encounter with the enemy.' Field Marshal Lord Wavell said in 1943: 'War is a muddle; it is bound to be. There are so many incalculable accidents in the uncertain business. A turn in the weather which could not be forseen; a message gone astray; a leader struck down at a critical moment. It is very rarely that even the best-laid plans go smoothly. The lesson is to realise this, and to provide, as far as possible, against the uncertainties of war – and not be surprised when they happen.' It would be foolish to imagine that the Normandy campaign might break this rule.

It is a sad fact that some great men seem to feel the need to emphasize their greatness publicly, and by so doing in fact reduce it. A certain humility, an acceptance that occasionally one may have been wrong, or that events, for any of a host of possible reasons, may have moved in other than exactly the direction intended, can enhance, rather than destroy a commander's reputation. After the war Montgomery was inclined to suggest that all his

neral Sir
rnard
ntgomery. As
n-C 21 Army
oup he was
erall land
ces
mander.
ghly
fessional and
cesful, but
th several
attractive sides
his nature.

operations went entirely as planned, in every detail. In doing so he did himself a disservice. As Wavell points out, much of the skill of the great general is the ability to sort out the inevitable muddle of war better and quicker than his opponent. If this was not Montgomery's strongest suit, though he was to prove an adept sorter of muddles in the later Ardennes battles, his preparation for battle was so thorough that the chances of muddle were rather less than those of most other generals. But he was not infallible. Certainly he expected the invasion forces to penetrate further inland on D and D+1 than in fact they did, especially in the Caen area. And, like others, he underestimated the difficulties of attacking through the *bocage* country. In consequence he had to adapt his operations to the take account of the situations confronting him. These are the inevitable facts of war, not culpable crimes. History might have been kinder to him if he had admitted this. But, and this is the key point, he never changed his overall operational plan.

Major General Sir Francis de Guingand, Montgomery's Chief of Staff since mid-1942, summarized his qualities:

> *'Number one factor was his wonderful ability to inspire confidence. This was simply terrific. Secondly, he was the real master of the art of high command in war. He knew everything about the handling of troops, planning a battle, training, logistics, and so much about every arm and service. He had devoted his entire inter-war existence to learning about the art of high command. He had virtually no hobbies except studying high command.'*

To successor generations Montgomery does not come across as a particularly attractive personality. Arrogant, self-important, supportive of his favourites but dismissive of others and lacking much personal warmth; it is not difficult to dislike him in principle without having taken the trouble to study his methods and achievements in any detail. And yet a study of Montgomery leads even the most biased critic to a grudging respect for his generalship. De Guingand, though loyal to his master, was not blind to his faults:

> *'I don't think you could ever call Monty a very humble man! He was always very proud of his achievements – and rightly so. And I think he was jealous of the success of others – but that probably goes for most dynamic, successful men.'*

The relationship between Montgomery and de Guingand is almost worthy of a book in its own right. The two men were such total opposites that it seems almost incredible that they combined so well throughout three years of war to form such a formidable command team. Montgomery, who never hid the image of the dedicated, almost puritanical, professional; de Guingand, whose true ability never concealed something of the playboy amateur. De Guingand was a student at the Staff College in 1935-36. The author's father, a fellow student, said this of him:

> *'Freddie was a really terrific chap. The moment the last period ended at Camberley you would see him, in a rather flashy sports car, heading for the bright lights of London. And while we more pedestrian folk probably had to give some time to preparing for the next day, Freddie would be having a whale of a party in London. He would return shortly before work started next morning,*

still in white tie and probably covered in lipstick, and yet be in his place on time, with all the correct answers.

'*Shortly after the course two students, de Guingand and Dunphie, were summoned to the War Office for interview by the Secretary of State as possible Military Assistants. Freddie won by a distance, and rightly so. He really was extremely able. But his enjoyment of a party never deserted him. I remember visiting him at Twenty-first Army Group in early 1945. The moment Monty retired for the night, out came the whisky, cigarettes and a pack of cards – and we had the hell of an evening. After the war Monty treated him outrageously. Having promised him VCIGS as a lieutenant general, when Monty became CIGS, he cancelled it at the last moment and retired Freddie as a major general because he did not want people to think that he could not operate without Freddie behind him. We remained close friends until Freddie died, and although he never hid his disappointment at his treatment by Monty, he never showed any bitterness. He was an immensely able man who could have risen to the top in any field. He was also a superb and loyal chief of staff. But above all he was such fun.*'

aj Gen Sir
ancis de
uingand,
ontgomery's
valuable
hief-of-Staff.

To other than students of military history the name of the fun-loving, extrovert de Guingand is almost unknown. Conversely Montgomery, the dedicated professional, remains the best-known of British Second World War generals. But his cultivation of publicity, especially during and after the desert war, must have seemed unnatural, even unattractive, to many of his contemporaries. In the first half of the twentieth century, military ambition and professionalism were normally kept well hidden. However, following the victory of El Alamein, before which the population of Britain had had little to celebrate, a small man in a succession of strange hats captured the public's imagination. He told people that he had and would continue to beat the Germans. And he then proceeded to do so. In factories throughout the United Kingdom workers identified with him: 'We are making bullets for Monty', was a not unfamiliar cry.

* * * *

So much of the success and failure in war comes down to personalities and how they work together. This is as true of the relationships between senior commanders as it is within a single tank crew. The personalities of the senior commanders are so important to the story of the Normandy campaign that it is worth considering briefly the strengths and weaknesses of some of the other key players. By the middle of 1944 the war had already lasted nearly five years for the British and Germans; for the Americans two and a half. It is hardly surprising that by this stage those who held senior command appointments were strong, determined leaders whose qualities had, for the most part, been honed and proved in battle. And where strong characters are thrown together, charged with the conduct of war, differences of opinion and clashes of personality seem almost inevitable.

Perhaps this is where the personality of the Supreme Allied Commander,

General Eisenhower, was to be so important. It might be assumed that a supreme commander for a vast, tri-service, multi-national operation would be a highly experienced battlefield commander, with a wealth of fighting experience at all levels of command behind him. In fact Eisenhower was the reverse of this blueprint. He had not seen active service in the First World War. His first taste of warfare had been as supreme commander of the Anglo-American force which landed in North Africa in November 1942. He had commanded neither brigade, division, corps nor army in peace, let alone in war. And yet he was to prove the ideal supreme commander for this, perhaps the most complex operation in the history of warfare.

Eisenhower's strengths lay in his personal qualities. Despite his lack of battlefield experience he proved to be a master at blending a collection of strong-willed and often difficult subordinates to make a formidable and lasting team. A man of huge charm, he possessed almost limitless patience and tolerance, which were frequently sorely tested by some of them, especially Montgomery and Patton. Eisenhower achieved what probably no-one else could have achieved – a continuity of command and purpose which was to last throughout the North-West Europe campaign, from D-Day, 6 June 1944, until VE Day, 8 May 1945. Contrast this continuity with that of his German opponents and Eisenhower's achievements become even more impressive.

Eisenhower's deputy was the British Air Chief Marshal Sir Arthur Tedder. As Air Officer Commanding-in-Chief Middle East Air Force, Tedder had worked alongside Montgomery's 8th Army in the North African desert campaign. After the battle of El Alamein in October 1942, with the Germans in full retreat, Tedder had advised Montgomery on the tactical handling of the land campaign. In particular he had suggested that rather than pursuing the Germans along the coast road, Eighth Army should follow the 1940 example of General O'Connor's Western Desert Force, strike across the Libyan desert and cut off the Germans south of Benghazi. To Montgomery this was intolerable. He was not the man to take advice on the conduct of his campaign from anyone, let alone an Air Force officer. At the end of the campaign in May 1943, while he was quick to promote the achievements of his Eighth Army, he paid less than fair tribute to the splendid support of the Desert Air Force. Tedder resented this; from then on the relationship between them was distinctly unfriendly. A sharp, intellectual officer, who seemed to possess a somewhat devious streak, he was to miss no opportunity to criticize Montgomery at Eisenhower's Supreme HQ. There were to be several occasions during the North-West Europe campaign, particularly just after Operation GOODWOOD, when Montgomery's lack of tact led to strained relations with Eisenhower, and where a 'friend at court' would have been

Supreme Allied Commander General Eisenhower.

Air Chief Marshal Sir Arthur Tedder.

invaluable. Tedder preferred to turn up the heat, rather than seek to turn it off. Before D-Day he had played a key part in the overall planning, in particular co-ordinating the preliminary air operations which were vital to the success of the invasion. But after D-Day, with no staff and no specific role, he was somewhat under-employed. Perhaps it left him time for scheming!

Next in importance at Supreme Headquarters Allied Expeditionary Force (SHAEF) was Eisenhower's trusted American Chief of Staff, Lieutenant General Walter Bedell Smith. Although, like many Americans, he seems to have disliked Montgomery personally, he was always extremely fair. In particular he had excellent relations, both officially and personally, with de Guingand, and it was this that so often saved the day when things became particularly tense between their two masters. De Guingand would later say that Bedell Smith's ever-open door was a source of real comfort in troubled times. Other than Field Marshal Sir Alan Brooke, Chief of the Imperial General Staff in London, to whom Montgomery always gave way immediately and without demur, de Guingand was perhaps the only person who could speak openly and critically to Montgomery. When the water became unreasonably choppy Bedell Smith would alert de Guingand who, in turn and alone, could persuade Montgomery of the need to apologize and adopt a less dismissive attitude with his Supreme Commander. The chemistry and frequent contact between the two chiefs of staff was to be an important factor in the success of the Allied command structure.

A further influential member at SHAEF was the Deputy Chief of Staff, Lieutenant General Frederick Morgan. Like Tedder, he proved to be no supporter of Montgomery. At the Casablanca Conference in January 1943 President Roosevelt and Prime Minister Churchill had decided to establish a joint Anglo-American planning team for D-Day. Morgan, a British general, was appointed to lead this team, titled Chief of Staff to the Supreme Allied Commander (designate) – (COSSAC). The COSSAC staff would in due course become the nucleus of SHAEF, once a commander had been appointed. Morgan started work in March 1943 and presented his findings at the Quebec Conference in August 1943. His plan, which proposed an invasion of Normandy rather than the more obvious assault in the Pas de Calais area, was accepted by the Combined Chiefs of Staff. It outlined an assault by three divisions along a forty mile front, with an airborne division being dropped in the Caen area. Planning progressed on this basis and it was not until January 1944, after Eisenhower and Montgomery had assumed their appointments, that the details of the plan were queried. Both considered the landing area too narrow and the force levels too small. The Germans might be able to concentrate sufficient forces, and in particular their panzer divisions, in time to defeat an invasion of this size and scope. Montgomery demanded an increase to five assault divisions, on a fifty mile front to include a landing at the foot of the Cotentin Peninsula (Utah Beach), with three airborne divisions dropped on the flanks. Morgan explained that his plan had been limited by the availability of shipping, in particular landing-craft, most of which would have to be provided from America. Montgomery stated that if more was needed to support a larger invasion, then more must be provided. It seems likely, bearing in mind Montgomery's personality and attitude to others, that he was less than tactful in dismissing the COSSAC plan. If this conjecture is true it is hardly surprising that Morgan, when he stayed on to become Eisenhower's Deputy Chief of Staff, proved, like Tedder, to be no friend of Montgomery.

Beneath Montgomery as Commander-in-Chief Twenty-first Army Group were two Army Commanders – Lieutenant General Omar Bradley of First US Army and Lieutenant General Miles Dempsey of Second British Army. Neither possessed Montgomery's flamboyant nature. Both were well liked and respected by those under their command, quiet and reserved by nature, and happy to allow their achievements to speak for them. And both had well proven operational command track records. Bradley, a strict disciplinarian from a quiet mid-west background, had commanded II US Corps in the final stages in North Africa and in Sicily. Montgomery had a high opinion of Bradley's professionalism and judgement – credits not lightly awarded. Dempsey had commanded a brigade in the 1940 campaign in France when Montgomery was a divisional commander, and XIII Corps in Montgomery's Eighth Army in North Africa, Sicily and Italy. He had been Montgomery's personal selection for command of Second Army. Bradley and Dempsey would prove to be highly effective and reliable Army Commanders in Normandy.

Although not on the stage by the time of Operation GOODWOOD, it is worth mentioning briefly one other senior commander, the American Lieutenant General George Patton, who was to appear on the Normandy scene just a few days after the battle, to take command of the newly-forming Third US Army, which would later lead the breakout and advance towards Germany.

Lieutenant General George Patton, Lieutenant General Omar Bradley and General Sir Bernard Montgomery – 'the remarkable simmering pot upon which General Eisenhower so successfully managed to keep the lid'.

Patton was to be one of the spicier ingredients of the remarkable simmering pot upon which Eisenhower so successfully managed to keep the lid. Alone among senior US commanders, Patton had had battle experience in the First World War in command of the only tank regiment deployed from America. Between the wars he had been a keen advocate, at times almost a lone voice, in promoting armoured warfare. Among those who had served under him between the wars and whose careers he had advanced was a certain Colonel Eisenhower, now, in Normandy, his Supreme Commander. A rich cavalry officer, from a background far removed from that of the humble Bradley, Patton had taken command of II US Corps in North Africa when General Lloyd Fredendall was sacked following the Kasserine fiasco. When, after six weeks, Patton left II Corps to form Seventh US Army and plan the invasion of Sicily, Bradley, his deputy commander and eight years his junior, took over II US Corps. In Sicily Bradley's Corps had served in Patton's Army. Now in Normandy Patton was to be an Army Commander under Bradley's command when, at the end of July, the latter was elevated to command Twelfth Army Group. Bradley did not like Patton. He disliked his flamboyant noisy outbursts, his frequent over-reaction and his offensive demeaning of others in public. Given the reversal of positions and the complete difference in character and style, theirs cannot have been an easy relationship. Nor can it have been made easier by the fact that Eisenhower and Patton had been close friends, when Eisenhower, five years younger, had commanded a battalion in Patton's brigade in the 1920s.

Patton was, perhaps, the complete obverse of the Montgomery coin, as is made clear by General de Guingand:

> 'Monty was a cautious commander in many ways, and he did play for safety. He used to argue with me, when perhaps I had suggested that we take a chance and have a bash: "No, Freddie, I can afford to wait a week or ten days. I shall be much stronger and can make absolutely certain of victory with fewer casualties." Monty really was the master of the set-piece battle; meticulous training of his troops and every detail of the battle worked out in advance.
>
> 'You can't really compare Monty with Patton. George Patton was, I always thought, a really magnificent general in his particular field, which was the fluid operation. He would take every sort of risk. He was right at the front himself, bashing his troops forward. He would do the most astonishing things. But I doubt that he would have been at his best in the methodical planning of the deliberate battle of which Monty was master. I could never see Monty doing the sort of things that George Patton did, but, nevertheless Monty had tremendous success and hardly lost a battle.' [1]

---

1. Following the rout of II US Corps at Kasserine in February 1943 it was decided that battle-experienced British officers should be posted to HQ II US Corps and its subordinate divisions as Assistant Chiefs of Staff, while the Americans found their fighting feet. Leader of this team, as British Chief of Staff to Patton and later Bradley, was the author's father, whose 26 Armoured Brigade had rushed forward and held the Kasserine Pass when Rommel put the American forces to flight. Despite Patton's welcome, 'I think you ought to know that I don't like Brits!', Dunphie subsequently got on extremely well with both Patton and Bradley. When II US Corps was selected as the assault corps for Sicily, in Patton's Seventh Army, which would land alongside Montgomery's Eighth Army, Bradley asked Dunphie to stay in post. To Dunphie's disappointment the British War Office had other plans for him, at which Bradley commented: 'A pity, Charles. You'll miss an interesting show – an opera with two prima-donnas!'

It is a remarkable fact, and a real credit to Eisenhower's personality, that the Allied command structure of forceful, yet so different leaders, was to remain intact, if not always harmonious, until victory was won. It is also a complete opposite of what happened 'on the other side of the hill'.

* * * *

On the German side the chain of command on D-Day looked, on the surface, secure and impressive. Yet despite its formidable dramatis personae it contained some real operational weaknesses. The Commander-in-Chief West, Field Marshal Gerd von Rundstedt, a sixty-nine year-old Prussian war-horse, was exercising command of his fourth operational theatre. Recalled from retirement in 1939 he had commanded the invasion of Poland. Next he led the brilliant Blitzkreig of 1940 which, in just a few weeks, overran the Low Countries and France and drove the British Expeditionary Force from the continent. He then commanded Army Group South for the invasion of Russia, driving through the Ukraine and capturing Kiev. Following defeat at Rostov he was transferred to North-West Europe, to command the defences from the Pyrenees to the Danish/German border. His experience of command at the highest level was unparalleled. His present area of responsibility was divided into two – in the north Army Group B, under Field Marshal Erwin Rommel, responsible for the defence of France north of the Loire and including the Low Countries; in the south Army Group G, under General Johannes von Blaskowitz, covering the rest of France.

Field Marshal Gerd von Rundstedt. Commander-in-Chief West until early July 1944.

Rommel, like Montgomery and Patton, was one of the Second World War commanders whose name and reputation was to become widely known, not just during the war but also to history. A recipient in the First World War of the Pour le Mérite, the German equivalent of the British Victoria Cross or the American Medal of Honor, Rommel's achievements in the desert in 1941-43 were the stuff of legends. Recognized as a favourite of Hitler, to whom he had direct access often over the heads of his military superiors, Rommel, a field marshal some sixteen years younger than von Rundstedt, must have been a difficult subordinate. Furthermore, personality problems apart, they differed on how to defeat the inevitable invasion.

Deployed in northern France, but not strictly under Rommel's operational command before D-Day, was Panzer Group West, commanded by General Leo Geyr von Schweppenberg. His responsibility covered the training of the panzer divisions, but it was expected that once hostilities started these divisions would pass to Rommel's command. However the two men disagreed on their use. Geyr von Schweppenberg held the traditional military view that it would be impossible to prevent the landings from taking place.

Field Marshal Erwin Rommel commanded Army Group B until he was seriously wounded on 17 July, just after alerting local German commanders to the likelihood a British armoured attack in the GOODWOOD area.

As soon as the main landing area had been identified, therefore, the panzer divisions, which should be held back initially, would then be rushed forward in a co-ordinated thrust to drive the invaders into the sea before they could consolidate their position. Since the invasion forces were likely to be light in tanks in the early stages they would be especially vulnerable to a major, concentrated tank counter-attack. Rommel disagreed. Based on his experiences in North Africa he was convinced that Allied air supremacy would make it impossible for the panzer divisions to reach the invasion area in time for decisive action. The only hope was to destroy the invasion on the beaches. This meant deploying the panzer divisions well forward and hoping that they were in the right places. He wished to site one in the Caen area and another near Carentan, and he wanted them under his command, ready for instant reaction.

The argument was taken to von Rundstedt, who, also lacking Rommel's recent experience, sided with Geyr von Schweppenberg. Rommel, as was his right as a field marshal, appealed to Hitler, whose compromise solution proved to be the worst of all worlds. Hitler decreed that 21st Panzer Division alone should be under Rommel's command, but that the rest should be held well back and must not be committed without his personal authority. And on the morning of 6 June 1944, when speed was essential, no-one dared to disturb the Führer's slumbers to seek their early release.

There was, perhaps, more to this disagreement than just a difference in tactical doctrine. It is understandable that Geyr von Schweppenberg, an aristocratic cavalry officer, should find it intolerable that, having trained the panzer divisions, he must then hand command of them to the upstart Rommel as soon as the battle started. Furthermore, real problems existed in command of German forces on the ground. In addition to the normal divisions under army command, there were a number of German Air Force divisions deployed in Normandy as infantry. These, and several battalions of 88mm anti-aircraft guns, came under air force, rather than army command. All AA guns carried anti-tank rounds, and some were about to play a vital part in Operation GOODWOOD. To have them deployed among army defences, but under a separate chain of command, was a recipe for confusion.

The contrast between the two command chains is stark indeed. For the Allies, complete continuity throughout the entire North-West Europe campaign, with even the rough water of periodic personality clashes smoothed over. For the Germans a high-level difference of views; a confused and illogical command structure – and then, when battle was joined, almost total instability among commanders. At the end of June, von Rundstedt, asked by Keitel, Hitler's right-hand man, 'What shall we do?' replied, 'Make peace, you idiots – what else can you do?' Perhaps not unsurprisingly he was replaced on 2 July, by Field Marshal Gunther von Kluge. Rommel, seriously wounded in an air-strike on 17 July, never returned to the front. Thereafter von Kluge acted as Supreme Commander and Commander Army Group B

General o Geyr von hweppenberg, mmander of nzer Group est.

eld Marshal unther von uge replaced n Rundstedt Supreme ommander fore mmiting icide.

until he too was replaced, for defeatism, on 17 August by Field Marshal Walther Model. Fearing that he would be accused of involvement in the attempt on Hitler's life on 20 July, von Kluge committed suicide in early August. General Friedrich Dollmann, commander of Seventh Army, concerned that he would be blamed for the loss of Cherbourg, died on 28 June of a heart attack brought on by worry, and was replaced by General Paul Hausser from II SS Panzer Corps. General Erich Marcks, the highly-respected commander of LXXXIV Corps responsible for the defence of much of Normandy – killed by aircraft attack on 12 June. Geyr von Schweppenberg, who had been wounded on 11 June, when his HQ, which had just been given operational responsibility for the Caen area, was bombed – dismissed by Hitler on 5 July and replaced by General Heinrich Eberbach. With several divisional commanders killed, the German command structure was a hopeless muddle, upon which Hitler frequently imposed ridiculous and usually unworkable orders.

Field Marshal Walther Model

The story of the Normandy campaign is the story of the German panzer divisions. Tanks are at their best when used for concentrated shock action. If they could be grouped together to strike at a vulnerable point before the Allies had built up sufficient forces in Normandy, they might have a significant, perhaps even decisive impact. Tanks are less effective used piecemeal, widely spread in defensive positions. But such was the pressure on the German defences in Normandy that each newly-arriving panzer division was quickly sucked into the defensive battle wherever it was immediately needed. Throughout June and July the Germans constantly sought to withdraw the panzer divisions from their ground-holding role, for centralized and offensive action. Equally constantly Montgomery was determined that this must not be allowed to happen. Ruthlessly and relentlessly he ensured that they were for ever being used to patch up the increasingly leaky bucket of the defence, and that they were ground down at the same time. Some have suggested that Montgomery only claimed this as his policy after the Normandy battle was over. This is misleading; there is ample proof of Montgomery's policy in the many letters and directives that he wrote at the time, spelling this out very clearly. It may not have been part of his pre-D-Day planning, but he quickly realised that the panzer divisions were being sucked into largely static defence, and he made the most of it. It is a pity that he did not later acknowledge this, thereby emphasising his operational flexibility, rather than suggesting later that it had always been part of his plan. Operation GOODWOOD was to be the final and largest example of this policy, as it pinned the German panzer divisions in front of the British in the east, thus easing the American break-out in the west. In GOODWOOD Montgomery achieved what the Germans constantly sought but never achieved – a concentration of armoured divisions used in a massive attack.

Chapter 2

ENLARGING THE BRIDGEHEAD – JUNE AND EARLY JULY

With hindsight it is possible to divide the Normandy campaign into three distinct phases; Phase One – D-Day Assault; Phase Two – Build-up of forces and wearing-down of the Germans; Phase Three – Breakout. Even if these were in the minds of senior commanders and their staffs, they would not have been obvious to those at the sharp end of the fighting. For the Allied front-line soldiers each successive action must have seemed like the hoped-for knockout blow – a blow which never seemed to land squarely on target as operation followed operation throughout June and early July.

D-Day had been, for the most part, a clear success. Its events have been too well chronicled to need more than very brief mention here. In the east, the British and Canadian beaches of Gold, Juno and Sword had all been successfully assaulted. Although none of the final objectives had been taken,

Map 2. The D-Day plan and achievements.

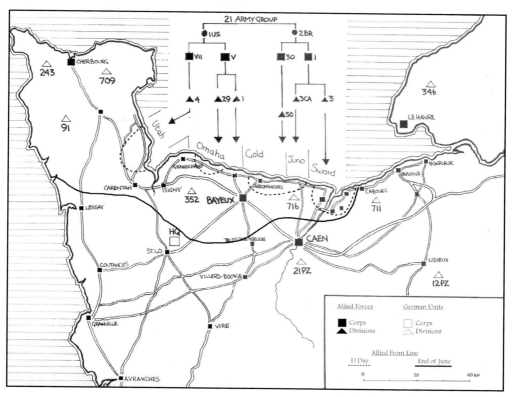

50th Infantry Division from Gold, and 3rd Canadian Infantry Division from Juno, were only a mile or two short of the Caen to Bayeux road. Inland from Sword, 3rd Infantry Division had been brought up short by German tanks as it advanced on Caen. But it had successfully married up with 6th Airborne Division, which had achieved all its key D-Day tasks east of the River Orne. At the American end things were rather less satisfactory. At Utah, near the foot of the Cotentin peninsula, 4th US Infantry Division had landed against relatively light opposition. By the end of D-Day it had met up with elements of 82nd and 101st US Airborne Divisions, which, despite chaotic and widely-dispersed parachute drops, had captured many of their objectives. Only at Omaha, the eastern American beach, where the 1st and 29th Infantry Divisions had suffered heavy casualties as they fought all day to get off the beach, was the success of the invasion ever in real doubt during the first few hours. By the end of D-Day even that beach seemed secure, though the area taken was small and there were ominous gaps between Omaha and its neighbours.

The conclusion of Phase One, the link-up of the beaches and the completion of the D-Day objectives, with the exception of Caen, lasted for about a week. After this, operations inevitably slowed down as the Germans brought more and better troops into the area. Throughout June and July, Phase Two was to prove the fiercest fighting of the entire North-West Europe campaign, as the Allies sought to grind down the German forces and expand the beachhead, both geographically and numerically, until, like some overfilled balloon, it burst. Launched at the end of July, Phase Three, the breakout, would be followed by a rapid drive across Northern France, through the Low Countries and into the heartland of Germany.

* * * *

Following the D-Day landings the first Allied priority was to link up the five beaches to form a continuous beachhead. In the east this was quickly achieved. Gold and Juno beaches were linked by the end of D-Day. Responsible for both Juno and Sword, but with a three-mile gap between them, I Corps Commander, Lieutenant General John Crocker, faced something of a dilemma. His main D-Day objective had been Caen, which had not been taken – hardly surprising since 3rd Infantry Division, with relatively few tanks, was quickly confronted by the tanks of 21st Panzer Division. On D+1 Crocker could either drive hard for Caen or concentrate on linking up Sword and Juno. He could not do both simultaneously. Critics of the failure to capture Caen quickly might have had stronger grounds for complaint if he had forged ahead, broken into the outskirts of Caen but handed to 21st Panzer Division the freedom to expand the wedge between Sword and Juno. Caen was to be a frustrating and unsolved problem for the next month, but Crocker was undoubtedly correct to give priority to linking-up his beachhead, which he achieved late on D+1.

By the end of 7 June, therefore, with the Americans from Omaha having met the British from Gold in the area of Port-en-Bessin, there was a continuous beachhead nearly forty miles long by between three and ten miles deep. But there was still a dangerous gap between Omaha and Utah, in the area of Carentan, where the Germans stubbornly refused to give ground. Eventually the link was achieved on 12 June, when 29th Division from Omaha captured Isigny, while 101st Airborne Division took Carentan.

Having linked-up its two beaches, First US Army could now turn its attention to two important targets – Cherbourg and St Lô. Bradley hoped to capture Cherbourg quickly as a working port. To do so he must first cut the Cotentin peninsula, thereby isolating the town from possible German reinforcement. Under Rommel's instructions the Germans had flooded the Douve and Merderet valleys. It took 82nd Airborne Division four days of heavy fighting, from 6 to 10 June, to secure the narrow causeway over the Merderet at La Fière. Thereafter, under the dynamic Major General J Lawton Collins ('Lightning Joe', one of the real 'stars' of the North-West Europe campaign), VII Corps struck west and reached the coast at Barneville on 18 June, thereby trapping three German divisions in the north. Collins closed in rapidly on Cherbourg; on 22 June he launched his final assault. Ordered by Hitler to defend it to the last round, the Germans fought doggedly. The result was never in doubt, but the battle, with close-quarter street fighting, took a full week. On 27 June General von Schlieben surrendered, and the battle was finally over on 30 June. By then more than 20,000 prisoners had been taken, but the Germans had had ample time to destroy the port facilities. It was not until September that Cherbourg was functioning again as a working port. Meanwhile, east of the river Vire General Gerow's V US Corps, having overcome the early horrors of Omaha beach, made rapid progress initially, capturing Caumont on 12 June. But thereafter the situation stuck.

The thick hedges and sunken lanes of the *Bocage.*

After the capture of Cherbourg Bradley turned his attention to St Lô, which he had always earmarked as the launch-point for his breakout battle. Slowed down by the bogs and floods near Carentan, the thick *bocage* country north of the town and resolute defence by the German II Parachute Corps, it took Bradley three weeks of hard fighting, and 11,000 casualties, to capture the town on 18 July. The *bocage* country was a defenders' paradise – a mass of small fields, often less than 100 yards wide, surrounded by thick hedges usually sited on high mounds, with the whole area interlaced with sunken lanes. Each hedge would prove to be a mental as well as a physical hurdle for the advancing infantryman. Would he be

The *bocage* country was a defenders' paradise. A German soldier armed with a *Fallschirmjägergewehr* 42 assault rifle lies in wait for the advancing allies.

confronted, as he broke through, by well-sited machine guns, which could not miss him at almost point-blank range? The tank, his constant and close friend, could offer little help. In this country the effect of its range and firepower was largely nullified. The tank commander, with his head just out of the turret, was an attractive target for the enemy sniper. The steep mounds were difficult obstacles for a tank. As it clambered over them it exposed its vulnerable base, at unmissable range, to any defender with even a light, hand-held anti-tank weapon. This difficult problem was only overcome through the ingenuity of Sergeant Curtis Cullin, of 102 US Cavalry Reconnaissance Squadron. He welded steel spars onto the front of a tank so that it could drive into the mound and lift it, like a farm tractor and loader. This solution was quickly and widely adopted. Ironically the steel was provided by Rommel – the redundant metal obstacles which, on his orders, had been positioned along the beaches to obstruct landings.

Nor could the artillery provide much support. Artillery fire is controlled by Forward Observation Officers travelling with the leading squadrons and companies. It is their job to identify targets and then call down fire on them. But when the field of vision is at most 100 yards, and the safety distance for troops advancing behind an artillery barrage is 200 yards, artillery is of little help.

Montgomery had planned and hoped for deep penetrations on D-Day. In the Caen area this did not happen. By the middle of June the Germans were

A US patrol clears the hedgerow.

feeding a constant supply of new divisions into the battle area. Although many of these suffered greatly from the attentions of the Allied Air Forces as they moved to Normandy, nevertheless the first rush of post-invasion success for the Allies was over. From about D+6 the shape of the campaign altered markedly. It became more a war of attrition than one of deep and spectacular thrusts, as the Germans sought to contain the invasion forces while the Allies poured in more troops and began to grind down the defenders. The Allied front line facing south was to move very little between 17 June and 18 July. The leading airmen, Tedder, the Deputy Supreme Commander, and Coningham, the Commander Second Allied Tactical Air Force, never seem to accept this fundamental change in the texture of the campaign. They considered that lack of ground-seizing success, so important in gaining space for airfields, meant lack of direction and drive.

Montgomery and Dempsey were keen to capture Caen, if possible without having to launch a direct and inevitably costly attack. Street-fighting requires large numbers of men and, if the defender fights stoutly, usually involves heavy casualties for the attacker – and the Germans clearly had no intention of giving up the city without a stiff fight. Caen was always a highly ambitious D-Day objective for a division which had undertaken an opposed beach landing and which was then quickly confronted by the only German panzer division in the landing area. Various unsuccessful outflanking attacks were launched in the hope of forcing the Germans to pull out. The first, soon after D-Day, involved three of Montgomery's favourite desert divisions in a pincer attack. 51st (Highland) Division would move into the bridgehead east of the river Orne, still held by 6th Airborne Division. It would then strike south, past Cagny, and secure the open ground astride the Caen-Falaise road. Meanwhile, west of Caen, 50th (Northumbrian) and 7th Armoured Divisions would seize Tilly-sur-Seulles, Villers-Bocage and the high ground just east of it. This operation never really got off the ground. Far from launching an attack, 51st Division was quickly sucked into a ground-holding battle in the airborne bridgehead, which was under constant attack from 21st Panzer Division. In the west Tilly, resolutely held by the excellent Panzer Lehr Division which arrived in the area on 8 June, withstood all 50th Division's efforts. 7th Armoured Division, in a wide right-flanking attack, did manage to capture Villers-Bocage and the high ground to the east, but was then forced back by a memorable German counter-attack. It was here that the remarkable Lieutenant Michael Wittmann, a company commander in 101 Heavy Tank Battalion, in a Tiger tank which was invulnerable to most British tank guns, managed to destroy the leading squadron/company group almost single-handed. It was an action which was to rate very high in the annals of tank warfare. By 14 June the planned pincer operation had been largely still-born.

The second attempt to outflank Caen was Operation EPSOM, 24-30 June. This proved to be no more successful. Lieutenant General Sir Richard O'Connor's newly-arrived VIII Corps would try to break through between Panzer Lehr Division in the Tilly-sur-Seulles area and 12 SS (Hitler-Youth) Panzer Division just west and south-west of Caen. 15th (Scottish) Division was to advance south from Le Mesnil-Patry, past Cheux and Mondrainville, and secure crossings over the river Odon in the area of Gavrus and Baron. Behind, ready to exploit success quickly, the tanks of 11th Armoured Division would then pass through the Scotsmen, cross the river Orne and secure the high ground astride the Caen – Falaise road. If this could be achieved the German positions round Caen would surely become untenable. But the weather was not kind to Operation EPSOM; rain and heavy cloud largely prevented flying which would have been so helpful to the attackers. Despite the excellent fire support from over 700 guns, 15th Division made slow progress against strong resistance from the Hitler Youth, and failed to reach the Odon. I SS Panzer Corps, with two newly-arrived panzer divisions, was rushed into the area alongside II SS Panzer Corps. On 28 June 11th Armoured Division, probing for gaps in the German defences, managed to find an undefended bridge over the river Odon near Baron. It quickly exploited this, with the tanks of 23rd Hussars and the infantry motor battalion of 8th Battalion The Rifle Brigade pushing on to secure Hill 112, about one mile south-east of Baron. For thirty-six hours the riflemen held this exposed hill-top against strong German counter-attacks. The British salient, about three miles by two, was now attacked on three sides by elements of five panzer divisions. With his flanks exposed and under increasing attack, Dempsey accepted that EPSOM could not succeed. He ordered a withdrawal to safer ground. On the night of 29/30 June the riflemen evacuated Hill 112. A small bridgehead over the Odon remained in the area of Baron, but neither side could claim ownership of Hill 112; its name still sends cold shivers down the spines of many Normandy veterans. A gentle rise across the fields from Baron, it is only when standing on the top that its significance becomes clear, with excellent views to the south and east. It was to be the scene of heavy fighting in early July.

With the failure of Operation EPSOM came the end of attempts to outflank the Germans in the Caen area. Caen must now be taken in a head-on attack. This task fell to Crocker's I Corps. Following a raid by 450 bombers, and with heavy artillery and naval gunfire support, Crocker attacked on 7 July. By 9 July all of Caen north of the Orne was in British hands, though much of the city was in ruins. But the Germans still held Fauberg de Vaucelles south of the river.

It is easy to understand why the Germans were so sensitive about Caen. Throughout June and the first half of July, misled by the success of Operation FORTITUDE, the D-Day deception plan, they expected another and larger invasion by the mythical First US Army Group, probably between the Seine and the Pas de Calais. A report from Rommel's Army Group B on 17 July, nearly six weeks after D-Day, states: 'The Second British Army is concentrated in the area of Caen and will carry out the thrust across the Orne towards Paris. First US Army Group – allowances must be made for a large-scale landing in the area of Fifteenth Army [Pas de Calais area] for operational collaboration with Montgomery's Army Group in a thrust on Paris.' Had this been true; had First US Army Group actually existed, it would have been logical for Montgomery's breakout to be launched from the Caen area, rather than, as Montgomery planned, from the US end of the Allied beachhead.

Chapter 3

THE SEEDS OF GOODWOOD

Montgomery's strategic plan for the Normandy campaign was simple. The whole Allied beachhead could be seen as a door, hinged at the eastern, British, end. At the vital moment it would spring open in the west, releasing the Americans against weakened German resistance. For this strategy to be effective 'the hinge', a phrase frequently used by Montgomery, must be maintained by constant pressure, thereby ensuring that the defending Germans were forced to keep the bulk of their forces, and in particular their panzer divisions in the east. In his book, *Normandy to the Baltic*, Montgomery wrote about the atmosphere in Normandy in mid-July, 'We were now on the threshold of great events. We were ready to break out of the bridgehead.'

On 10 July he summoned his two Army Commanders, Bradley and Dempsey. All seemed to be coming into place. Caen had at last fallen. Cherbourg and the Cotentin peninsula had been taken, while the bulk of the German armour still confronted Second British Army in the east. Detailed planning for the breakout must now be undertaken. But Bradley was not yet ready. He had yet to secure the St Lô – Périers road, which he had selected as

In Caen a British 6-pounder anti-tank gun commands a street.

the start line for his breakout offensive. And he felt that he did not have sufficient stores stockpiled to sustain what should become, once the breakout had been achieved, a very fast moving advance. Once he had broken through the crust of the German defence he must maintain the pressure; it would be inexcusable if opportunities presented themselves but could not be exploited through lack of transport, fuel, ammunition or other vital stores. Bradley asked for ten more days.

It was hardly surprising that the Americans needed more time. Fighting in the *bocage* country had proved much harder than had been envisaged by anyone before D-Day. Furthermore, from 19 to 21 June there raged in the Channel the worst summer storm in forty years. For three days eight feet high waves lashed the two pre-fabricated Mulberry harbours, which had been floated over from England and positioned off the French coast. One hundred and forty thousand tons of supplies were lost and many ships beached or sunk. The British harbour at Arromanches, with every section anchored and afforded some natural protection by the coastline, survived. Following repairs it regained full capacity by the end of June. But the American harbour at St Laurent, with only one anchor to every six sections and totally exposed to the full force of the storm, was wrecked beyond repair. Thereafter all the American reinforcements, supplies, etc., had to come over the open beaches. The achievements of the American logistics staffs were truly remarkable, but it was not surprising Bradley felt that he needed more time.

'Take all the time you need, Brad,' was Montgomery's reply. The master of the set-piece battle himself he would not pressurize a subordinate to attack before he was ready. He told Dempsey to continue his offensives, keeping the German forces, and especially their armour, pinned down in the east, while Bradley prepared to launch the eventual breakout in the west. After the meeting Dempsey suggested quietly that if Bradley was stuck the Second British Army should launch the breakout in the east. But Montgomery would hear none of it; the plan was quite clear and he was not a man to change his mind.

Throughout late June it seemed, looking at a map, that the Americans had achieved far more than the British. The press, and in particular the American press, unaware of the operational concept, were suggesting that the Americans were doing the bulk of the fighting, while the British failed to play their proper part. It must have been exceedingly irritating for Dempsey to read implied and even open criticism that his army was not pulling its weight. It was also quite incorrect; wars are won by defeating the enemy's army, not just by overrunning countryside. Besides, the American advances had mainly been heading north up the Cotentin peninsula towards Cherbourg. Once the peninsula had been cut on 18 June the Germans defenders were, in effect, bottled-up, with no chance of escape or reinforcement. The result was never in doubt. The American advances south had been no greater than those of their British neighbours. But the press

General Sir Mi Dempsey, Commander 2 British Army.

looked only at real estate liberated as a measure of the fighting, and the liberation of the Cotentin peninsula looked good on the map. These press reports were read by politicians in Washington and London. Criticism of the British mounted as June gave way to July.

In fact most of the press criticism was levelled at Montgomery, not Dempsey. Unlike Montgomery, Dempsey was not a self-publicist. It is an interesting fact that he, almost alone among senior Second World War commanders, never wrote any memoirs. Montgomery, on the other hand, openly courted publicity. The press, always keen to tilt at someone who suggests that he is invincible, largely overlooked the presence of Dempsey as Commander Second Army. In their eyes criticism of the British was criticism of Montgomery.

Caen had eventually fallen on 9 July, the day before the three generals met. This at last offered opportunities which had not previously existed. Dempsey felt that if his armoured divisions could break through onto the high open plateau south of Caen, astride the Caen to Falaise road, there was no telling how far they might penetrate. With Bradley delayed for ten days, he might, given the chance, win a significant victory, silence the unfair critics of his army's achievements and fighting qualities, and even present his Commander-in-Chief with a de facto breakout. It must have been a tempting thought.

Although he firmly turned down Dempsey's suggestion, Montgomery readily accepted that an operation by Second Army's three armoured divisions would be an invaluable precursor to Bradley's offensive, since it would continue to pin down the German panzer divisions in the east, and thereby ease Bradley's subsequent breakout.

* * * *

The idea of an armoured thrust east of the Orne was not new. Background planning for such an operation had been undertaken in mid-June, but Operation DREADNOUGHT, as it had been called, was never launched. It was now resurrected in mid-July as Operation GOODWOOD. On 10 July, following his meeting with his Army Commanders, Montgomery sent a written Directive to Dempsey which includes these sentences:

> 'The Army will retain the ability to be able to operate with a strong armoured force east of the Orne in the general area between Caen and Falaise. For this purpose a Corps of three armoured divisions will be held in reserve, ready to be employed when ordered by me. The opportunity for the employment of this Corps may be sudden and fleeting; therefore a study of the problems involved will be begun at once.'

Three days later Dempsey issued Operation Instruction No. 2, which outlined widespread attacks by all corps. XII Corps was to attack south-west on the night of 15/16 July to secure the high ground south of Evrecy – Operation GREEN LINE. On the morning of 16 July XXX Corps would attack south towards Fontenoy Le Pesnil and Noyers – Operation POMEGRANATE. Both these attacks would be carried out by infantry divisions, supported by independent armoured brigades. Then on 18 July VIII Corps, with three armoured divisions, would cross the Orne into the D-Day bridgehead now held by 6th Airborne and 51st (Highland) Divisions, 'attack southwards and establish an armoured division in each of the following areas: Bretteville-sur-Laize, Vimont/Argences and Falaise'. I Corps would advance on its left along the Bois de Bavant ridge, and II Canadian Corps on its right capturing Fauberg de Vaucelles (that area of Caen south of the Orne). The codeword for this operation was GOODWOOD. It would be preceded by the heaviest air raid ever mounted in support of a ground attack.

By launching GREEN LINE and POMEGRANATE west of the Orne, and then GOODWOOD east of it only two days later, Dempsey's aim was to unbalance the German defence. He hoped to force the enemy 'to bring divisions across and be able to hit them with our airforce in the process when they are particularly vulnerable'. Dempsey called this 'tennis over the Orne'.

Things were gathering pace. Next day, 14 July, Montgomery wrote to Brooke, the CIGS in London:

> 'Second British Army is now very strong; it has reached its peak and can get no stronger. It will, in fact, get weaker as the manpower situation begins to hit us. Also the casualties have affected the fighting efficiency of the divisions. The original men were very well trained; reinforcements are not so well trained, and this is becoming apparent and will have repercussions on what we can do. The country in which we are fighting is ideal defensive country; we do the attacking and the Boche is pretty thick on the ground. I would say we lost three men to his one in our infantry divisions.
>
> But the Second Army has three armoured divisions – 7, 11 and Guards. They are quite fresh and have been practically untouched. Having got Caen my left flank is now firm; my whole lodgement area is very secure and is held by infantry divisions supported by eight independent armoured brigades with a tank strength of over 1,000 tanks. So I have decided to have a real show-down on the east flank, and to loose a Corps of three armoured divisions into the open country about the Caen – Falaise road.'

Manpower was indeed a real problem for the British. Whereas the Americans had a seemingly endless supply of men and formations which continued to flow into Europe almost until the end of the war, for the British the cupboard was bare. There was no reserve of manpower left. Five years of war had bled the country dry – a fact which the Americans never seemed to understand. On 5 July Dempsey had been informed by the War Office in London that there were no further trained infantry reinforcements available in the UK. He would have to cannibalize his existing infantry divisions in order to maintain fighting strengths. But there were plenty of tanks. All the armoured regiments were fully equipped and by mid July there was already a pool of 500 tanks held in reserve in Normandy, ready to replace battle casualties. It seemed almost obvious that the next major offensive should be a predominantly tank affair.

In parallel with his letter to Brooke, Montgomery sent another Directive to Dempsey dated 15 July, extracts of which are below:

NOTES ON SECOND ARMY OPERATIONS
16 July – 18 July

1. **Object of the Operation.**
   To engage the German armour in battle and 'write it down' to such an extent that it is of no further value to the Germans as a basis for battle. To gain a good bridgehead over the River Orne through Caen, and thus improve our positions on the eastern flank.
   Generally to destroy German equipment and personnel.

2. **Effect of the Operation on the Allied policy.**
   The eastern flank is a bastion on which the whole future of the campaign in North West Europe depends; it must remain a firm bastion; if it becomes unstable the operations on the western flank would cease. Therefore, while taking advantage of every opportunity to destroy the enemy, we must be careful to maintain our own balance and ensure a firm base.

3. . . .

4. . . .

5. **Initial Operation VIII Corps.**
   The three armoured divisions will be required to dominate the area Borguebus – Vimont – Bretteville, and to fight and destroy the enemy, but armoured cars should push far to the south towards Falaise, and spread alarm and despondency, and discover 'the form'.

6. **II Canadian Corps.**
   While para 5 is going on, the Canadians must capture Vaucelles . . . and establish themselves in a very firm bridgehead on the general line Fleury – Cormelles – Mondeville.

7. **Later Operations by VIII Corps.**
   When 6 is done, then VIII Corps can 'crack about' as the situation demands.

Although Dempsey's Directive of 13 July specifically mentioned 'establishing a division in the area of Falaise', it is of interest that this did not feature in Montgomery's plan, although the possibility of armoured cars ranging that far forward was retained. It seems clear that Montgomery envisaged a rather more limited operation than was originally in Dempsey's mind. Perhaps, based on the Intelligence picture of what confronted him, outlined later, Dempsey still hoped for more.

On 17 July Dempsey met his corps commanders and briefed them fully. He supported this with a Directive which outlined the tasks of the three corps. It stated that:

'VIII Corps will establish armoured divisions in the areas:
   (a) Vimont.
   (b) Garcelles – Secqueville.
   (c) Hubert-Folie – Verrières.

The task of these three divisions will be to get their main bodies so established that there can be no enemy penetrations through the ring; to destroy all enemy troop concentrations and installations in the area; to defeat enemy armour which may be brought against them. Main bodies of the three divisions will not be moved from the area (a), (b) and (c) without reference to me.'

Some have suggested that GOODWOOD was an attempted breakout that failed, and that Montgomery only outlined the limited nature of it after the event. But all the documents produced in the run up to GOODWOOD spell out the objectives quite clearly. The object of the operation quoted above is quite unambiguous. It was never Montgomery's intention that the breakout should be launched in the east. Nor would a meticulous commander like Montgomery invite a corps to breakout with the imprecise order to 'crack about as the situation demands'. And yet GOODWOOD was indeed part of the breakout battle – the first phase of a two-phase attack by Twenty-first Army Group. General de Guingand makes it all quite clear:

'You must remember that Monty was CinC 21 Army Group, not Commander Second British Army. GOODWOOD was Phase 1 of Twenty-first Army Group's break-out; COBRA, Bradley's break-out, was Phase 2. Most of the German tanks were opposing the British. It was imperative to keep them there when General Bradley broke-out. That was how I saw GOODWOOD as Monty's Chief of Staff.'

In his memoirs General Bradley makes the same point, dealing, too, with the press criticism:

'Monty was spending his reputation in a bitter siege of Caen. Had we attempted to exonerate Monty by explaining how successfully he had hoodwinked the Germans by diverting them towards Caen, we would have given our strategy away. We desperately wanted the Germans to believe that Caen was the main objective.'

But if Montgomery, Bradley and Dempsey were clear about the overall strategy and the link between GOODWOOD and COBRA, and if the subordinate commanders fully understood the aims and objectives of the operation, it seems likely that those above were less clear. Responsibility for this must lie, to a large degree, with Montgomery. He was not a man to waste time with those who he did not respect. His letters, in particular those to Brooke, show that whatever his views of Eisenhower's personality he did not respect him as a battlefield general. This is hardly surprising; other than Brooke, Montgomery clearly did not respect the generalship of any of his other superiors, such as Alexander and Wilson in the Mediterranean. He was happy enough to work under them nominally, so long as they did what he wanted and did not seek to interfere with his detailed conduct of the campaign. GOODWOOD was a classic example of this. Montgomery himself gave neither the time nor the trouble to ensure that Eisenhower was fully aware of the aims and objectives of the operation. Eisenhower and his HQ were still in England; Montgomery had been in France since 8 June. Communication between them was remote. But de

Guingand has said that he personally briefed Eisenhower about GOODWOOD and was surprised when it emerged later that the Supreme Commander clearly expected far more from the operation than Montgomery planned. Perhaps the explanation for this confusion lies elsewhere.

At SHAEF Tedder, Eisenhower's deputy, was singing from a different hymn-sheet. The job of deputy, or second-in-command, is always likely to be frustrating and rather unsatisfactory. It usually has no executive authority, and often involves dealing with the less important subjects for which the commander does not have time or interest. Yet in the build-up to D-Day Tedder's role of ensuring close co-ordination of all air force assets, and in particular the strategic bomber forces, was vital. Following D-Day his main concern was that of acquiring good airfield sites so that the Allied Expeditionary Air Force, which provided air cover over the beachhead, could deploy on French soil, rather than have to mount its operations from the UK. The *bocage* country west of the Orne was thoroughly unsuitable for the creation of airstrips, but the wide open plains south of Caen offered exactly what the Air Forces required. Had Caen fallen as planned on D or D+1, with the Allied armies some fifteen to twenty miles deep into northern France within the first week, as suggested by the Phase Line map, all the real estate needs of the airmen would have been met. It was now five weeks after D-Day and the position on the ground seemed to have improved little. In a small beachhead, into which a never-ending flow of men and equipment seemed to be crammed, there was little space for airfields, and those that were constructed were within range of German heavy artillery. Tedder must have clutched at the mention of Falaise. If GOODWOOD could reach that far the Air Forces' problems would be solved. The subsequent achievements of GOODWOOD were to give Tedder powerful ammunition in his anti-Montgomery murmurings at SHAEF.

Furthermore, Morgan, during his COSSAC planning, had always envisaged the breakout being launched from the Caen area, this being the most direct route towards Paris. He, too, would stir the pot at SHAEF. Despite a visit from de Guingand to explain the concept, Eisenhower was clearly surprised and disappointed by the achievements of GOODWOOD. Perhaps the hopes of Tedder and the views of Morgan persuaded him to expect more.

Over in France things looked rather different. During the week 10 to 17 July the embryo of an idea had been discussed and developed until the assault divisions had clear and limited objectives and had already started to move towards their assembly areas. There was an air of expectancy among the participants. And even if higher commanders were constantly refining objectives, none of this was evident to the soldier at the front. Whether a plan is for a breakout, a limited attack, or just a feint, matters little to him. The village or hill to be captured, the fire support available, the ground and the likely enemy resistance are more than sufficient to concentrate the mind of the front-line soldier. Nor would it be prudent to tell him, even if it was true, that the attack which he is about to undertake, and which may well cost him his life, is only a deceptive curtain-raiser to the main event, in this case the breakout by First US Army some fifty miles west.

Chapter 4

THE GOODWOOD PLAN

The main problem confronting the British armour was lack of space. VIII Corps, consisting of 7th, 11th and Guards Armoured Divisions, which were all deployed west of the Orne, must move east, cross the Caen canal and the Orne, and move into the small bridgehead now held by 6th Airborne and 51st (Highland) Divisions. This bridgehead, which measured just five miles by three and had seen heavy fighting since D-Day, would be the launch-pad for the assault. With two infantry divisions already in the area, and another two due to deploy before advancing south, it would be impossible to conceal one armoured division, let alone three, in an area this size. In the interests of security, therefore, the tanks of the leading division must not enter the Orne bridgehead until after dark on the night before the attack. Unfortunately nights are very short in mid July; there would be precious little sleep for the attackers before they crossed the start line on the morning of 18 July. The attack would have to be preceded by two difficult and exhausting night moves.

The leading division would advance south as far as Cagny, which it would bypass to the west and swing south-west towards the key ridge-top villages of Bourguébus, Hubert-Folie and Bras. Behind it, the second division would follow closely, take Cagny and swing south-east towards Vimont. This would leave room for the third to come up in between, as the central prong of the trident, and take the villages of La Hogue and Secqueville. Once the Bourguébus ridge-line was secure, and the three armoured divisions were operating in line abreast, Intelligence believed that they would have broken through the main German defences. It was important that this should happen quickly, before the Germans had time to bring forward their reserves. If this was achieved, the opportunities for exploiting the success would be considerable, with armoured car regiments free to 'crack about as the situation demands'.

The first few hours of the operation would be vital. To help the leading division during the early stages, Twenty-first Army Group asked for a massive aerial bombardment to precede the advance. The bomber barons in England initially rejected the application. In their views anything that removed aircraft from bombing Germany was detracting from the real war-winning effort. They pointed out that on the two previous occasions in which bombers had been used to support a ground attack, at Cassino and Caen, results had been disappointing. The bombing had not eliminated the opposition and our own troops had been hampered by cratering and rubble-blocked roads. In reply the Army stated that GOODWOOD was to be a rural, not urban, attack, and that fragmentation, rather than high explosive bombs would be required along the axis of the advance. Air Vice Marshal Coningham, as Commander Second Tactical Air Force, the senior airman deployed in France, returned to UK and managed to convince the Commander-in-Chief Allied Expeditionary Air Force, Air Chief Marshal

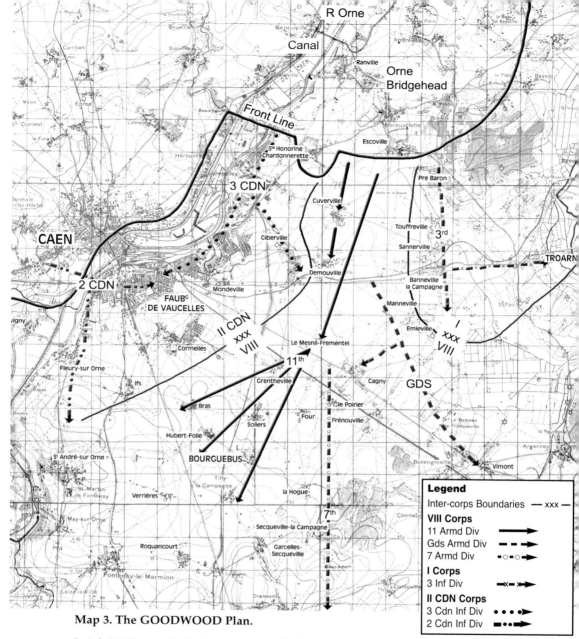

Map 3. The GOODWOOD Plan.

Legend

Inter-corps Boundaries — xxx —

VIII Corps
11 Armd Div ⟶
Gds Armd Div - - ->
7 Armd Div ○○○⟶

I Corps
3 Inf Div ×—×⟶

II CDN Corps
3 Cdn Inf Div •••⟶
2 Cdn Inf Div ■••⟶

Leigh-Mallory, of the importance of the bombing. With his support, the request was reluctantly accepted. It was to produce the largest bomber raid ever launched in direct support of a ground attack.

From 5.45 to 6.30 am, 1,056 Lancaster bombers of RAF Bomber Command would drop high explosive bombs on the flanks of the corridor and on Cagny. From 7.00 to 7.45 am, 482 medium bombers from IX USAAF would saturate an area about two miles square, along the axis of the armoured advance, including the villages of Cuverville, Démouville, Giberville and up to half a mile south of the Caen to Troarn railway with fragmentation bombs. From 8.30 to 9.00 am, 539 heavy bombers from IX USAAF, also using fragmentation bombs, would bomb the villages along the Bourguébus ridge. In the early stages of planning it was arranged that a second bombing raid would be launched onto the Bourguébus ridge in the early afternoon, and that the leading division would be held in the Cagny area until this had occurred. But as planning advanced this proposal seems to have been dropped – a pity, as events turned out.

It was hoped that this vast bombing raid would destroy most of the Germans on the flanks, and so undermine the morale and resilience of those in the centre of the corridor that they would be largely ineffective, at least during the first vital hours of the advance.

The advance would also be supported by a massive artillery fire plan. The leading tanks would follow closely behind a rolling barrage fired by eight field regiments of 25-pounder guns. The barrage, on a frontage of just 2,000 yards, would advance at a speed of 150 yards per minute. Just south of the Caen to Troarn railway it would pause for fifteen minutes while the leading division crossed the railway line and expanded the width of its advance, whereupon the barrage would continue for a further mile. But once the tanks had reached the small hamlet of Le Mesnil Frémentel they would be beyond the range of the supporting field artillery regiments. Thereafter they must rely on the fire of their own divisional artillery moving closely behind the leading troops. Meanwhile, medium and heavy regiments would fire concentrations on selected flank and depth villages.

* * * *

The commander of VIII Corps, Lieutenant General Sir Richard O'Connor, was already something of a legend. He had emerged from the First World War a twenty-nine year old lieutenant colonel with two DSOs, an MC, nine Mentions in Despatches and an outstanding reputation as a fighting soldier. As Commander, Western Desert Corps in Egypt in 1940 he had planned and led the force which swept a greatly superior Italian army from Libya. But the arrival of the Germans under Rommel in early 1941, and the reduction in British forces to allow divisions to be sent to Greece, had tilted the balance firmly the other way. In the resulting retreat O'Connor, by then GOC Egypt, had been sent hurriedly forward to hold the hand of his successor in Libya. By a stroke of bad luck the two generals had run into a German patrol and been captured. After two and a half years as a prisoner of war in Italy, O'Connor had escaped and returned to England. A much liked and respected commander, he now had the task of launching the three armoured divisions into Operation GOODWOOD.

O'Connor's plan had to take account of the fact that the corridor of the advance was so narrow that there would only be room for one division to advance at a time. He selected 11th Armoured Division to lead, with orders 'to establish itself in the area Bras, Verrières, Rocquancourt and Bourguébus'. The advance was to be conducted in three phases. In Phase One 29th Armoured Brigade was to cross the start-line west of Escoville and advance south, bypassing Cuverville and Démouville to the east, and then, just north of Cagny, swing south-west to secure Le Mésnil Frementel. Meanwhile, in a separate

Lieutenant General Sir Richard O'Con KCB, DSO, MC Commander V Corps at GOODWOOD much respected 'fighting Gene

operation, 159th Infantry Brigade would capture Cuverville and Démouville.

In Phase Two 29th Armoured Brigade would continue south-west to attack the villages on the Bourguébus ridge. In Phase Three 159th Brigade would come forward to establish a firm defensive position in the area captured by 29th Armoured Brigade, hopefully as far forward as the villages of Verrières and Rocquancourt.

Speed was essential. 11th Armoured must get clear of the Cagny area as quickly as possible in order to allow Guards Armoured and finally 7th Armoured to come up into line. Commanding 11th Armoured was Major General Pip Roberts, at thirty-seven the youngest general in the British Army. As Brigade Major 4th Armoured Brigade, in the rank of Captain, he had served in Lieutenant General O'Connor's corps in the 1940 desert offensive. Less than two years later he was commanding 22nd Armoured Brigade in the desert battles of Alam Halfa and El Alamein. In early 1943 he commanded 26th Armoured Brigade in the final battles in Tunisia. Eighteen years younger than O'Connor and about ten years younger than most other divisional commanders, Roberts was in fact younger than both his brigade commanders and most, if not all the regimental commanders in his division. Small, neat, wiry and quiet; but three DSOs and an MC from the desert campaign told their own tale. There was an aura of the utmost calmness and confidence in his manner, which communicated itself to all ranks in the division. Quite simply, they knew that they were commanded by the best armoured commander in the British Army; a man with a steel core of toughness and an uncanny eye for ground; a superb judge of both risk and opportunity, but someone who would never squander soldiers' lives heedlessly, nor order them to do anything that he himself would not do. If anyone could launch GOODWOOD with the necessary drive and purpose, it was surely Roberts – doubtless that was why O'Connor selected 11th Armoured to lead the advance.

But Roberts was not happy with the detailed plan given to him:

Major General Pip Roberts, the thirty-seven year old commander of 11th Armoured Division. Undoubtedly the outstanding British armoured commander of World War II – with three DSOs and an MC to prove it.

'Right from the start my two brigades were to be tied up in two quite separate battles. It was essential that 29th Armoured Brigade should get on as quickly as possible so the Guards and 7th Armoured could come up into line. But because of my orders to take Cuverville and Démouville I would not have 159th Infantry Brigade available to help clear villages etc for the tanks. I felt that this was wrong, so I raised it with the Corps Commander, verbally and on paper. He replied, "Well, Pip, if with all your experience you think it is an unsound plan, then I'll have to get another division to lead." So we led!!

'I was also told to take Cagny. I felt that this was rather off my centre-line, and with my infantry brigade tied up in Cuverville and Démouville, I felt that this was too much. So again I represented this to General O'Connor. He said, "Alright, but you must leave an armoured regiment to mask Cagny until the Guards come up." As the story unfolds you will see how unfortunate it was that I lost the argument over Cuverville and Démouville, but won it over Cagny – but that is how things happen in war!'

* * * *

There were considerable differences between the three armoured divisions of VIII Corps. 7th Armoured Division was brimful of experience, having fought with great distinction throughout the North African campaign and in Italy. But on return to England in late January 1944 many felt, not without real justification, that they had 'done their bit', and that others would doubtless pick up the baton for the forthcoming North-West Europe campaign. In England 9th Armoured Division, untried in battle, was longing for the chance to show what it could do. But Montgomery always liked to surround himself with those who have proved themselves in his earlier battles. Three of his favourite desert divisions were to be included in the Normandy line-up. 50th (Northumbrian) Division was to be the assault division on Gold Beach; 51st (Highland) Division was one of the first follow-up divisions ashore; 7th Armoured, the famous Desert Rats, the first armoured division to land. But the fighting conditions in Normandy were very different from those of the open desert. In particular the dense *bocage* country west of Caen, with visibility often no further than fifty to 100 yards, proved a mental, as well as physical hurdle which some desert veterans found it difficult to overcome. 51st and 7th Armoured Divisions were to prove disappointments in Normandy – both were to have their divisional commanders sacked before the campaign was over. Roberts himself was a former regimental and brigade commander in 7th Armoured. His loyalty to his old division was real, but he would later describe the Desert Rats in Normandy as 'canny – they seemed to look for problems in every opportunity, rather than opportunities in every problem'.

Guards Armoured Division was almost the opposite of 7th Armoured. It had never been to war before, and, as the last arrived of the three armoured divisions, GOODWOOD was to be its first taste of battle. Furthermore, Guardsmen are traditionally infantrymen. It was a complete change of role for them to convert to serving in tanks. 'Yet,' to quote Roberts again, 'what the Guards lacked in experience they more than made up in dash and drive.'

11th Armoured was somewhere between the other two. Normandy was its first campaign, but many of the senior commanders had fought in the desert. In addition to Roberts, Brigadier Roscoe Harvey, Commander 29th Armoured Brigade, had commanded a regiment and brigade in the desert where he had won two DSOs, to which he would later add a third. Most of the regimental commanders also had battle experience. And shortly before D-Day two organizational changes were to add considerably to the division's bank of experience. 3rd Royal Tank Regiment, which had fought at Calais in 1940, in Greece in 1941, throughout the desert campaign (with Lieutenant Colonel Pip Roberts as its commanding officer for much of 1942) joined 29th Armoured Brigade. It was also decided that each regiment should have at least one squadron leader with battle experience, so a number of high quality majors were selected and posted into the division. Voices of experience were thus spread throughout the division.

Like the other armoured divisions, 11th Armoured consisted of two brigades, 29th Armoured and 159th Lorried Infantry Brigades. 29th Armoured Brigade had three armoured regiments of Sherman tanks, 3rd Royal Tank Regiment, 2nd Fife and Forfar Yeomanry and 23rd Hussars and a motor infantry battalion, 8th

Battalion The Rifle Brigade. All three armoured regiments had very different origins. 3rd Tanks was a regular army unit which had already fought at Calais, Greece and in the North African desert campaign. The Fife and Forfar Yeomanry was a territorial army regiment from Scotland, while 23rd Hussars was one of six armoured regiments formed in 1941 just for the duration of the war. Neither had been in action before Normandy. 159th Lorried Infantry Brigade contained three infantry battalions, 3rd Battalion The Monmouthshire Regiment, 1st Battalion The Herefordshire Regiment and 4th Battalion The King's Shropshire Light Infantry. They would move forward in lorries, but fight on foot. For artillery support the division also contained two field and one anti-tank artillery regiments, 13th Regiment Royal Horse Artillery (Honourable Artillery Company), with its self-propelled 25-pounder Sextons supporting 29th Armoured Brigade, 151st Field Regiment (Ayrshire Yeomanry), with towed 25-pounders, supporting 159th Infantry Brigade, and 75th Anti-tank Regiment.

GOODWOOD was not 11th Armoured's first taste of battle. Having arrived in France between 14 and 17 June the division took part in Operation EPSOM and the fierce fighting round Hill 112. Montgomery's comment to Brooke on 14 July that the three armoured divisions were 'quite fresh and have been practically untouched', was not the way it was seen by those at the front. Lieutenant David Stileman, the twenty year-old commander of 11 Platoon, G Company, 8th Battalion The Rifle Brigade, the motor infantry battalion in 29 Armoured Brigade, felt rather differently about his first taste of war:

> *'We had the bloodiest possible battle inoculation on Hill 112.'*

Following EPSOM there was an almost inevitable bill to pay. It is easy, when outlining the course of a battle, to dwell on the experiences of those who prosper – easy, but misleading. However well trained a unit may be, that first encounter with someone whose sole aim is to kill you comes as a real shock. Some, indeed most, are able to cross their personal Rubicon, as described by Stileman, who was ordered to investigate a wooded area ahead:

> *'I moved slowly forward at the head of the leading section. Suddenly, without any warning, there was a huge flash and something fired at us at virtually point-blank range. Instinctively I threw myself on the ground. As I started to withdraw I was horrified to see that almost all the Riflemen with me had been*

11 Platoon, G Company, 8th Rifle Brigade, shortly before leaving for Normandy. Lieutenant David Stileman (centre) with Sergeant Henry on his right and Sergeant Dedman on his left.

wounded, some obviously severely.

'*Among them was Sergeant Dedman, who was horribly wounded. I did my best to drag him to his feet – in vain. He couldn't stand and implored me to leave him. From that day until he died some thirty-five years later he was paralysed from the waist down. And several others in the section had gaping wounds from that shell-burst, or whatever the cursed projectile had been.*

'*Feeling wretched I started to sort out this mayhem when, out of the blue, Michael Lane, who commanded 10 Platoon, appeared at my side and asked what had happened. Lying as flat as I could I tried to point out to him where the weapon was concealed. He wanted to identify it clearly for himself, so he knelt beside me and searched the area through his binoculars. As I urged him to get down there was another monumental explosion, followed by a small groan beside me. I turned to look at Mike. Most of his throat had been ripped away and blood belched from a hole in his chest. He died a few days later.*

'*I returned to Mick McCrae, G Company Commander, and explained that, yes, there were enemy in that hedge. I then took myself off, away from the others, and in peaceful isolation, sobbed my heart out. This did me a power of good, because after a few minutes I was as right as rain. Indeed I honestly felt that I could have taken on the entire 21st Panzer Division single-handed, and was totally ready for round two, whatever that might be. And I did not have to wait long to find out.*'

Stileman's war was not destined to last long. Only ten days after Operation GOODWOOD he was hit between the eyes by a bullet, which blew out the side of his face. Miraculously, he survived. For others the first taste of battle can prove too much, as General Roberts made clear when addressing British Army officers in later years:

'*After EPSOM I had to make one or two changes in command. I had to get rid of one brigade and two battalion commanders. You may wonder why I didn't do it beforehand. Well, I can only tell you that it is damned difficult to tell if a chap is going to be up to taking war or not. If he has done well on training, given out sensible orders, etc, it is very difficult to say that he won't be able to stand up to heavy shell-fire. In two cases this was so. During EPSOM we had been shelled by "moaning minnies" – those multi-barrelled mortars which make a terrible noise. One brigade commander put a tin hat on his head, got down in the bottom of his trench and never moved – quite hopeless, so of course he had to go. Now if, as a commander, you find that some of your subordinates are not up to the job, you've got to get rid of them quickly, or you'll start losing battles and men unnecessarily. It isn't nice, but you've got to do it.*'

GOODWOOD was going to need dynamic leadership at all levels. The first division must be 'goers', determined to push on despite casualties, taking risks where necessary so that the later divisions could come up into line and put intolerable pressure on the German defences. Roberts and his 11th Armoured Division were the obvious ones to lead, and were raring to go, as Stileman makes clear:

'*Despite our unpleasant experiences on Hill 122, morale in 11th Armoured was simply terrific. This is not surprising because, as in all good organisations, morale stems from the top, and we knew that in General Pip Roberts we had the finest divisional commander in the British Army.*'

Chapter 5

THE GROUND AND THE GERMANS

VIII Corps' advance was to be launched from the small bridgehead east of the Orne. The ground in front was to have a profound effect upon the detailed plan and the progress of the advance. From the ridge-top villages of Amfréville and Bréville, just east of Pegasus Bridge, it is possible, on a clear day, to see the Bourguébus ridge some eight miles south. Once there, the ground opens out to become a high, wide plateau, almost ideal country for exploiting the speed and flexibility of armoured forces. But in between these two ridges the country is rather less

Map 4. The GOODWOOD country – 'a pin-board of well-built villages up to a mile apart' – and the three railway lines.

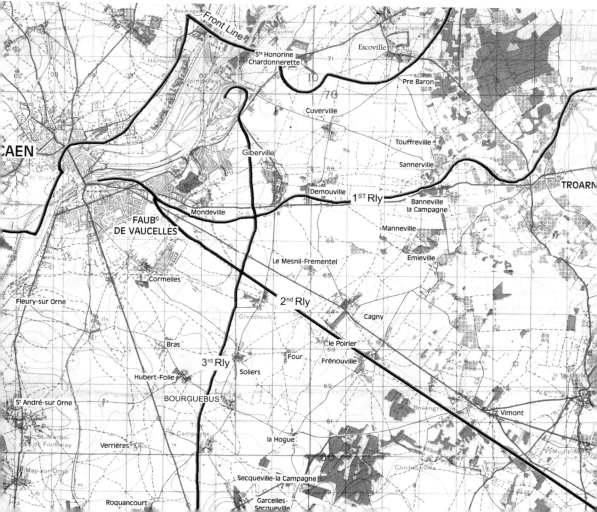

inviting. The armour must advance down a corridor about two miles wide initially, widening to five miles south of Cagny. To the east is the densely wooded Bois de Bavant ridge, along which 3rd Infantry Division would advance. But at walking speed they would quickly be left behind by the tanks. In the west, the axis of 3rd Canadian Infantry Division, the advance would be confined, for the first few miles, by the river, canal and the industrial area of Colombelles, where the tall chimneys would provide the Germans with splendid observation over the whole area. And ahead the gently rising slopes of the Bourguébus ridge offered 'dress circle' views over the 'amphitheatre' of the advance. Although in 1944 the ground was for the most part open, it was studded with a pin-board of compact and well-built stone villages and hamlets, up to one mile apart, each surrounded by woods, orchards and high walls. To the military eye it suggested a defence which conformed to most of the recognized principles – mutually supporting, sited in depth, with good all-round defence and good concealment. South of Cagny the constricting flanks of the corridor fell away, and the ground opened out, rising gently up to the Bourguébus ridge.

To complicate things further a number of railway lines crossed the axis of advance. The first two, Caen to Troarn (since removed) and Caen to Vimont, ran east to west across the line of the advance, the former just south of Démouville the latter south of Cagny. The third railway, which connected the mines and quarries of Potigny and Hautmesnil with the port of Caen, ran north-south along a steep embankment [the embankment remains but the line is no longer in use]. While these might not significantly impede the tanks, their raised banks could pose considerable difficulties for the half-tracks and carriers of the supporting infantry motor battalion, and the wheeled logistic support vehicles.

The rise from the lowest point to the Bourguébus ridge is rather less than 100 feet. It sounds insignificant. But stand, for example, on the edge of Bras or Hubert-Folie, looking north, and it is immediately evident that this is dominating ground, with long fields of view and fire. This ridge was to prove the vital ground of the battle. If the British armour could seize it the German gunners would be denied observation over the area, thereby making defence extremely difficult. Once established on the Bourguébus ridge, three armoured divisions would be a formidable, hopefully an unstoppable striking force. Conversely, if the Germans could hold the ridge long enough to bring forward their reserves, with their markedly superior anti-tank weapons making good use of the long fields of fire, they would surely take a heavy toll of the British tanks.

Speed was therefore essential. The leading tanks must by-pass the villages, and press on to secure the Bourguébus ridge as quickly as possible, leaving follow-up echelons to mop up by-passed German positions. It was hoped that the shock effect of the aerial bombardment would unsettle the defenders long enough to ensure this. If so, the success for which Dempsey hoped might well occur. But life can be very uncomfortable for tanks by-passing villages which are held by resolute defenders with anti-tank weapons, at relatively short range. Much depended on the enemy – how they were deployed, what weapons they had, and how quickly they would come to life after the bombing.

* * * *

There is a marked difference between training and reality in the business of Intelligence. In training the exercise author usually gives sufficient information to the players that if they draw sensible deductions from it they are likely to take decisions which will lead to the exercise following the correct, planned course. There is a sureness and confidence over Intelligence during training. Reality is quite different. The commander and his staff have no idea whether the Intelligence that they have is five, fifty or eighty per cent of the enemy picture. Indeed they do not even know whether what they 'know' is correct or not. GOODWOOD was to prove this point.

The enemy picture painted by Intelligence staffs was distinctly encouraging. It suggested that the German defences lay in two belts, about four miles deep. In front was thought to be 16th German Air Force Division. Following the battle for Caen in early July, in which it had sustained heavy casualties, its two forward regiments, 32nd and 46th GAF Regiments, thought to number about 900 men each, had been clearly identified holding the ground from the Orne to Escoville. Just behind them, the division's third regiment, 31st GAF Regiment was estimated at only about 300 strong. This thin and exhausted line of defence would hardly impede the advancing tanks. On the right, running north from the Bois de Bavant to the coast, was 346th Infantry Division, with two weakened regiments in the line.

The identity and location of the second line defences had not yet been confirmed, but was probably based on 21st Panzer Division. This division consisted of one panzer (tank) and two panzer-grenadier (mechanized infantry) regiments, each of two battalions. It was thought that either 192nd Panzer-Grenadier Regiment or Battle Group Luck (a reinforced 125th Panzer-Grenadier Regiment), was probably deployed in the Fauberg de Vaucelles, south of Caen. Both these regiments were thought to number about 1,200 or 1,300 men. The nearest German tanks would be the Mk IVs of 21st Panzer Division's tank regiment, 22nd Panzer Regiment, probably in the Argences – Vimont area, some ten miles distant. 21st Panzer Division, which also had between thirty and forty anti-tank and anti-aircraft guns, twenty-five artillery and thirty-five assault guns, was expected to be a formidable opponent. Doubtless it would quickly be sucked into the battle, but once through it and the way should be open.

The true picture was very different. Throughout early July Rommel had become increasingly concerned about the area east of Caen. On several visits to troops and headquarters in the area he had said that he expected the next major British attack to be an attempt to break through here. On 15 and 16 July, during visits to 346th Division, Panzer Group West and LXXXIV Corps, he actually warned of a likely attack on 17 or 18 July, probably led by British armoured divisions. It is not surprising that by 18 July the German defences in this area were strong and alert. What is surprising is that Allied Intelligence failed to realize this. Whatever the reason for this, the soldiers who crossed the Start Line at 7.45 am on the morning of 18 July expected a very different reception from that which actually awaited them.

In fact the German defences lay in four belts and ran to a depth of about ten miles. At the front was indeed 16th GAF Division. Its three weak regiments were now under command of 21st Panzer Division, which, having been made responsible for the defence of the entire area, was much further forward and in greater strength than British Intelligence estimated. Behind the forward battalions, the second line of defence was based on the two panzer-grenadier regiments of 21st Panzer Division. On the left Colonel Rauch's 192nd Panzer Grenadier-Regiment, with two battalions, stretched from the Orne to just west of Cuverville. Rauch was also responsible for the defence of Vaucelles (Caen south of the river). On his right, from inclusive Cuverville to Pré Baron, Battle Group Luck would bear the brunt of the British advance, at least in the early stages. It consisted of Colonel von Luck's two panzer-grenadier battalions of 125th Panzer-Grenadier Regiment, fifty assault guns of Major Becker's 200th Assault Gun Battalion and a considerable assortment of tanks and anti-tank guns.

Also in the area was the tank element of 21st Panzer Division, Colonel von Oppeln-Bronikowski's 22nd Panzer Regiment. In theory it should have consisted of two battalions each of up to fifty Mk IV tanks. But 2nd Battalion was away being re-equipped with Mk V Panther tanks, and their place was

German Mk VII King Tiger. At sixty-nine tons, twice the weight of a Sherman, with an immensly powerful gun and frontal armour which no British anti-tank weapon could penetrate (see Annex B).

A six-barrelled *Nebelwerfer*, the 'moaning minnie' – an alarming and effective weapon.

filled by Captain Fromme's 503rd Heavy Tank Battalion. With two companies each of ten Mk VI Tigers and one of ten Mk VII King Tigers, 503rd Tank Battalion was a most powerful force whose presence was quite unknown to the British. Located in the woods near Emiéville and in the grounds of the Chateau de Manneville, 1st Battalion 22nd Panzer Regiment and 503rd Heavy Tank Battalion also formed part of Battle Group Luck. Knowledge of their presence, and especially that of Tiger tanks, invulnerable to most British tank guns and sited just on the flank of the main advance, would not have been encouraging to those at the front of the advance.

The Caen to Vimont railway line marked the beginning of the third line of defences. Just south of it 7th Werfer Regiment, with some 270 *Nebelwerfer* launchers, was sited in the area of Grentheville and nearby villages. Known to the British as the 'moaning minnie', due to the terrifying noise that it made in flight, the *Nebelwerfer* was a multi-barrelled mortar which fired a salvo of projectiles, weighing between seventy-five and 250 pounds, out to a range of 8,000 yards. A battalion of these alarming weapons, which had no equivalent in the Allied armoury, was in direct support of von Luck. Further south, sited in the villages along the Bourguébus ridge, was a screen of forty-four 88mm anti-tank guns from 200th Tank Destroyer Battalion (not to be confused with

200th Assault Gun Battalion, of which more later) and in excess of sixty artillery guns. And throughout the area, under Air Force rather than Army command, were several batteries of 88mm anti-aircraft guns, all of which carried anti-tank rounds with them.

Still further behind were the tanks of 1st and 12th SS Panzer Divisions. Following heavy fighting, both were somewhat reduced in strength. But they had already acquired formidable reputations – in the case of 12th SS, the fanatical Hitler Youth. Following the recent arrival in the area of several infantry divisions, they had been withdrawn from the line for use in co-ordinated offensive operations. Intelligence had located neither of them, and it was not envisaged that they would be available to oppose the GOODWOOD advance. 1st SS Panzer Division was to prove this assumption to be very wrong.

The overall effect was that behind the thin crust of 16th GAF Division the Germans had built up a framework defence based on mutually supporting villages, each of which was held by a force of infantrymen and anti-tank guns in well-prepared and concealed positions with good fields of fire. With a powerful tank force on the eastern flank, a mass of anti-tank guns along the Bourguébus ridge and two SS panzer divisions not far away, the defences were formidable indeed. This was hardly surprising. Local commanders had heeded Rommel's warning and were ready. The same 17 July report from Rommel's HQ, quoted in chapter 2, states: 'The large-scale attack of the British Second Army with the object of breaking through to the SE is expected from the evening of 17 July.'

* * * *

VIII Corps' chief opponent, at least in the early stages of the attack, would be Colonel Hans von Luck, a doughty fighter with a wealth of battle experience behind him. Now aged thirty-three, he had served in 1940 as a company commander in 37th Panzer Reconnaissance Battalion, part of Rommel's 7th Panzer Division. When, during the advance across northern France, the battalion commander was killed, Rommel ordered von Luck to take command. He led his battalion, and Rommel's division, to its final objective, Cherbourg. Having reverted to command of his company again, he was, in 1941, selected as chief of staff of 7th Panzer Division for the invasion of Russia. In April 1942, at the personal request of Rommel, von Luck was summoned to North Africa to take command of 3rd Panzer Reconnaissance Battalion in 21st Panzer Division. As a bright young commander, who had clearly caught the eye of the Desert Fox in the early days of the war, his fortunes seemed inexorably bound up in Rommel's success.

In late March 1943 von Luck was sent by General von Arnim, who had succeeded Rommel in North Africa, as a personal messenger to Hitler. The end of the campaign was no longer in doubt. Von Arnim proposed that all Axis forces should be withdrawn to mainland Europe while still intact, rather than face elimination or a chaotic Dunkirk-type evacuation. But Hitler would

Colonel Hans v Luck – the dynamic commander of 125th Panzer Grenadier Regiment, who personality and leadership had great effect on Operation GOODWOOD.

hear none of it and insisted that they fought for the last yard of African soil. Where the generals had manifestly failed, it was hoped that a young battalion commander, straight from the front, might be able to persuade the Führer. Von Luck was sent as emissary to Berlin. In the event he never even gained access to Hitler. General Jodl made it clear to him that evacuation was out of the question. Despite the failure of his mission von Luck was at least spared the fate of the rest of the Axis forces in North Africa. When on 12 May 1943 von Arnim and more than 275,000 men surrendered, von Luck was still in Germany.

In early May 1944 he was appointed to command 125th Panzer-Grenadier Regiment in 21st Panzer Division in northern France. On D-Day von Luck's regiment was south-east of Caen; throughout June and early July he led numerous attacks to try to eliminate the British bridgehead east of the Orne, captured on D-Day by 6th Airborne Division and then reinforced by 51st Highland Division. On several occasions he managed to penetrate the British defences, but was never able to hold onto the ground seized for long. By mid July von Luck and his men knew every inch of the ground over which the forthcoming battle would be fought. This is a very strong card in the hands of any worthwhile defender. Von Luck and his battle group did not waste it.

To the casual tourist the finer points of 'ground' seem almost unimportant. To the frontline soldier they are vital. The field of view of an infantryman, in a trench at ground-level, is quite different from that of a tank commander, in the turret of his tank some ten feet or so higher. The infantryman may be able to see only 100 yards; the tank commander several thousand. A dip of just a few feet can reduce the infantryman's ground-level view to almost nothing; it can also provide a hull-down position for the tank, where its weapons are just as effective but it is less vulnerable to anti-tank fire. Weapons can only be effectively sited at the height at which they will be fired, so detailed knowledge of the ground is an important tool for the defender. This is, of course, denied to the attacker.

* * * *

The story of 200th Assault Gun Battalion is one of remarkable ingenuity. Following the North-West Europe campaign of 1940 Captain Alfred Becker, an engineer by profession but then commanding an artillery battery, decided to experiment by fitting his artillery guns onto Carden-Lloyd chassis, captured during the advance across France. When deployed to the Russian campaign as part of 227th Division, Becker's battery proved to be the only armoured, self-propelled artillery battery. Its 105mm guns, normally indirect fire weapons, earned a high reputation against the powerful Russian T34 tanks, in a direct fire role. This success came to the ears of Hitler and in mid-1942 Becker was ordered to take one of his guns to Berlin to show off its capabilities.

The demonstration was a clear success and Becker was ordered to construct thirty of his self-propelled guns within three weeks for deployment

Major Becker – a pre D-Day inspection of 200th Assault Gun Battalion by Field Marshal Rommel, who is talking to Major General Feuchtinger, Commander 21st Panzer Division.

to North Africa, where Rommel's advance had just reached the Egyptian border near a small, hitherto unknown place called El Alamein. The order proved impossible to fulfil, but by the end of the three weeks fifteen guns were on their way to the desert. Becker now turned his energies to further development. First he tried fitting 105mm guns on the chassis of Mk IV tanks, and captured Russian anti-tank guns onto Skoda tank chassis. Then he heard of Hotchkiss chassis in a number of French factories. He decided to try converting them into armoured, self-propelled guns.

By June 1944 200th Assault Gun Battalion had been formed, with Becker, now a Major, as commanding officer. Originally planned to have six batteries, only five had been completed and deployed by D-Day. Each battery, with a strength of 116 men, consisted of six 75mm guns on Hotchkiss chassis and four 105mm guns on Mk IV chassis. In addition there was a battery command tank, a radio tank and six tracked or half-tracked armoured ammunition vehicles, also Becker's inventions. Becker's battalion HQ, split into command

and administrative groups each 200 strong, also possessed a rocket platoon of four sixteen-barrel 80mm *Nebelwerfer* launchers, an anti-aircraft platoon of two four-barrel 20mm guns and a pioneer platoon. All of these were similarly armoured and self-propelled. This unusual organization had no equivalent in the British forces; indeed it is impossible to imagine the British Procurement Authorities ordering anyone to design, construct and then command his own battalion.

Like von Luck's 125th Panzer-Grenadier Regiment Becker's battalion had taken part in most of the fighting east of the Orne since D-Day. They, too, knew the ground well. This powerful and extraordinary force was to play a most significant part in the battle that was about to unfold.

Von Luck had deployed his forces with care. On the left, behind 16th GAF Division, he sited his 1st Battalion in Cuverville, Démouville and Giberville, with its HQ in the small hamlet of Le Mesnil Frémentel. His 2nd Battalion was in Touffréville, and Emiéville. Bolstering the defence of the panzer-grenadiers were Becker's batteries. 1 Battery, under Captain Eichhorn, was in Démouville, just east of Captain Foerster's 2 Battery in Giberville. Behind them were 5 Battery under Lieutenant Schreiner in Le Prieuré and Captain Röpke's 4 Battery covering the gap between Le Mesnil Frémentel and Cagny. Further back still, Captain Nösser's 3 Battery provided defence for a battalion of *Nebelwerfer* launchers sited in the orchards around Grentheville. At the start

75mm (long) of Major Becker's 200th Assault Gun Battalion. It is easy to understand how they could be mistaken for tanks by the advancing British.

General Sepp Dietrich. Commander I SS Panzer Corps, inspects a 105mm assault gun of Becker's battalion, shortly before D-Day.

of GOODWOOD Becker's battalion HQ was sited just south-west of Cagny, between the parallel road and railway, while he himself was in a forward command post between 4 and 5 Batteries on the road north from Cagny.

The tanks of 22nd Panzer Regiment and 503rd Heavy Tank Battalion were to provide flank protection in the east, and be available for immediate counter-attack, from their positions in the woods and orchards of Emiéville and the Chateau de Manneville. Nearby, in the village of Frénouville, was von Luck's regimental HQ – the nerve-centre of this deep and well co-ordinated defence.

Chapter 6

'TWO DREADFUL NIGHT MOVES'

The bridgehead east of the river Orne had been under almost constant attack from Colonel Hans von Luck's 125th Panzer-Grenadier Regiment since D-Day. The village of Ste Honorine la Chardonnerette, for example, had changed hands several times during six weeks of heavy fighting. To strengthen its defences 51st Highland Division had constructed a dense minefield along its southern flank of the bridgehead. Gaps must be made through this minefield before any advance south could be launched. In theory minefields are carefully plotted when laid. It should be possible, based on the records made at the time, to open up gaps with little difficulty. However these mines had been laid hastily, often under fire and in bad weather. In the subsequent shelling many had been detonated or displaced in the standing corn. It therefore proved impossible to locate the individual mines with any degree of accuracy. Minefields which cannot be systematically 'lifted' must be 'breached' – a complicated, dangerous and time-consuming business for the Royal Engineers. Furthermore, the breaching operation must be carried out without alerting the Germans. Under cover of darkness, for several nights, Royal Engineers worked like beavers creating gaps through the minefield. When General Roberts visited HQ 51st Division on 17 July, he asked that the home side of the minefield should be marked by a high fence, liberally draped with white tape which would be easily visible to tank crews moving forward in the dark. By 4.15 am on 18 July 51st Division reported 'all gaps, marking and signing complete'.

* * * *

Following the end of Operation EPSOM and the withdrawal from Hill 112 on 30 June, 11th Armoured Division licked its wounds in the area of Cully, a few miles inland from Arromanches, while General Roberts effected his 'few changes in command', and replacements arrived to fill the gaps in both men and equipment which Epsom had produced. On 16 July began a series of complicated moves to ensure that the three armoured divisions were in place for the attack. The main difficulty was that the Lines of Communication for Second British Army ran north to south, from the beaches to the battlefront. VIII Corps must move 900 tanks, 30,000 men and several hundred vehicles from west to east, a distance of some twenty miles across these lines, without unreasonably impeding the essential flow of men and stores to the front.

A move such as this, conducted under cover of darkness and without lights, in the interests of security, offered endless potential for chaos. Co-ordination demanded the very highest levels of efficiency, both in planning and execution. HQ Second Army therefore laid down times at which sectors of the Army Lines of Communication were to be frozen, to allow lateral movement of the armoured divisions. Responsibility for conducting the move was then devolved to HQ VIII Corps. Brigadier Sir Henry Floyd, Brigadier General Staff VIII Corps, and his staff planned the selection, signing and policing of routes, to ensure a continuous flow of traffic. They also organized for recovery of broken-down vehicles and re-routing in the event of a route becoming blocked. It must have been a staff officer's nightmare – and yet, with one or two inevitable hiccups, it worked admirably.

The leading division, 11th Armoured, consisted of two brigades, 29th Armoured Brigade with three armoured regiments, each of sixty-five tanks, and a motor infantry battalion, and 159th Lorried Infantry Brigade with three infantry battalions each of about 800 men. On the night of 16/17 July 159th Brigade and the headquarters of 11th Armoured Division and 29th Armoured Brigade would move into the Orne bridgehead, to be concealed by first light on 17 July. It would clearly be impossible to hide the tanks and half-tracks of 29th Armoured Brigade in the area during daylight, so they would move to a holding area near Beuville just west of the Orne that night. They would lie up concealed there throughout the daylight hours of 17 July and then cross into the Orne bridgehead during the night 17/18 July, just a few hours before launching the attack south.

Behind 11th Armoured, Guards Armoured Division would move from its location near Bayeux, arriving at the Hermanville to Beuville road by dawn on 18 July, ready to cross the Orne as soon as 11th Armoured started its advance south. Still further behind, 7th Armoured was to move from its area north of Tilly-sur-Seulles, timed to reach the Hermanville to Beuville road at 6.45 am, by which time Guards Armoured should be moving forward towards the Orne bridges. To complicate things further two flanking divisions, 3rd Infantry on the left and 3rd Canadian Infantry on the right, also needed to be in place in the Orne bridgehead, ready to start their advances. By dawn on 18 July the Orne bridgehead would be so full of men and vehicles that even a random shell fired into the area must surely find a target.

All who took part in Operation GOODWOOD remember those two night moves. Captain Douglas Hutchison, second-in-command of A Squadron, 2nd Fife and Forfar Yeomanry, an armoured regiment in 29th Armoured Brigade:

'I shall always remember those two dreadful night moves. It had been rather dry weather, so our tanks churned up a terrific dust. Then there was a sort of misty drizzle that came down as we moved, so that when we arrived in our harbour area on the early morning of 17 July the tanks were absolutely covered, inside and out, with a fine muddy sludge. We had a hell of a job getting them all clean.'

If the moves were unpleasant for the tanks, they were even worse for the following motor infantry. Lieutenant David Stileman of 8th Rifle Brigade:

'We followed the tanks in our half-tracks and carriers. Much of the journey was along farm tracks and it really was most unpleasant. The choking volumes of dust made it impossible to see the route signs. The appalling grit and grime clogged ears, eyes, nose and throat – it was just like munching a never-ending

A half track and carrier. With a thin armoured skin on the sides, these open-topped vehicles were very vulnerable to shell-fire – and dust!'

oatmeal biscuit! It was with intense relief that early on 17 July we met up with our Harbour Party in a delightful orchard near Beuville. Immediately we set about camouflaging our vehicles, under the watchful eyes of some unmistakably artistic gentlemen. Ere long our efforts would have done justice to any float at the Lord Mayor's Show! We were all dead tired after the night's drive, but were delighted to welcome the ever-faithful Colour Sergeant Pratt, who arrived with the mail, daily papers and NAAFI supplies – all gratefully received. This included our first sight of English beer – most welcome and rapidly consumed. It proved to be a beneficial change from the Normandy cider and Calvados which was beginning to play havoc with the 'inner man' of some of the riflemen! Noel Bell, who had taken over command of G Company after Mick McCrea was wounded during EPSOM, told us all to get our heads down and then went off to receive orders from Colonel David Silvertop, CO 3rd Tanks. At about 4 pm we were roused from our blissful slumbers. Having given out formal orders to the platoon commanders, Noel then collected the whole company and briefed them all. Out came letters from home, cigarette packets and pencils, and the riflemen took down the details of the entire 'menu' – the bombing waves, artillery plan and so on. By doing this Noel made every rifleman a shareholder in the business, right from the start. Rested and fully briefed, morale was sky-high'

Major Bill Close, commanding A Squadron 3rd Royal Tank Regiment, was a veteran of many battlefields. As a sergeant in 1940 he had been one of few who escaped from Calais. Promoted to staff sergeant he had fought in some of the early desert battles, and also in Greece, where once again he had to escape. When the Germans overran the country Close and a few others walked across the Peleponnese, stole a small boat and sailed into the Aegean. Picked up by a British destroyer, they were bombed and then set ashore on Crete. After briefly joining the infantry defending Crete he and all other trained tank crew were ordered to try to get back to Alexandria – his third escape. By chance Close was still carrying his squadron's pay, so he 'bought' a small Greek boat and its family crew. Accompanied by about 100 others, he sailed half the length of the Mediterranean to Alexandria. His reward – promotion to squadron sergeant major. In mid 1942 he was commissioned in the field by the Commanding Officer of 3rd Royal Tanks, one Lieutenant Colonel Pip Roberts, and by the end of the North African campaign he was a major commanding A Squadron, an appointment which he was to hold until the end of the war. By then Close, who had been continually in action since May 1940, had been knocked-out of eleven tanks and wounded several times. Having been awarded a Military Cross in the desert he was to receive a bar to the award later in the North-West Europe campaign.

Major Bill Clos MC – 'at the front of every tank battle sinc the Crimea!' – commanded A Squadron 3rd Royal Tanks – photographed a a Captain in North Africa.

> 'On arrival in the first harbour area I told the tank crews to have a meal and get some rest. About 3 o'clock in the afternoon I was called to my CO's O Group. I then learned the details of Goodwood and that we in 3rd Tanks would be leading the attack, with my squadron on the right, B on the left and C in reserve, and with our friends of G Company 8th Rifle Brigade as our supporting infantry. We had seen some very good photographs of this area. I remember being pleased at the thought of operating in open country, after the close country of Operation EPSOM, west of the Orne. But of course we knew that good tank country was usually good tank-killing country too – not that that worried us too much. It would be nice to be at the front, following up closely behind the air and artillery bombardments. With luck we would be able to burst through the German defences before they recovered.'

While 29th Armoured Brigade lay up for the day in the orchards near Beuville, 159th Infantry Brigade had already crossed the Orne and moved into its concentration area near Ranville. Not for them the peaceful relaxation of a fine Normandy day, as Major Ned Thornburn, commanding D Company 4th Battalion The King's Shropshire Light Infantry, recalls:

> 'We arrived overnight 16/17 July to find an ever-increasing crowd of men and vehicles. Great emphasis had been placed on silence so as not to reveal our move to the enemy. We dug ourselves in before dawn in a swampy area near Ranville Church. The area was so small that our vehicles, heavily camouflaged, stood nose to tail. We shared this smelly location with a veritable army of mosquitoes which, encouraged by the sultry heat, plagued the life out of us for the next twenty-four hours. As Jack Clayton, commanding B Company said, "They died in their millions, but still they came on. Not a man but bore the marks of that affray." '

As soon as it was dark on 17 July 29th Armoured Brigade started its second move, across the Orne, towards its final assembly area. This proved to be just as trying as the first, and was accompanied by sporadic German shelling. By the time the regiments had reached their allocated areas even those who had taken full advantage of the day's sleep were again dog-tired. Captain Peter Walter, second-in-command of C Squadron, 23rd Hussars, had been an actor before the war. Like many, Normandy was his first campaign and Operation EPSOM had been his first taste of battle.

> 'I suppose that I could be described as the complete antithesis of the gallant Bill Close. He was a professional soldier and, as far as I can see, he had been at the front of every tank battle since the Crimean War! I, on the other hand, was not a soldier at all. I had simply joined up for the duration – and that went for most of us in 23rd Hussars. In view of my background I suppose it was natural that the colonel should appointment me as regimental camouflage officer. I attended a marvellous course run by the well-known stage designer, Oliver Messell. So my first job for GOODWOOD was to run the regimental harbour party for those two night moves. I went ahead by day and set out the next harbour area, and the rest of the regiment followed that night. But when they got their heads down next day, I was off again on my next recce. Following two days and nights on the go, I was, by the start of GOODWOOD, feeling distinctly short of kip. This didn't worry me too much because this was clearly to be an important show, which is probably why I found myself as second-in-command of the reserve squadron of the reserve regiment! I thought that my place at the back of this vast tank armada would give me an ample chance to catch up with some kip. I planned to tell my driver, a splendid cockney, Trooper "Mush" Wright, to "Follow that tank". I would then let down my seat in the turret and have a little snooze.'

Leading the second night move was Major Bill Close:

> 'We arrived in the assembly area at about 1 o'clock in the morning, and found the area crammed full of crashed gliders from the airborne drop on D-Day. In the dark they seemed like ghostly outlines; it really was a most weird sight. At about 2.30 am Noel Bell, G Company Commander, and I walked down to recce the route through the minefield. I remember the smartly dressed Provost staff, who were able to show us the taped lanes, so I was quite happy that we would have no problems getting through. I returned to the squadron, gave final orders to my crews, got them into their tanks and, just before first light, we moved slowly down towards the minefield.'

Chapter 7

'DRIVER, ADVANCE'

Lack of space meant that Brigadier Roscoe Harvey's 29th Armoured Brigade would have to advance with only one armoured regiment forward in the early stages. Each of his three armoured regiments had a motor company from 8th Rifle Brigade, to provide infantry support, and an artillery battery from 13th Regiment Royal Horse Artillery (Honourable Artillery Company). 3rd Royal Tank Regiment would lead, with G Company and H Battery, and with additional support from a squadron of flail (mine-clearing) tanks of 22nd Dragoons and a troop of engineers from 26th Assault Engineer Squadron. Immediately behind would come Harvey's own tactical headquarters, followed by 2nd Fife and Forfar Yeomanry with F Company and I Battery, and finally 23rd Hussars with H Company and G Battery. Only after crossing the first railway line just south of Démouville would the ground widen out sufficiently for Harvey to be able to bring the Fife and Forfar Yeomanry up into line alongside 3rd Tanks. Thereafter he would advance on a two regiment front, with 23rd Hussars held in reserve behind, to be called forward when needed.

Shortly before dawn the infantrymen of 51st (Highland) Division, who were holding the southern sector of the Orne bridgehead from which the attack would be launched, were quietly withdrawn 1,000 yards north, to ensure that they were not at risk from wayward bombs. Then at 5.45 am on 18 July, led by marker planes of the Pathfinder Force, the RAF's heavy bombers arrived over the battlefield. Major 'Monkey' Blacker, second-in-command of 23rd Hussars, watched events unfold:

'Dawn broke mistily on 18 July; it was obviously going to be another gloriously sunny day. Gradually, as the light grew stronger, we could see the whole armoured brigade drawn up in its full battle array. Tanks, guns, half-tracks, carriers – it really was a most impressive, indeed thrilling sight. As the mist rolled away we heard in the distance the drone of a vast number of bombers. And then, appearing over the horizon behind us and coming in an apparently never-ending stream, were the big black Lancasters of the RAF, while high above them Spitfires twisted and rolled. The bombers passed over our heads and began to unload their bombs on the villages which flanked our advance. Immediately the whole area erupted in grey and brown clouds of dust which completely obscured our view. Next came the Marauders, the medium bombers, white and glistening in the sun, flying straight down the middle of the corridor, dropping fragmentation bombs along the path of our advance. Again the whole area disappeared in a tremendous swirl of dust. By this time all the chaps were tremendously excited, waving, cheering and shouting at the tops of their voices. And then tragedy – one of the Marauders dropped a bomb short and killed a complete crew. This sobered everyone up. We settled down into our tanks and got ready to advance.'

Most of those who witnessed the bombing would agree with Lance Corporal Farmer of F Company, 8th Rifle Brigade, attached to 2nd Fife and Forfar Yeomanry, waiting on the start line:

> 'Surely nothing and nobody could survive this. No-one who saw this raid will ever forget it. Paris next stop, surely!'

Although many Germans did indeed survive and fight vigorously throughout the three days of GOODWOOD, the immediate effect of being under that immense bombardment was profound. Lieutenant Richard von Rosen commanded 3 Company, 503rd Heavy Tank Battalion, stationed in the grounds of the Chateau de Manneville, near Emiéville, on the east flank of the planned armoured advance. Commanded by Captain Rolf Fromme, the battalion, which had arrived in Normandy from the Russian front in early July, had not been identified by British Intelligence. It had three companies, each consisting, in theory, of fourteen tanks; 1 Company equipped with the vast sixty-nine ton King Tiger MkVII tank, 2 and 3 Companies with the no less formidable MkVI Tiger, each armed with two machine-guns and one 88mm gun, the most formidable anti-tank weapon of the entire war. On 18 July von Rosen had twelve tanks serviceable, in well-concealed positions in the grounds of the chateau. Sited a few miles behind the front, they were tasked, as von Rosen described it, as 'an intervention reserve'. The crews had dug fox-holes underneath their vast tanks, and must have felt entirely safe from any bombardment. Most of them were asleep when the bombers arrived. Von Rosen's account of the next few hours is graphic indeed:

> 'I was awakened early in the morning by engine noise, and saw the first bomber waves approaching. From then on we were subjected to heavy air bombardment which lasted for two and a half hours without interruption. It was like hell, and I am astonished that I survived it. I was unconscious for a while after a bomb exploded just in front of my tank, almost burying me alive. Another tank, about

A Mk IV tank overturned by the bombing which preceded GOODWOOD.

thirty yards away, received a direct hit, which set it on fire instantly. A third was turned upside down by the blast – a Tiger weighed fifty-eight tons and yet it was tossed aside like a playing card. It shows what sort of hell we found ourselves in. It was so nerve-shattering you couldn't even think.

'Then suddenly the bombing ended and the following silence was uncanny. Two Tigers were completed destroyed, and two so severely damaged that they could not be used. All the rest were completely covered by earth and had to be dug out. The engines were full of dust and the air-cooling systems were not functioning. All weapons were put out of adjustment by the shock effect. Fifteen men in my company were dead. Two, who could not stand the terrific nervous strain of the bombardment, had committed suicide. Another had become insane and had to be sent to an asylum.

'The bombing was followed by heavy fire, but this came almost as a relief, although the shells fell all around us. Eventually I received orders to establish a defence line south of Manneville park. After about an hour's work we had the majority of the tanks combat-ready. The move to our new position was very difficult because the whole area was full of craters – some as wide as fifteen metres. In my view this was the worst day of the entire war, and I say that in spite of three years of war in Russia.'

* * * *

At 6.10 am, under cover of the bombing, 3rd Royal Tanks started to move forward towards the minefield gaps, through which they passed without difficulty. In their wake followed G Company 8th Rifle Brigade, with Lieutenant David Stileman commanding the half-tracks of 11 Platoon:

'As we were about to move forward we were attacked by a swarm of mosquitoes. I think that had been feasting on the blood of the KSLI at Ranville and decided to change diet to the riflemen of G Company. They were a bonus we could well have done without, so we were delighted to get moving.'

Sherman tanks moving forward to the GOODWOOD start-line. In the background Ranville Church.

A Sherman tank negotiating, with difficulty, the narrow turning to Escoville, in Herouvillette, on the way forward to the start line. The beamed house was removed in the 1980s, and the road junction widened.

As the bombers wheeled away to return to England, so the ground in front of the waiting tanks erupted as more than 700 artillery guns opened fire. It was now 7.45 am – H Hour. Eight field regiments of 25-pounder guns started the rolling barrage, fired on a front of 2,000 yards and advancing at a speed of 150 yards per minute, while two field, six medium regiments of 5.5inch guns and two heavy regiments of 7.5inch guns fired on targets on the flanks of the armoured corridor. Meanwhile to the east, supporting I Corps' advance along the Bois de Bavant ridge, one field and three medium regiments opened up, while a further two medium regiments supported II Canadian Corps' advance on the west.

On the start line just south-west of Escoville by shortly after 7.00 am, most of the tank crews were ready. But somehow there always seems to be a mass of last-minute business to conduct just before launching an attack. Unfortunately one or two of the tank crews were outside their tanks when the barrage started, and a few artillery rounds fell short. Major Peter Burr, who had been a troop leader in the desert campaign and was now commanding the C Squadron of 3rd Tanks, was killed, as was Second Lieutenant Peter Pells, an eighteen year-old troop leader in A Squadron; tragic, and seemingly so avoidable, but that is the almost inevitable nature of the messy business of warfare.

'Move now.' The order echoed over 3rd Tanks' command radio net. And ' over the tank intercoms, 'Driver, advance.' Leading was A Squadron and Major Bill Close:

> 'I had nineteen tanks in the squadron, four troops of four tanks each and my HQ of three. For the most part we had 75mm guns on the tanks but each troop had one with the more powerful 17-pounder, the Firefly, the only weapon we had that would guarantee to knock out a German tank. With its different turret and longer gun barrel it was an obvious target for the German anti-tank gunners, so the two troops in front of me moved in arrowhead formation, with their Firefly tucked in behind.
>
> 'We set off after the barrage which advanced ahead of us. Control was fairly easy initially, but with the tremendous dust and the explosions only 100 yards ahead, it became increasingly difficult. Tanks were about thirty yards apart. I was in between and just behind my leading troops, with my third and fourth troops behind me. On my left was B Squadron. I suppose our regimental frontage was about 600 yards. Soon we met the first dazed and shaken German infantry who tried to give themselves up. We rather gaily waved them back where the motor platoons of G Company had their hands full rounding up parties of bewildered Germans and pointing them to the rear. I clearly remember seeing David Stileman behind me, like a florid cockerel marshalling his chicks. As we got level with Cuverville on our right there was a small amount of anti-tank fire, so I told my two right-hand troops to brass up the hedgerows with their machine guns, just to keep the enemy's heads down, while we pressed on towards the first railway line.'

Stileman and his half-tracks were just behind:

> 'Initially we just followed faithfully behind the tanks, with little to do except try to keep up and look after prisoners. This proved quite a problem as we could not spare men to shepherd them back. Fortunately in 11 Platoon we had the revered and popular Rifleman Grossman, the G Company tailor. His ancestors came from the Promised Land and he had no difficulty in persuading German prisoners, entirely properly but forcefully, to obey his instructions. Sadly he was killed two weeks later at the same time that I was clobbered.'

Commanding 4 Troop, A Squadron, was Sergeant 'Buck' Kite. A veteran of many battles, he had won the Military Medal in the desert and was to win a bar to it on GOODWOOD. Later in the war he was to win a second bar, an almost unique achievement:

> 'I was fairly surprised by the lack of opposition we encountered at the start. I could see the enemy's front line positions, but there was only spasmodic fire coming our way. Then suddenly I found myself looking down the barrel of a self-propelled anti-tank gun, with the crew and some infantry milling around. My heart was in my mouth for a minute or two until I realized that the bombing and barrage had done such a good job that the enemy were still too dazed to offer any resistance. We pushed on, knowing that the Rifle Brigade behind would mop them up, hopefully before they regained their senses and shot us up from the rear.'

Each regiment was organized in three waves. Following the two leading tank squadrons was the commanding officer's group, the Stuart tanks of the

Sergeant 'Buck Kite.

Reconnaissance Troop and a carrier platoon of infantry from the attached motor company of 8th Rifle Brigade. Wave three consisted of the reserve squadron, the rest of the motor company and the self-propelled artillery battery of 13th RHA.

Lieutenant Colonel David Silvertop had plenty of battle experience. He had won a Military Cross in the desert serving with the 14th/20th Hussars, before being posted to command 3rd Royal Tanks. Moving just behind A and B Squadrons, he was close enough to be able instantly to see what was happening ahead, but not so close that he would get sucked into the leading squadrons' battles. The art of command in battle is a very personal business which each commander must work out for himself. Soldiers are quick to judge their commanders. They will not respect the one who hangs too far back, seeming unwilling to face the dangers he requires of them. Nor will they feel comfortable with the other who always wishes to be at the very front, doing the job of the leading corporal. The really good battlefield commander has an innate ability of being at the right place at the right time, where he can 'read the battle' instantly, thus being able to bring his personality and influence to bear when and where it is needed. Somehow he always seems to appear just when his soldiers most want to see him. And once a commander has earned his soldiers' respect, they will follow him anywhere. Colonel Silvertop was just such a commander, as all those who served with him bear ready witness. [Sadly, he did not survive the war, being killed in Holland in early 1945.]

Silvertop needed two men at his elbow – Major Noel Bell of G Company 8th Rifle Brigade, to provide infantry to clear enemy positions which might impede the advance, and Major Bill Smyth-Osborne of H Battery 13th Royal Horse Artillery to bring down instant fire support where necessary. Throughout GOODWOOD their vehicles would never be more than a few yards from the colonel's tank. Silvertop watched A and B Squadrons set off after the artillery barrage.

The Reconnaissance Troop consisted of thirteen Stuart tanks, nicknamed Honeys, with Lieutenant Robin Lemon as second-in-command. A nineteen year-old whose arrival in the troop just before GOODWOOD was greeted with 'My God, they're bringing on the children!', this was to be Lemon's first taste of action. The Honey had a high turret and a rather ineffective 35mm gun. As Lemon put it, 'The HE shot could just about knock a brick out of a wall, while the AP shot could only ricochet off a tin chamber-pot'. But remove the turret, cover up the gap with metal engine plates from knocked-out Shermans and mount Browning machine-guns on the plates, and the Honey proved to be a fast and elusive reconnaissance vehicle, with a low silhouette which made it easy to conceal. Lemon was not far behind his colonel's command team:

'As we passed Cuverville and Démouville I remember having a machine gun shoot at several targets, though observation was difficult through the dust and smoke. At one point an aggressive German suddenly appeared out of the corn only a yard or two away from my tank. He had a grenade in his hand and

appeared to be about to throw it. I used my revolver for the first time, and in spite of our bumpy movement I think I cut him down because he fell and never came up. From then on my eyes were everywhere and my revolver immediately ready as a grenade could so easily be lobbed into our open hatch.'

At 8.05 am the leading squadrons reached the first railway which ran parallel to the Caen to Troarn road, just south of Démouville. This posed no significant problem for the tanks, but G Company's half-tracks and carriers found crossing it to be more difficult, until an Armoured Vehicle Royal Engineers [built on a Churchill tank chassis, the AVRE's 290mm petard mortar fired a powerful forty-pound high-explosive charge, nicknamed the 'Flying Dustbin', a distance of eighty yards], from 3rd Tanks attached engineer troop, blew holes in the bank. By now it was 8.30 am, and the artillery barrage had reached the end of its first phase, a line 300 yards south of the railway. The plan allowed for a fifteen minutes pause, to allow 2nd Fife and Forfar Yeomanry to cross the railway and come up in line with 3rd Tanks, before the barrage resumed in a south-westerly direction for a further 2,000 yards. The advance would then continue on a two regiment front, Fife and Forfar left, 3rd Tanks right. However, with the delay caused in crossing the railway, this all took rather longer than expected, so the pause in the artillery fire was extended for a further five minutes. Even then, the two leading regiments were not fully ready, and thereafter they found it increasingly difficult to catch up with the rolling barrage.

Meanwhile, the third phase of the air bombardment had started, with US planes dropping fragmentation bombs on all the villages along the Bourguébus ridge. And 159th Infantry Brigade was underway towards its unwelcome task of capturing Cuverville and Démouville.

M3 Stuart ' Honey' tanks moving forwards towards Escoville. An effective reconnaissance vehicle when the turret gun was removed.

Chapter 8

SLOW BUT SURE – CUVERVILLE AND DÉMOUVILLE

Brigadier Jack Churcher had commanded 1st Battalion The Herefordshire Regiment during Operation EPSOM. But following General Roberts' hasty removal of the commander of 159th Infantry Brigade, Churcher, who had performed well, had been promoted to command the brigade. GOODWOOD was to be his first operation in command, with the initial task, which Roberts had tried so hard to avoid, of capturing the small villages of Cuverville and Démouville. To provide some

Map 5. 159th Infantry Brigade's attack on Cuverville and Démouville.

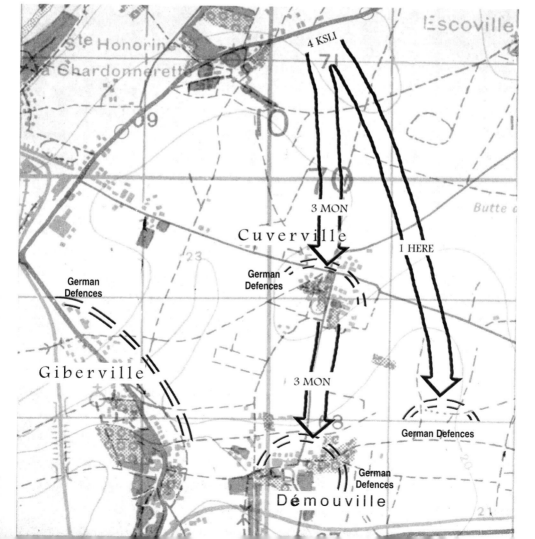

tank support for Churcher's brigade, Roberts gave him the Cromwell tanks of the divisional reconnaissance regiment, 2nd Northamptonshire Yeomanry.

Churcher planned a three phase operation. Phase One would be a two-battalion attack. On the right 3rd Battalion The Monmouthshire Regiment would capture Cuverville, with C Squadron 2nd Northants Yeomanry in support. On the left 1st Battalion The Herefordshire Regiment, supported by B Squadron, would bypass Cuverville to the west and capture a small orchard area about 500 yards south-east of the village, equidistant between Cuverville and Démouville. The plan for Phase Two, the capture of Démouville, was flexible. If the Monmouths encountered little or no opposition in Cuverville, they would continue straight on to Démouville. Similarily the Herefords must be ready to seize Démouville if they had captured the orchards unimpeded and the Monmouths were still dealing with Cuverville. The third battalion, 4th Battalion The King's Shropshire Light Infantry, would wait in reserve near the start line, but they, too, must be ready to pass through and take Démouville. A Squadron 2nd Northants Yeomanry was to provide west flank protection for these attacks, in particular preventing any enemy in the Giberville area from interfering. The start line for the advance was about 500 yards east of Ste Honorine La Chardonerette, just south of the Hérouvillette road.

At 7.45 am on 18 July 3rd Monmouths crossed the start line and advanced through the chest-high corn, supported by the tanks of C Squadron. By 8.45 am the leading companies, A and B, had entered Cuverville, having encountered nothing more than some hastily-evacuated trenches and a few scattered machine-gun posts, manned by soldiers who seemed so battered by the bombing that they were quite happy to surrender after only token resistance. As they were clearing the village they came under a brief but heavy artillery bombardment and sustained a few casualties. But by 10.20 am, and having taken more than fifty prisoners from 16th German Air Force Division, Lieutenant Colonel Hubert Orr reported to Churcher that Cuverville was secure.

Similarly 1st Herefords' advance went much as planned. The commanding officer, Lieutenant Colonel Bob Turner-Cain, recently promoted from second-in-command on Churcher's departure, first ordered D Company, with the tanks of B Squadron, to secure an almost imperceptible ridge about 800 yards east of Cuverville astride the Sannerville road. This area would then be the firm base for the rest of the battalion to pass through, cross the road, and, still supported by B Squadron, press on to secure the main objective, the orchards 500 yards further on.

D Company moved fast, and by 8.20 am reported that the ridge was secure. Turner-Cain quickly brought the rest of the battalion forward, through D Company and on towards the orchards, with two companies up, B right, C left. Lieutenant Ken Crockford was tasting action for the first time, having only recently arrived from England as a battle casualty replacement. The warmth of his welcome by C Company commander, Major Jack Phillips, rather surprised him, until it emerged that all the platoon commanders in C Company had been wounded during EPSOM. Only slightly disconcerted by this news, he assumed command of 15 Platoon:

> 'Having received the company commander's orders on 17 July, the enormity of the situation hit me. Here was I, aged twenty-one and one day, who had never seen a dead person, taking nearly forty soldiers, all of whom had recently been under fire and seen death and injury at close quarters, into action. Fortunately this was the first and last time such thoughts occurred. Thereafter I was far too busy to think about it.
>
> 'We were the left forward platoon and had advanced about 500 yards when there was a loud "crack" beside me. I glanced right and saw the upright body of a soldier, minus his head. He seemed to hover for a second or two before collapsing into the corn. It was impossible for the stretcher-bearers to locate casualties in the high corn, so the drill was that you stuck the casualty's rifle into the ground by the bayonet, with their steel helmet on top. Of course we had to push on. We advanced with two sections up, in arrowhead formation and platoon HQ in between. Suddenly shells began to fall between me and my reserve section, which was disconcerting, but caused no casualties, fortunately. On our way to the main objective we came upon about fifty of the enemy, most of them totally shell-shocked and keen to surrender. As we were

Cuverville – the battered remains of the village, after the battle.

disarming them a shell exploded in the trees above our heads. I was sent spinning to the ground by a large piece of wood, much to the amusement of some of the Germans, who were quickly "corrected" by Sergeant Lobb. We sent them to the rear and pressed on the final few hundred yards to the orchard. Having secured the objective without trouble, we immediately started to dig shell-scrapes.'

By 10.15 am Turner-Cain reported that his objective was secure and that he had taken over fifty prisoners. He, too, was ready for Phase Two.

In view of the ease with which the Phase One objectives had been taken, Churcher ordered 3rd Monmouths to be ready to push on to take Démouville. Although 11th Armoured Division's original Operation Order had stated that once Cuverville had been cleared 'it need not be held', for some inexplicable reason a plan had been made between the chiefs of staff of I and VIII Corps that a unit of 51st Highland Division would move up and relieve the Monmouths in the village before they moved on. This was surprising; it was also a pity. With 29th Armoured Brigade already several miles further south by the time Cuverville was taken, and with the Canadians and 3rd Infantry Division advancing on the flanks, there can have been no real threat of a German counter-attack on Cuverville.

At 10.45 am Orr reported that the Monmouths would have handed over Cuverville and be ready to launch Phase Two 'in about half an hour's time'. However, at about 11.00 am a German artillery concentration fell on Cuverville, just before the relieving Scotsmen were due to arrive in the village. Lieutenant Joe How was commanding a platoon in D Company which, having been in reserve for the attack, was brought forward to the village as soon as A and B Companies had cleared it:

'Suddenly very heavy artillery fire came down on us. Shells exploded against the sides of the house and in the rubble that lay everywhere, throwing bricks and shrapnel in all directions. A corporal standing beside me was hit and lay on the ground in great pain, shouting loudly. We had great difficulty putting him onto a stretcher as one leg was almost severed and caused him great pain when we moved him. He knew he was going to die and asked us to take off his gold ring and send it to his wife.'

In view of this fire Churcher decided that it would be foolish to risk two battalions being in the village at the same time. At 11.10 am, therefore, he ordered the relief to be postponed. Surprisingly, perhaps, he did not then amend his plan by ordering the Herefords, ready and waiting in the orchard area less than one mile away, to press on to Démouville. Nor did he call forward 4th KSLI, who were still back in the area of on the start line.

With the advantage of hindsight these might seem obvious options. Perhaps Churcher felt that 4th KSLI, whose commanding officer had also been removed during Operation EPSOM, and who were now temporarily in the hands of the second-in-command, Major Max Robinson, pending the arrival of a new colonel, should not be bounced into a sudden change of plan. Following Churcher's promotion, the Herefords were also under a

Démouville Church – infantrymen clearing the rubble of the village – and today.

new commander. Perhaps, in his first operation commanding a brigade, Churcher was feeling his way gently. Whatever the reason, having ordered 3rd Monmouths to take Démouville, he decided to stick to that plan rather than risk changing it.

It was not until 12.00 pm that 7th Battalion The Argyll and Sutherland Highlanders had taken over Cuverville. At 12.10 pm, therefore, the Monmouths set off again, with C Company left and D Company right. This time How was at the front of the attack:

'We were fired on almost immediately but ran forward. About 100 yards further on about a dozen German soldiers rose up from the corn and surrendered. We ran on and got into the village without further trouble, but C Company, on the left, had a hard time with an anti-tank gun and infantry in the gardens and houses on the edge of the village. My platoon was soon involved in confusing minor battles with German infantry amongst the ruins. I had some casualties from someone shooting from the church tower. I entered the church with a couple of men, found the door to the narrow winding stairs to the tower, and shouted in very bad German for whoever was there to come down. When I got no answer I started to climb, which was difficult as the stairs were old and worn and there was not much room for a big man in army equipment. About half-way up a noise made me stop, and two young German soldiers came down and surrendered, quite pleased that the war was over for them.

Lieutenant Colonel Huber Orr, command 3rd Monmouth He was killed Holland in September 194

It was difficult to keep control, even of a platoon, when fighting amongst the streets and gardens. German soldiers kept appearing – we fired at them, they fired at us, all very inaccurate and hurried. We pushed them back along the road towards Giberville but, as I had so few men, having lost touch with some of my platoon and the rest of the company, I did not get beyond the last farmhouse. Eventually the battalion concentrated at the southern edge of the village.'

By 2.30 pm Colonel Orr reported that they had secured the village and were mopping up. Meanwhile B Squadron 2nd Northants Yeomanry passed by and dealt with some infantry and anti-tank guns in the orchards just to the south.

Once Démouville was secure Churcher ordered 4th KSLI to move forward to a defensive position about half a mile east of the village. This was achieved without opposition, so by shortly after 3.30 pm 159th Brigade had secured all its objectives. Surprisingly, it was not until 5.10 pm that Churcher reported to Roberts that his brigade was ready to move forward to join the armoured advance.

A post-war photograph of Brigadier (late Major General Jack Churcher. Newly promoted to command 159t Infantry Brigade, he wa feeling his wa during GOODWOOD

In later years General Roberts, with typically self-critical modesty, said:

'I considered this operation to be something of a chore and to pose no real problems. So I left the brigade commander to his own devices. You could say that as it was his first operation in command of a brigade I should have held his hand a bit, but I honestly thought that there was no great problem. The most important thing was for 29 Armoured Brigade to get on quickly so that the other divisions could come up into line. So I went with the armour. If I

had been here I might have persuaded the brigadier to use one of his other battalions on Démouville, leaving the Monmouths in Cuverville. But I wasn't here! Anyway, this operation took a hell of a lot longer than it ought.'

The effect of this slow and rather laborious operation was that, as he had always feared, General Roberts did not have his infantry brigade available to help 29th Armoured Brigade clear some troublesome villages further ahead. As unfolding events will show things might have been very different if the battalions of 159th Brigade had been available to move forward from shortly after midday.

Cuverville and Démouville proved costly to the Germans. The battalions of 716th Infantry Division had been easily overrun in Cuverville and the leading companies of von Luck's 1st Battalion, having given a stern account of themselves in Démouville, had been wiped out. Lost with them were the guns of 1 Battery of Major Becker's 200th Assault Gun Battalion.

Military policemen interrogate German soldiers captured at Démouville.

* * * *

General Roberts was essentially a front-line commander. He was not one to sit back at his main headquarters relying on radio reports from his brigade commanders to keep him abreast of the progress of the battle. Leaving main division headquarters in the orchards near Amfréville he set off to follow the advance with a small tactical headquarters of just three tanks. In the bowels of his own tank was a staff officer to man the radios – the forward link to the brigade commanders and main headquarters and the rear link to O'Connor's VIII Corps Headquarters. The second tank was that of Brigadier Frizz Fowler, Commander Royal Artillery. Aged forty-five, Fowler was eight years older than the general, but an MC won in the First World War and a DSO in the desert campaign were proof that he was a highly experienced and efficient gunner officer. With him in his tank was his brigade major, manning the radios which controlled the vast artillery barrage. The third tank, commanded by Roberts' ADC, Captain Charles Pidduck, was the alternative command tank, available for Roberts to take over in the event of his own being hit or breaking down. In addition there was a protective troop of four tanks.

Following closely behind 29th Armoured Brigade this small group moved through the minefield, across the start line and paused briefly in the field just south. Ahead Roberts could see the rear of the armoured brigade passing to the left of Cuverville and moving on towards the first railway line just south of Démouville. To his right 3rd Monmouth were advancing through the high corn towards Cuverville:

'As soon as we halted we came under artillery fire, so we moved on a few hundred yards – and so did the fire. So we moved a few hundred yards left, and again the fire followed us. Indeed it became pretty intense, so much so that a piece of shrapnel sliced the CRA's mapboard, which was on top of his turret and just a few inches from his face, completely in two. He got a bit upset by this as he was trying to control our own artillery barrage, so I decided to move well forward towards the front of the battle, which was much quieter! We followed the tanks on past Démouville to a small hedgerow north of Le Mesnil Frémentel. Here I deployed the protective troop facing north where they had quite a good shoot at Germans in Démouville which of course had not yet been attacked by 159th Brigade.

'Now my ADC's main job in battle was navigation for my tactical HQ. But he had been terribly badly bitten by those wretched mosquitoes near the start line, and his eyes were almost completely closed. So I had to do the navigation. But when we halted near the hedgerow he suddenly jumped out of his tank, dived in to a nearby German slit-trench and emerged with a magnificent pair of Zeiss binoculars, just what I had been looking for for ages. So he was immediately returned to his normal duties!'

Chapter 9

A Thorn In The Side – Cagny

At 8.50 am the rolling barrage, having paused for twenty minutes just south of the first railway line to allow 29th Armoured Brigade to expand onto a two-regimental front, started to move forward again, now heading south-west. Behind it the advance resumed, with 3rd Royal Tanks on the right and 2nd Fife and Forfar Yeomanry on the left. Commanding the Fife and Forfar was Lieutenant Colonel Alec Scott. Like Silvertop in 3rd Tanks, Scott, who had also won an MC in the desert campaign, was a regular officer imported from the cavalry, in this case the 5th Royal Inniskilling Dragoon Guards. He deployed his regiment with two squadrons up, Major Sir John Gilmour's B Squadron on the left, Major John Powell's A Squadron on the right, while C Squadron under Major Chris Nicholls was in reserve.

Tucked in behind Scott's command group was Lieutenant Philip Noakes, the regimental Intelligence Officer, most of his work done in the build-up to the battle:

> 'I was in the RHQ scout-car, with the somewhat ill-defined instructions – "Keep up, keep in touch, be ready to identify prisoners." Identification would be important as confirmation of what enemy armour had been drawn onto our front and away from the Americans. Like traffic released at the lights, we were off, lurching, swaying, grinding along through dust and smoke, always trying to catch up with the artillery barrage – and never quite making it.'

By 9.05 am the artillery barrage had run its course, at a line running through the small hamlet of Le Mesnil Frémentel. From now on 29th Armoured Brigade must rely on the eighteen Sexton 25-pounder self-propelled guns of 13th Regiment, Royal Horse Artillery. Lieutenant Colonel Robert Daniell travelled with Brigadier Roscoe Harvey's small tactical HQ, while his battery commanders were never far from their respective armoured regimental commanders. Still further forward were Forward Observation Officers with the leading squadrons, in radio contact with the battery commander and the guns. These FOOs could also call on fire support from the 5.5inch Medium Regiments, still west of the Orne, whose longer range and greater hitting power could reach out to the Bourguébus ridge.

At 9.10 am HQ 11th Armoured Division informed HQ VIII Corps: 'Two leading armoured regiments crossed the railway south of Démouville. Third regiment crossing now. Infantry clearing up Cuverville.' This was followed fifteen minutes later by an equally cheerful message: 'Leading troops 800 yards north of Cagny; little opposition except infantry.' This was quickly conveyed to the army commander, General Dempsey, who had moved his tactical headquarters close to HQ VIII Corps in order to be in instant touch with the progress of the advance.

* * * *

Having crossed the first railway line without encountering any serious opposition, 29th Armoured Brigade had indeed broken through the first line of the German defences. Based on the Intelligence picture painted before the battle, those at the front must have felt that the Bourguébus ridge would shortly be secured without too much difficulty. But they were about to encounter unexpected resistance of an altogether different quality. Major Alfred Becker's 200th Assault Gun Battalion was now directly in the path of the British advance. Warned to expect an advance, Becker had, at 4.30 am, moved his tactical HQ forward to a position north of Cagny, near the track between Le Mesnil Frémentel and Le Prieuré. 1 Battery in Démouville had been badly mauled by the bombing and was about to be over run by 159th Infantry Brigade. But from 8.00 am onwards the battery commander, Captain Eichhorn, managed to provide Becker with a clear running commentary on the British advance as it passed east of the village. He reported a vast armada of tanks but, as far as he could see, no accompanying infantry (he seems not to have recognized the half-tracks and carriers of 8th Rifle Brigade as infantry). Becker had two batteries directly in the path of the advance. On the left was Captain Röpke's 4 Battery, with two sections, each of three 75mm guns, in the cornfields astride the Cagny road, between Le Mesnil Frémentel and Le Prieuré. The four 105mm guns of his third section were a few hundred yards back, concealed in the orchards along the northern edge of Cagny. On the right, Lieutenant Schreiner's 5 Battery was well concealed in the then-extensive orchards of Le Prieuré, with the four 105mm guns at the track junction about 500 yards south of the hamlet.

Although an outstanding engineer, battlefield command was not, by all accounts, Becker's forté. But he was supported by excellent battery commanders, who he played 'on a loose rein'. His instructions to Schreiner and Röpke left much to their own initiative, 'withdraw into Cagny if necessary'. Learning from Eichhorn that the advancing tanks were not accompanied by infantry will have been reassuring. His batteries had the weapons to destroy advancing tanks, and they knew all the best fire positions in the area. What they could not withstand would be an infantry attack. Fortunately for them, none seemed likely.

* * * *

Following the direction of the artillery barrage 11th Armoured Division's axis now swung south-west. On the right 3rd Tanks passed west of Le Mesnil Frémentel. They could see German troops in the hamlet, but, as the enemy's fire was only light and spasmodic, the tanks brassed up the hedgerows and swept by. Colonel Silvertop was keen to push on, and by 9.20 am his leading squadrons had reached the Caen-Vimont road. About 400 yards ahead was the second railway line and beyond it they could see the orchards surrounding the small village of Grentheville. On their left, 2nd Fife and Forfar Yeomanry also made excellent progress, its leading squadrons passing

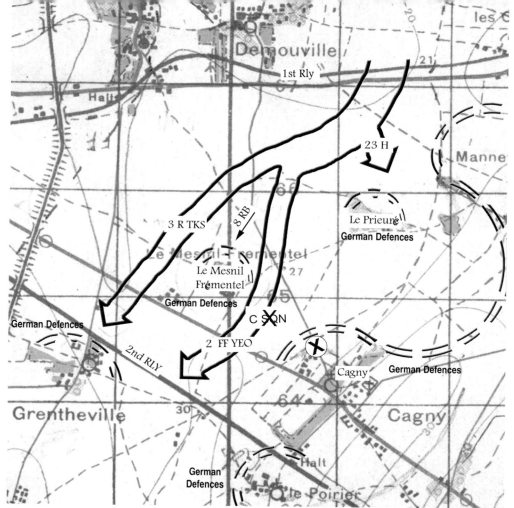

Map 6. 29th Armoured Brigade's advance to the 2nd railway showing where C Squadron 2nd Fife and Forfar Yeomanry was destroyed by 88mm AA guns deployed by von Luck at X. Also shown is the attack by 8th Rifle Brigade on Le Mesnil Frémentel.

between Le Mesnil Frémentel and Cagny without difficulty. By 9.35 am both regiments reported that they had reached the second railway line.

While the two leading regiments were crossing the second railway 23rd Hussars, in reserve, were just clearing the first and trying to catch up. Major Patrick Wigan's A Squadron was on the left:

> 'We were moving forward when my leading troop commander reported Tiger tanks in the area of Le Prieuré, a small hamlet surrounded by orchards about half a mile on our half-left.'

This posed something of a problem for the Hussar's commanding officer, Lieutenant Colonel Perry Harding. The orders were to press on and avoid getting caught up in local time-consuming skirmishes, but he could hardly neglect the threat of Tiger tanks, of which Intelligence had given no indication, on his left flank. He ordered A Squadron to provide fire support, while C Squadron, hitherto in reserve, tried to outflank the enemy and force them to withdraw. Major Bill Shebbeare moved C Squadron slightly east, but then came under fire from the woods east of Le Prieuré. Any movement further east risked the danger of being drawn away from the main axis of advance and becoming sucked into a battle with tanks and anti-tank guns which should become the responsibility of the later divisions. Shebbeare halted his squadron, and for the next hour and a half 23rd Hussars carried out its own private shooting match with Schreiner's 5 Assault Gun Battery, well concealed in the orchards of Le Prieuré. Doubtless it was glimpses of the high profiles of these unusual guns which had led Major Wigan's leading troop commander to report the presence of Tiger tanks. At this stage the Tigers of Lieutenant von Rosen were still trying to dig themselves out of the post-bombing morass.

Eventually Schreiner's battery was forced to pull back to Cagny, but not before 23rd Hussars had lost two tanks. While Shebbeare was directing the fire of C Squadron onto Le Prieuré, his second-in-command, Captain Peter Walter, looked ahead:

> 'I got my glasses out and started scanning the whole area, when suddenly I saw a most horrific sight. Pretty well the entire rear squadron of the Fife and Forfars, which was just about a mile ahead of us, suddenly went up in a sheet of flames, almost simultaneously.'

Colonel Scott of 2nd Fife and Forfar Yeomanry had planned that once A and B Squadrons had crossed the second railway line, he would pass C Squadron through, to lead the assault onto the Bourguébus ridge. C Squadron's initial advance, tucked in behind the leading squadrons, should have been safe and straightforward. And yet it had suddenly turned into an unexpected and blazing nightmare, with a dozen tanks hit in just a few horrifying minutes. The first tank to be hit was Major Nicholls', followed shortly by that of his second-in-command, Captain Miller. Among those caught up in this mayhem was Lance Corporal Ron Cox, a young radio operator in 3 Troop:

The heart of the GOODWOOD battlefield. 2nd Fife Forfar Yeomanry of 11th Armoured Division crossed left to right, between Cagny and Le Mesnil Frémentel. Guards Armoured Division's advance was halted between Chateau de Manneville woods and Le Prieuré 2nd Grenadier Guards eventually captured Cagny attacking from Le Prieuré.

CHATEAU DE MANNEVILLE WOODS   LE PRIEURÉ

GDS ARMD DIV'S DIRECTION OF ADVANCE   11TH ARMD DIV'S DIRECTION OF ADVANC

'I did not see Major Nicholls' tank hit; it was out of sight of my periscope. But I did see what happened to the 2ic's tank. It brewed as soon as it was hit, and the three turret crew baled out, the gunner and radio operator both with their clothes smouldering. Then Lieutenant Sammy Millar, our troop leader, whose tank was halted just in front of us, was the next to be hit. Our crew commander, Sergeant Wally Herd, could see the carnage going on around him as he stood huddled down with his head just above the turret. My view, through the periscope, was more limited. I sat glued to the eyepiece; there was nothing else to do. There were no identifiable targets to engage, so no gun loading to be done; nothing intelligible was coming over the radio. And it hardly seemed the moment for my other normal duty – making the tea and spreading jam on biscuits! The whole crew remained perfectly calm and almost totally silent, apart from the occasional "Bloody hell!" as another tank went up.

'After what seemed hours but was probably only a few minutes Wally Herd, whose coolness, I'm sure, saved our lives that day, ordered "Driver, reverse." The tension was electrifying. I remember thinking "Good old Wally, he's getting us out." There was absolutely no cover, except the uncertain billows of smoke that might obscure us one moment and reveal us the next. Suddenly there was a tremendous crash and the tank shuddered and rocked. The driver, Charlie Kent, came over the intercom "We've been hit; track broken." We were now stranded, in the sights of a German gun. The next shot would surely follow as soon as the gunner had reloaded. Still retaining his imperturbability, Wally gave the order for the gun to be turned, thus moving it from being over Charlie's hatch flap, and ordered "Bale out", as calmly as if on an exercise. We crouched behind the tank, relieved that all of us were unhurt. As we were deciding which way to go the tank was hit a second time – on the left hand side, just where I had been sitting.'

It was ironic that the first tank to be hit should be that of the squadron leader, Major Nicholls. When Montgomery had insisted that each of those regiments that had not yet been in action should have at least one battle-experienced squadron/company commander, Nicholls, who had served with The Staffordshire Yeomanry in the North Africa, was posted into 2nd Fife and Forfar Yeomanry. His was the voice of experience, there to help those tasting the brutality of war for the first time. And he had been a splendid selection.

CAGNY   C SQN 2FF YEO DESTROYED   BOURGUÉBUS RIDGE   LE MESNIL FRÉMENTEL
IN FIELD HERE   (in distance)

He had quickly earned the trust and respect of his men, and at Operation EPSOM had shown a confidence in command which had greatly impressed them. They knew that they could rely on his judgement and his tactical reading of the battlefield. But now, just at the moment that he was most needed, Nicholls was dead, and his second-in-command, Captain Miller, was also knocked out. C Squadron, with twelve of its tanks burning and devoid of leadership, played no coherent part in the rest of Operation GOODWOOD.

Just ahead of C Squadron, in the regimental scout-car, Lieutenant Philip Noakes was finding it difficult keeping up with his colonel's group:

'Suddenly two tanks on the left were hit; they must have been C Squadron. They just stopped and blew up as only a Sherman could. It wasn't christened "the Tommy Cooker" for nothing. Then more ominous columns of smoke to left and right. Clearly the German tanks and anti-tank guns, so neatly marked in chinagraph on my map, were there alright, waiting for us charging forward towards them "like bloody driven grouse" as Sergeant Hutcheson so picturesquely put it from the bowels of the scout-car. I just hoped that scout-cars were out of season, or too small.

'Scout-cars are not good over rough country, ditches and banks – and they're dreadful over railway lines. Sergeant Hutcheson had somehow bounced us over the first railway line, but now, on the second we came to a grinding halt, firmly stuck on the lines, totally exposed to fire from any direction. The driven grouse had suddenly become the sitting duck! I jumped out to inspect the damage. The main shaft was broken and the rear axle bent. I went round to the front of the scout-car to speak to Sergeant Hutcheson, when, to my complete surprise, something hit me very hard in the face, fortunately at such an angle that the bullet went through my parted lips, across my lower jaw and out through my left cheek. I felt more affronted than anything else.

'By now the leading squadrons and RHQ were out of sight, so I reported my vehicle and myself as casualties on the regimental net. There was an ominous silence. I doubt whether anyone heard. As we took stock of a thoroughly unpromising situation, just to our left another Sherman blew up. Hit amidships, there was a terrific explosion, with flames and smoke wooshing up from the turret. A few seconds later out popped the flaming torch of a man, Trooper Sedgebeer. Sergeant Hutcheson and I seized the fire-extinguisher from our scout-car, rushed over to him and sprayed him from head to foot. Somehow we managed to put him out. He was horribly burnt. It was impossible to get near the burning tank, which was already beginning to glow. There was no chance of any other survivors. This frenzied activity had rather taken my mind off my own problem, but I was bleeding copiously and beginning to feel rather light-headed.

'Then one of our tanks arrived heading north, crammed with wounded. It was still a runner but I think it had a bent gun. We bundled Sedgebeer onto it and I clambered on too. I hung on to a side-rail with one hand and Sedgebeer with the other as we lurched our way north. We passed several smouldering Shermans. And there was the all-pervading, never-to-be forgotten smell of the

Normandy battlefield – the reek of hot metal, the stench of dead animals, acrid smoke and the sickly sweet smell of growing corn crushed under tank tracks. Eventually we reached the regimental aid post, where I handed over Sedgebeer and I was patched up a bit.'

Noakes described his evacuation to England as 'the model of efficiency'. It was to prove far harder to return to his regiment, having recovered from his wound. A few days after he rejoined them in November he received the following letter:

29/11/44

Dear Sir,

For the past few months I have tried to get in touch with you and now I am informed by one of my pals from A Squadron that you are now back with the regiment. On 18 July I was lucky enough to escape from a tank, in which I was the only survivor. I was badly burned and eventually brought to England. After numerous skin and bone grafts I am now almost normal, although I have lost my right hand.

However, my purpose in writing this is that at all the hospitals I have been told that I owe my life to the prompt action taken at the time of the accident. Perhaps you don't remember assisting me in any way because, after all, I was only one injured person among thousands, but during my stay in hospital I have had lots of time to think over the last few months, and I would like to take this opportunity to express my very sincere thanks for your assistance on that fatal day.

It is possible that I may never see you again, and a letter of thanks does not compensate my debt to you, but in the future I hope that you are always given that help which you so readily gave me.

I am just learning to write with my left hand and I trust you are able to read it.

All the very best of luck.
Yours very sincerely,

J Sedgebeer.

* * * *

Colonel Hans von Luck missed the start of GOODWOOD. A few days earlier he had been summoned to HQ I SS Panzer Corps where General Sepp Dietrich had told him that he had been awarded the Knight's Cross and that he was to take a few days leave. Von Luck, who expected a British attack very shortly, protested that he would prefer to remain with his battle group. But his protestations were swiftly over-ridden. 'So, having filled my car with Normandy produce, I set off for Paris, for a few days with my "femme de chambre".'

Shortly after dawn on 18 July von Luck left Paris to return to Normandy. It was a fine sunny morning. At about 8.45 am he drove down the slope from

Vimont towards his HQ at Frénouville. All seemed quiet and peaceful, though he kept a wary eye out for the ever-present Typhoon aircraft which made movement so dangerous for the Germans. He could see some dust in the distance, perhaps from the wind or routine British artillery fire. After a leisurely breakfast he would change into his battle uniform and re-assume command:

'What I found was quite different. I asked the commander of my 1st Battalion, who I had left in command, for a report on what was happening. He told me about the tremendous bombing and the attack. I asked him about news from the battalions or from the tanks, but he knew nothing. I asked if he had sent out patrols to try to find out the situation, but he had done nothing. I immediately relieved him of command, sent for my Mk IV tank and drove to Cagny, hoping to get over to the HQ of my 1st Battalion in Le Mesnil Frémentel. As I came out from the village, through the orchards, the sight I saw was absolutely disappointing. I saw thirty to forty British tanks which were crossing the main road out of Cagny and advancing towards the railway line. It was immediately clear that this was a break-through and that there was now a large gap between my left flank and 192 Regiment south-west of Caen.

'I couldn't get any radio contact with Division, nor with my 2nd Battalion, nor with the tanks at Emiéville, so I decided to return to my HQ. As I drove back through Cagny I saw a battery of 88mm anti-aircraft guns in position near the church, with their guns pointing up in the air. It must have been part of the screen of anti-aircraft guns we had round Caen. I stopped and went to see the

Colonel Hans von Luck. This was taken shortly before GOODWOOD – with his adjutant.

commander, a Captain. "What are you doing here?" I asked. "I am looking for aircraft to shoot at," he replied. "Do you know what is happening on the left flank outside Cagny?" I asked. "No," he replied, "that is your job. I am under Air Force command." I informed him of the situation and ordered him to get into position immediately and to fight the British tanks. And I got a flat refusal. So I took out my little pistol and I asked him whether he would like to be killed or to get a decoration. And he decided for the latter. So I gave him clear orders to take his guns to the north edge of Cagny and to shoot the tanks. And I told him quite clearly "In half an hour I will be back."

'I returned to my HQ and tried to contact my divisional commander, General Feuchtinger, but I could get no communications. So I contacted the CO of my 2nd Battalion and told him to build up a strong defensive screen on the right flank, between Emiéville and Cagny. I also saw Major Becker and told him to co-operate with the 2nd Battalion. And I sent a young officer to see what had happened to the tanks. I said that if any tanks were available they were to reinforce the screen, which they did later on. And I sent a section of my HQ Company to reinforce the 88s in Cagny.

'I then returned to Cagny to see what was going on. I found the battery in full action and absolutely fascinated in what they were doing. There were many tanks burning and more withdrawing slowly north. I told the captain that if he was heavily attacked by infantry or tanks he should destroy his guns and

German Mk IV tank, with the Mk V Panther, the backbone of German Panzer Divisions. Colonel von Luck commanded his battle group from a Mk IV tank.

withdraw. Finally I returned to my HQ and informed the divisional commander about the situation. I told him that I was very concerned about the area Frénouville – Vimont and asked for assistance to secure this sector. But he told me that was not possible – the recce and engineer battalions of the division were involved protecting the artillery and anti-tank guns on the Bourguébus ridge.'

It must have been the leading squadrons of 2nd Fife and Forfar Yeomanry that von Luck saw as he tried to make his way to Le Mesnil Frémentel. By the time he had 'encouraged' the 88mm battery to join the battle, these squadrons had moved on to the second railway line, and it was C Squadron which took the full force of the German fire.

In fact the issue is not quite so clear cut as von Luck's story suggests. It must be remembered that he had been away from the battlefield for several days, and that the briefing he received on return, from a deputy whose inaction had led to his removal, was doubtless shallow and incomplete. It seems likely that von Luck was unaware of the locations of Becker's guns.

Trying to reconstruct the jigsaw of a battle inevitably requires an element of conjecture. Alerted by Eichhorn that the British tanks were advancing south, bypassing Demouville to the east, Becker and his battery commanders will have been watching carefully. They could hardly have missed the vast columns of dust thrown up by the rolling barrage and the following tanks. Before the leading tanks reached the area Becker had withdrawn his command vehicles into Cagny. It seems entirely logical that, in accordance with his instructions, Röpke had also withdrawn his 75mm sections, moving to join the 105mm section in the cover of the orchards north of Cagny. From Eichhorn's reports it was clear that the British were moving fast, bypassing villages as they went. The cover provided by the orchards of Cagny would be the ideal place from which to engage them as they swept by.

Perhaps Röpke's 75mm sections were still moving into position as the leading squadrons of the Yeomanry passed. But it seems highly likely that his battery of ten powerful anti-tank guns, manned by battle-experienced men, played some significant part in the destruction of C Squadron.

* * * *

Not far behind the advance the divisional commander, General Roberts, was, as ever, keeping a close eye on the progress of 29th Armoured Brigade. Brigadier Harvey had his tactical HQ in a small clump of trees just north of Le Mesnil Frémentel. Roberts joined him there:

'Shortly after this incident I came up to see Roscoe Harvey. The Fife and Forfar squadron was burning in the field ahead and there was quite a lot of mortaring coming down in the area of the village in front. As I arrived I heard Alec Scott of the Fife and Forfar tell the Brigadier that he was ordering his motor company of 8th Rifle Brigade to attack Cagny. He was pretty certain that the fire had come from there. But you will remember that I had specifically asked to be relieved from having to take Cagny. We had 23rd Hussars in reserve looking

75mm (short) of Major Becker's 200th Assault Gun Battalion – capable of knocking out any British tank.

after the left flank until the Guards Armoured arrived very shortly. So I told Harvey to cancel any attack by the motor company and to concentrate on getting forward onto the Bourguébus ridge. Hans von Luck says that at the time the village was held by only a battery of 88s. Had I not told Harvey to cancel the attack, the company would have virtually walked straight into Cagny. In the event it was to take the Guards the rest of the day to capture the village after a considerable battle. How unfortunate it was that I arrived just in time to cancel Scott's attack, but that is the sort of thing that happens in war'.

The facts about Röpke's battery being in Cagny only emerged after General Roberts' death. But even if F Company 8th Rifle Brigade might not have had the easy walk into Cagny that he envisaged, they would surely have secured the western part of the village. This would have been an invaluable lever for the guardsmen who were just arriving in the area and for whom Cagny was to prove a tough nut.

There frequently comes a moment in battle when the situation changes, suddenly and dramatically. This was just such a moment. So often the presence of one man, of any rank, who seizes the pendulum of battle and pulls it firmly his way, seems to affect the whole course of events. It is perhaps too much to suggest that von Luck's actions alone prevented GOODWOOD from becoming the tactical success for which its authors hoped, but there is no doubt that the withering fire which destroyed C Squadron 2nd Fife and

Forfar Yeomanry in front of Cagny, had a marked effect on the subsequent course of the battle. Commenting on the battle in later years General Roberts always emphasized how unfortunate it was that he lost his argument about having to leave 159th Infantry Brigade to capture Cuverville and Demouville, but won it over not having to take Cagny. Had it been the other way round; had he had his infantry brigade tucked in behind the tanks, available to be committed quickly when required, Roberts had little doubt that Cagny would have been captured by midday or soon after. As it was, it was evening before the village was taken.

The effect of Cagny holding out until the late evening was that the Guards Armoured Division never managed to clear the centre of the battlefield and swing south-east towards Vimont. Behind them, 7th Armoured, which should have come up in between 11th and Guards, hopefully by late morning or early afternoon, never joined the battle that day. In consequence the Germans were able to concentrate their reserves, which they brought forward very quickly, along a front of just three miles, facing 11th Armoured Division at the western end of the Bourguébus ridge, instead of having them strung out thinly against three armoured divisions in full cry, along a ten mile front. History is full of 'if onlys', but, as GOODWOOD was to play such an important part in Montgomery's reputation, it is intriguing to imagine what might have happened had Cagny fallen by midday or shortly after on 18 July.

Chapter 10

UNORTHODOX SUCCESS – LE MENSIL FRÉMENTEL

Although 29th Armoured Brigade bypassed the villages as it pushed on rapidly towards the Bourguébus ridge, Brigadier Roscoe Harvey was naturally concerned about the small hamlet of Le Mesnil Frémentel. 2nd Fife and Forfar Yeomanry had passed left of it and 3rd Royal Tanks, passing to the right, had lost two tanks from anti-tank weapons concealed in the orchards. Harvey decided that he could not leave it uncleared, an island of opposition in the mainstream of his advance, posing a real threat to the soft-skinned logistic vehicles which must get forward quickly and safely to resupply the tanks further forward after dark. Clearly the small hamlet must be taken. Harvey therefore ordered 23rd Hussars to clear the area with the minimum of delay. But Colonel Harding replied that his regiment was already fully occupied with the enemy at Le Prieuré; he could not undertake another operation at the same time. Harvey therefore had no option other than to call on Lieutenant Colonel Tony Hunter of 8th Rifle Brigade.

Aged only twenty-eight, this was to be Hunter's first operation in command. His arrival, in early July, following the departure of the previous commanding officer after Operation EPSOM, had caused a minor stir to Lieutenant David Stileman:

> 'I saw this youth advancing towards me. Assuming that he was
> a replacement subaltern, after our EPSOM casualties, I was
> about to address him in familiar subaltern terms, when I
> noticed, at the last minute, that the top 'pip' on his shoulder
> was in fact a crown and that he already wore the ribbons of MBE
> and MC won in the desert campaign. I was therefore dutifully polite
> to my new commanding officer!'

The commanding officer of a motor battalion in an armoured advance like GOODWOOD has very few toys with which to play. None of Hunter's three rifle companies was available to him. They were forward, under command of the three armoured regiments, each with sections of the anti-tank and mortar platoons from Support Company. Flexibility is one of the key principles of war, and Hunter was about to prove this point. Ordered to take Le Mesnil Frémentel with whatever force he could lay his hands on, he collected a distinctly ad hoc team. The infantry element was formed by the two medium machine-gun platoons, about twenty men each, from Major Tony Rowan's Support Company and a few men that Hunter could spare from his own headquarters. For armoured support he borrowed the squadron of flail tanks of 22nd Dragoons which General Roberts admits that he had somewhat

The Sherman 'flail' tank, though not needed for minefield clearance, had a gun which was used to real effect during 8th Rifle Brigade's attack on Le Mesnil Frémentel.

reluctantly agreed to accept:

> 'Shortly before the battle General Hobart, who commanded 79th Armoured Division, came to see me and said that he hoped I was taking some of his flail tanks. I told him that I wasn't, as I did not expect there to be any mines. "My dear boy, you'll look pretty stupid if the whole advance gets held up because of mines," he said. I was pretty confident that there wouldn't be any – after all the Germans had been running all over that bit of country for weeks. But Hobo had been a major general commanding an armoured division, and a pretty terrifying one at that, at the beginning of the war when I was only a captain. Admittedly we were now the same rank, but it seemed much simpler to agree! I couldn't think what we would use them for, but actually they proved very useful to 8 RB at Le Mesnil Frémentel, though not as mine-clearers!'

Mounted on a Sherman tank, flails normally beat a path through minefields, exploding the mines with heavy chains which rotated on a drum held by two arms well in front of the tank. But they also had a 75mm gun. Hunter was to use this to good effect. He also managed to acquire the 75mm self-propelled anti-tank guns of 119 Anti-tank Battery, Royal Artillery, and a troop of AVREs from 26 Assault Squadron, Royal Engineers. For none of this motley force was the clearing of an enemy held village a normal operation.

At 10.30 am the attack went in. The machine-gun platoons, mounted in their carriers, advanced from the north, using the cover of a thick hedge. On the flanks the flail tanks provided excellent supporting fire with their machine-guns. The scene was one of considerable devastation. Huge craters littered the area and many of the trees that had received direct hits, either from the bombing or the rolling artillery barrage had either been uprooted or blown to pieces. It seemed unlikely to Captain Nat Fiennes, Hunter's adjutant, travelling with the colonel just behind the two machine-gun platoons, that anyone could have survived the fire which had rained down upon them. As they reached the orchards the riflemen dismounted from their carriers, charged through the orchards and on to the farm, behind the blanket of machine-gun fire from the flail tanks. There was surprisingly little resistance, doubtless due to the speed and drive of the assaulting riflemen and the effectiveness of the covering fire.

In very short time they reached the southern end of the village, where Hunter quickly gave orders for his unlikely force to take up defensive positions. The anti-tank battery, which had followed close behind the assaulting riflemen, was soon sited facing south and south-east towards Cagny, against the very likely possibility of a counter-attack from that direction. For the next hour the riflemen went back to carry out a detailed search of the buildings and woods, rounding up groups of Germans, who emerged, dazed and confused, from trenches and dug-outs, many of which had been partly covered or collapsed by the bombardment. As soon as he was happy that the battle was over Hunter tucked his battalion headquarters under the trees just north of the farm buildings. Satisfied that the headquarters was properly sited, Fiennes became inquisitive:

> 'Armed only with a pistol I decided to investigate a number of trenches near battalion HQ. My German was very limited, but waving my pistol in what I hoped was a menacing manner and shouting "Aus, aus" seemed to have the desired effect and a number of bedraggled Germans emerged. They did not seem keen to fight. I suppose that the bombardment and the speed of our advance had undermined their morale. But I remember thinking how odd it was that on a fine, hot July morning almost all of them seemed to be wearing long trench-coats. By 11.30 am we had cleared the whole area and taken 134 prisoners from 1st Battalion 125th Panzer Grenadier Regiment. We sent them off with a small escort heading north.'

Military wisdom has it that the attacker should ensure, if possible, that he outnumbers the defender by three to one. And yet this small and unorthodox force with not more than fifty riflemen on their feet had cleared a well-prepared defensive position held by one company and battalion headquarters of panzer-grenadiers – an indication of what can be achieved with decisive leadership and drive, against an enemy somewhat demoralized by the heavy pounding they had taken.

Task done, Hunter asked for permission to move forward to rejoin the advance. However, Harvey insisted that the riflemen stay at Le Mesnil Frémentel until the Guards Armoured Division came up and took over the area. He did not want any chance of the Germans reinvesting the hamlet again. But Hunter felt that his place was near the brigade commander, so leaving Rowan and Fiennes firmly in control, he left to rejoin the brigadier's tactical headquarters.

By 2.30 pm, when the likelihood of counter-attack seemed to have receded, 119 Anti-tank Battery was called forward, followed about 5.00 pm by the flail tanks. Fiennes was champing at the bit to get forward to join his colonel, but it was not until late evening that he was ordered to bring the machine-gun platoons forward to meet up with Hunter in the Grentheville area.

Among those captured at Le Mesnil Frémentel was Lieutenant Gerhard Bandomir, who commanded the panzer-grenadier company in the hamlet. Like others, his lasting memory of GOODWOOD was of the bombing raid:

'We just sat and waited to die, unable to do anything. Thanks to our well-built trenches and overhead cover our personnel losses were relatively low, but the psychological effect of bombing was very strong. The bombing was followed by heavy artillery fire, which virtually ploughed up every square yard of the ground. My command post was hit two or three times. A wild rabbit fled into my bunker, jumped into my arms, drank, quite petrified, from my cup of coffee and chewed a hole in my sleeve! It was unlike anything I had ever experienced before, and I had served in France and in Russia as far as Moscow and part of the way back.

'Surprised to find ourselves still alive, we looked over the edge of our trench. I saw many tanks approaching. I scaled a wall, hoping to find some of my company, but nobody came back from the forward positions. So we decided to leave the village and try to head south to rejoin the regiment. We passed a sunken road bordered with trees, where there were many dead and wounded soldiers. Then we hid in a cornfield hoping to wait for the dark. But the enemy found us there, so finally I released the soldiers to surrender. It was shortly after 12 noon that the war ended for me and my company. I remember the infantry who came behind the tanks. What made a great impression on me was their freshness – clearly first-rate men.

'18 July 1944 was a hot and sunny day in Normandy. But for me and my company it was the most dismal and depressing day in all our operations, because we were powerless to do anything.'

Chapter 11

So Near And Yet So Far –
Bras And Hubert-Folie

Having met little serious opposition so far, 3rd Royal Tanks reached the second railway line by 9.35 am, crossed it quickly and pushed on towards Grentheville, a small village surrounded by rather ominous-looking woods, only a few hundred yards ahead. Major Bill Close's A Squadron was still leading:

> 'We were about 2-300 yards short of Grentheville when we came under very heavy AP fire from well-concealed guns in the orchards on the north-west edge of the village. Almost immediately I lost about five tanks, and I could see that John Watts' B Squadron on my left was also having casualties. Several of his tanks were already brewing. It really was an extremely unpleasant position. There was no real cover at all, though my leading tanks managed to get some sort of protection under the lea of the high railway embankment on our right. Fortunately I had a Gunner FOO from H Battery with me, travelling in a Honey tank. I called him over and I told him in no uncertain terms to get some fire down on the village as quickly as possible. Once that happened, which it did very quickly thank goodness, things eased up a bit. I myself managed to find a small dip by some bushes and was able to engage a couple of anti-tank guns on the edge of the village, which we knocked out.'

The practice of having artillery Forward Observation Officers with the leading squadrons was general throughout the army, and vital. The FOO would identify the target, and work out its map location. A few quick words on the radio from Close's FOO and the Sexton, self-propelled guns of H Battery 13th RHA, travelling just behind the tanks, were quickly in action. Warrant Officer II Ernest Powdrill was with them:

> 'We had just crossed the railway when we were ordered to bring our guns into action quickly. We did so but we were shelled and sniped at and had casualties among the gun crews almost before we started firing.
> 'Sergeant Davies of E Sub-section was shot by a sniper in the neck and was in a pretty bad way. I placed him on a stretcher strapped onto my bren-carrier and set off to find the First Aid post. Shortly after, I found two more of our wounded lying in the corn. Gunner Jones was in a very bad way, but there was little I could do because I had used my morphine on Davies. Sadly he died. I managed to get Davies to the First Aid post, where the MO was doing wonders for both our and German wounded. I saw him attend to a German, a boy of about seventeen, who had most of a leg missing. I left Davies in good hands and started to make my way back. Finding an ammunition truck in the area I loaded my carrier with as much 25-pounder ammunition as it could take, and set off back to the guns. By the time I got there they had gone – I had no idea

Major Bill Close's drainpipe! The bridge under the railway embankment, west of Grentheville, through which Close led his tanks.

where. It took me a long time to find them again.'
3rd Tanks, with G Company and H Battery, had indeed moved on. Tucked in beside the railway embankment, Major Close was feeling distinctly exposed:

> *'At the same time as we were involved with the enemy in Grentheville my CO, Colonel David Silvertop, came up on the air and told me very clearly to get my squadron over to the far side of the railway embankment as quickly as possible. The embankment was high and steep, and I didn't want to scramble over the top, where we would be silhouetted. But there were a few openings, farm tracks, that sort of thing, under the railway, so I told my chaps to get through the nearest one and into cover on the far side. But despite several attempts to get them to move, nothing happened, so I thought I'd better lead the way. I stood up in my tank, took off my beret, waved it above my head, ordered "Conform to me" on the radio, and shot up the nearest hole like a rat up a drainpipe. As I did so I remember hoping it wasn't mined. There was no time to worry about that, and fortunately it wasn't. To a man the squadron followed and we emerged out onto the far side, into a scene of absolute peace and calm. No sign of enemy or war, just an ocean of golden corn, waving gently in the breeze. Ahead was a gentle slope and at the top, about a mile or so away, were our objectives, the two villages of Bras and Hubert-Folie. I remember thinking "This is it. This is where we really get going". But how wrong I was.'*

To allow room for the other squadrons to follow and shake out into battle formation, A Squadron moved on about half a mile west towards Cormelles. As they approached it Lieutenant Johnny Langdon, commanding 1 Troop, reported a Mk IV tank in the village, which he duly destroyed. But Close, whose eye was on the ridge villages, did not want to be diverted by side issues. He quickly ordered Langdon to break off contact and move to a

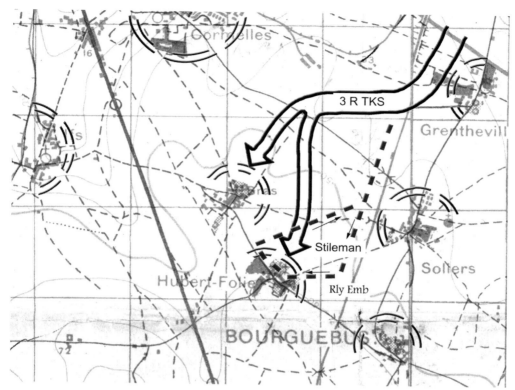

Map 7. 3rd Royal Tanks first attack on the ridge villages, and the route of Lieutenant Stileman's patrol through Hubert-Folie.

position as the forward left troop facing the ridge. Colonel Silvertop, ever keen to push on, was not far behind. By shortly after 10.00 am all three squadrons were through Close's 'drainpipe' and deploying in line abreast for the advance towards the ridge. C Squadron, hitherto in reserve, came up on the left, with orders to keep parallel with and close to the railway embankment. B Squadron, in the middle was to advance on Hubert-Folie. On the right A Squadron was to aim for Bras. The regiment was now on a frontage of about a mile, just a mile and half from the ridge villages. Bras and Hubert-Folie looked peaceful and unoccupied – hardly surprising, since pre-battle intelligence suggested that they were now through the German defences. If he could secure them, Silvertop knew that he would be able to dominate the entire ridge and then press on to the Caen-Falaise road beyond. There seemed to be the prospect of rich pickings just ahead.

3rd Tanks started its advance up the slope. The ground was completely open; a gentle slope, entirely devoid of any cover. Nowhere to conceal a tank – fine, as long as the advance was unopposed. For about a mile all went without incident. With just half a mile to go the two villages seemed to be almost within touching range. But it was a touch which would not be made for another thirty hours. Suddenly, the regiment was hit by devastating fire from several directions. The villages of Hubert-Folie, Bras and even Ifs well off to the right, all seemingly so peaceful a few minutes earlier, had, without warning, sprung into violent life. High velocity shells seemed to be flying in all directions. To Close's amazement he was even taking casualties from the area of Bourguébus, at least 2,500 yards away to the left. On all sides tanks were hit, erupting into spirals of smoke and flame, with the horrific sight of burning crewmen struggling to escape from the inferno.

Sergeant Eric Whittaker, a troop sergeant in B Squadron, was in a Sherman Firefly heading for Hubert-Folie:

'As we got near the village we suddenly started losing tanks from 88s and tanks well concealed on the ridge. To my immediate left Sergeant Dickson was brewed-up by a gun hidden in a haystack, which I immediately eliminated. To my rear Corporal Taffy Richardson was also hit. On getting to the ridge I was hit twice. On baling out I found that my driver, Jack Turner, had been killed, the operator/loader, Harry Palmer, badly wounded in the leg, and the gunner, Titch Everett, had his foot blown off. Nearby Sergeant Bob Lawton's Firefly had been struck on the gun mantlet, which had put his elevating gear out of

75mm Sherman – the workhorse of the Guards and 11th Armoured Divisions at GOODWOOD. Its gun lacked the punch to penetrate the front armour of most German tanks.

order, so we got my two wounded men on bedding rolls on the back of his tank and got them back to the MO, Captain Macmillan.'

Inevitably, the advance halted. The leading troops withdrew slowly down the slope, each tank commander desperately seeking any dip in the ground which might afford some protection from the withering fire, and also provide a good position from which to try to identify and engage the unseen enemy. Suddenly and brutally the pendulum of battle had swung.

There comes a time in battle where movement gives way to fire, as both sides struggle for supremacy. Further advance may only become possible if the attacker can win that fire fight, forcing the defender to give ground or at least take cover. But first he must locate the enemy. On the ridge the German anti-tank guns were in well concealed positions, while the Sherman tanks were easy targets, at unmissable range, in the vast open field. For the tank crews of 3rd Tanks the situation, which only a few minutes earlier had seemed so encouraging, had dramatically altered. Exposed in open country devoid of any cover, vulnerable to fire from superior weapons, it was almost impossible to identify targets to engage. And as every minute passed yet another tank erupted in a violent explosion of fire and smoke. This is the sort of moment when the personality of the commanding officer is vital. If he can regain the initiative quickly, and drive the attack forward again, then success may follow. But if not failure is a real possibility. All those who served with Colonel David Silvertop have described him as a truly outstanding tank regimental commander. He was certainly not one to sit back and allow the initiative to slip from his hands without a real effort to regenerate the attack. To do so he must find out quickly where the enemy were sited and whether there were any weaknesses in the defence which he could exploit. The immediate problem, therefore, was to find out if all of the villages were strongly held. If he could break into just one of them he might be able to use it as a lever to prise open the position. This was not a job for tanks, but nearby was G Company 8th Rifle Brigade and Lieutenant David Stileman:

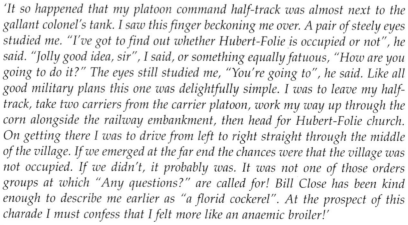

'It so happened that my platoon command half-track was almost next to the gallant colonel's tank. I saw this finger beckoning me over. A pair of steely eyes studied me. "I've got to find out whether Hubert-Folie is occupied or not", he said. "Jolly good idea, sir", I said, or something equally fatuous, "How are you going to do it?" The eyes still studied me, "You're going to", he said. Like all good military plans this one was delightfully simple. I was to leave my half-track, take two carriers from the carrier platoon, work my way up through the corn alongside the railway embankment, then head for Hubert-Folie church. On getting there I was to drive from left to right straight through the middle of the village. If we emerged at the far end the chances were that the village was not occupied. If we didn't, it probably was. It was not one of those orders groups at which "Any questions?" are called for! Bill Close has been kind enough to describe me earlier as "a florid cockerel". At the prospect of this charade I must confess that I felt more like an anaemic broiler!'

Lieutenant
David Stileman
G Company,
8 Rifle
Brigade, shortly
before leaving
for Normandy.

While Stileman was contemplating his distinctly unattractive task he was joined by the reassuring presence of his company commander, Major Noel Bell. Stileman outlined the plan and was given by Bell an excellent air photograph of the area, from which he could clearly identify the route to, and the geography of, the village. This was certainly encouraging. Even more so was the suggestion from Major Bill Smyth-Osbourne that the guns of H Battery could provide fire support to cover Stileman's approach to the village. The last round, and the signal to 'go', would be a single phosphorous smoke round fired in the area of the church.

Stileman duly took over his carriers and explained to the crews the details of this seemingly mad enterprise. It was at about 10.45 am that they set off and edged gingerly forward beside the railway embankment to an area of a dense hedge, just north of the road from Soliers to Hubert-Folie. Stileman then gave the order to swing half-right and climb the slope towards the village, the two carriers hull down in the high corn with only the heads of the commanders showing above it. Meanwhile the fire of Smyth-Osbourne's guns rained down on the village ahead:

> 'We made our way up towards the east side of the village, and sure enough, the smoke round landed smack on the church tower. That was the signal to go. I gave the order to my driver, Rifleman Butler – and we didn't loiter! We went flat out straight down the road through the middle of the village, between the orchards and the houses, which are now much as they were then, out the far end, swung right and came straight back down the slope. I then reported that we hadn't seen any enemy and that since I had returned I didn't think it could be occupied. But how wrong can one be, because we discovered shortly afterwards that the place was simply groaning with Krauts.'

Hubert-Folie was indeed held, and in some strength, by 88mm anti-tank guns of 200 Tank Destroyer Battalion (not to be confused with Becker's 200th Assault Gun Battalion), the guns of 2nd Battalion 155th Panzer Artillery Regiment and panzer-grenadiers of 192nd Panzer-Grenadier Regiment. And yet Stileman and his carrier patrol emerged not only unscathed but even unengaged. The explanation is probably quite simple and reflects the way in which the reality of war differs from logical armchair judgement. Logic suggests that Stileman and his riflemen should have met a very quick and noisy end as soon as they entered the village. But the majority of the defenders were on the northern edge of the village, their attention and the muzzles of their weapons pointing down the slope towards the tanks which they had just so successfully halted in the field in front. The main road runs laterally through the back of the village. Stileman, with his carriers hull down in the tall corn, approached undetected from the east, as the fire of Smyth-Osbourne's guns kept the Germans' heads down. Stileman's mad cavalcade must have crossed behind the main Germans defensive positions and been through the village before they realised what was happening. It takes time, perhaps only a few seconds in the case of a rifle but longer for a machine-gun or anti-tank gun, to turn round and engage an enemy coming from behind. The fleeting target of two carriers, crossing flat out, behind,

Hubert-Folie. The last phorphorous round of the artillery barrage hit the church tower before Lieutenant David Stileman and his carrier patrol came up the road from the right, turned right at the small hall (still there today) and sped through the village.

along the lateral village road, would have been too quick and too unlikely to allow time for the Germans to engage them. Never was the maxim 'If you are going to go, go hard and go fast' better proved.

What is perhaps more surprising is that Stileman was not shot up as he made his way back, down the slope, to report to Silvertop, passing the now blazing tanks which had just been knocked out and which were very clearly in the German sights. Perhaps the height of the corn almost concealed the two carriers. But it was certainly with considerable and understandable relief that Stileman reported the success of his mission and reverted to command of the half-tracks of 11 Platoon. Doubtless based on Stileman's report, Silvertop ordered his tanks forward. Once again they advanced through the corn which in places had now caught fire from burning tanks. This time they managed to get right up to the top of the ridge. Lieutenant Johnny Langdon, leading A Squadron's 1 Troop even managed to cross the Bras to Hubert-Folie road:

'*I was ahead of the rest of my troop, and had just crossed the road between Bras*

The dreaded 88mm – probably the most effective battlefield weapon of the Second World War.

and Hubert-Folie when I was knocked out, I think from Bras. The tank immediately caught fire. My gunner, Trooper Hume, was very badly wounded, and Troopers Pickering and Millington, the co-driver and wireless operator, were slightly wounded. Corporal Latimer, the driver, and I were untouched. With great difficulty we managed to get Hume out of the tank and into a shallow ditch by the roadside. Both his legs were shattered above the ankles. I gave him a shot of morphine, but his pain was so intense that I doubt whether it relieved his sufferings much.

'The ammunition in the tank was starting to explode, and as we were crouching just alongside it we had to move without delay. But we were at least 200 yards from the nearest cover, which was the uncut corn we had just come through. And the ground we had to cross was completely open. We picked up Hume and carried him across the open ground. We must have been in full view of the enemy in both villages, but not a shot was fired at us.

'On nearing the corn we met my troop sergeant, Sergeant Lennard, who had also been knocked out, but had been sent forward by Major Close to assist us. With his help, and now in the cover of the corn which was nearly shoulder high, we managed to get Hume back down the slope to the remains of the squadron near the railway embankment and then on to the Regimental Aid Post. There Hume, Millington and Pickering were treated by the MO, Captain Macmillan, and then evacuated. Sadly Hume died shortly after. I then went back to the squadron and took over command of my troop corporal's tank.'

Major Close, too, was in the thick of the battle:

'We came under a merciless hail of fire from Bras and Hubert-Folie. It is extraordinary but true that you could actually see an 88mm round coming

Lieutenant Johnny Langd – a troop leade in A Squadron 3rd Royal Tan – in the thick the fighting throughout GOODWOOL

your way. Fired just above the level of the corn, it caused a wake like a shallow torpedo. It was even possible, if you happened to be looking in the right direction at the right time, to take avoiding action. Almost immediately about five of my tanks went up and, as I was just taking stock of the situation, there was a hell of a crack in my own tank. A stentorian voice from the bowels of the tank shouted "Bale out". Once on the ground I could see that the back of the tank had been almost completely blown off. I sent the crew back through the corn towards the railway embankment, while I ran over to one of my HQ tanks, to try to take over command, only to find that it had also been knocked out. But my corporal's tank was still operating, so I turned him out, took over his tank and resumed command of the squadron.'

All three squadrons had been struck. Sergeant Jim Caswell of B Squadron had a nightmare experience:

'Most of the tanks around me had been knocked out. I ordered my driver to swing half left so that we could engage some enemy near Bourguébus. Then I saw a terrific flash from a German tank, and I was certain he was ranging on me. I ordered "reverse", but we had not got far when there was another huge flash and we were hit. The blast inside the tank was terrific. On collecting my wits I found that the turret gunner was dead, and the wireless operator had collapsed on the floor. I only had a bang on my right knee. I spoke to the driver on the intercom, but there was no response, although we were in fact reversing broadside across the line of advance.

'Inside a Sherman it is not possible for the commander to see through to the driving compartment. Thinking that the intercom must be out of order I crouched down and shouted through to the front. But there was no reply, and we were still reversing. I climbed out of the turret onto the front of the tank, but couldn't open the driver's hatch. Getting no response, I felt sure that the driver and co-driver had been killed, and yet the tank was still moving. I couldn't find any way of stopping it, and we were now careering across the slope towards the enemy positions on the right. I had no option but to abandon the tank. So I climbed back into the turret, dragged up the wireless operator and somehow got him out. I lowered him over the side into the corn. I then had another go at trying to lift the front crew's hatches, but couldn't open them. Again I got into the turret, had another look at the gunner – although he was clearly dead I could see no sign of wounds – and I baled out. I waved my tank goodbye as it reversed helplessly across the slope.

'I then followed the tank tracks back through the corn to look for my operator. When I found him he seemed to have no visible wounds, but his legs were useless. So I humped him over my shoulder and carried him back, down the slope, for about a mile until eventually I found the RAP. I handed him over and meant to look for regimental HQ. But I must have collapsed then, because I can remember nothing for the next five or six weeks.'

On the right of A Squadron was Sergeant Buck Kite's troop:

'Suddenly, from a small copse on top of the ridge to my right there were gun flashes, and I could see a tank taking up a firing position. I engaged what I

think was a Panther, and I saw the crew bale out. Then one of Johnny Langdon's tanks was knocked out on my left by one of three dug-in guns in the copse, one of which I managed to destroy. There seemed to be more tanks appearing on the ridge, and I knocked out another. But it was now getting very sticky, and we were ordered to pull back slowly, which we did, making best use of the ground – not easy in that open country.

'As we did so we came across one of Johnny Langdon's baled-out crews. One of them, Jock Wilson, was terribly badly wounded. Both his legs were shattered below the knee, and hanging on by pieces of sinew. I got him on the back of my tank and gave him some morphine. As we continued to reverse I spotted the MO's scout car. We handed Wilson over, but I'm afraid to say he died that evening.'

With all three squadrons shot to bits, there was little that Silvertop could do. When in early afternoon Brigadier Harvey told him to have one more try at the ridge in an attempt to cut the Caen to Falaise road, Silvertop was forced to admit that there was little chance of success. Throughout the afternoon 3rd Tanks tried repeatedly to get forward, but every troop and every tank that moved was greeted by a hail of fire. The regiment was firmly pinned down in open ground, exchanging fire with an enemy who was well concealed, held the dominating ground, had superior weapons and who was being steadily reinforced. Like sheep on a highland moor, using even the shallowest dip to provide some shelter from the driving storm, tank commanders sought places to conceal at least part of their tank. A hull-down position might make the difference between life and death. At 3.30 pm Silvertop reported that the position was steadily deteriorating, but that he would hold on in the area as long as possible.

But Silvertop was not one to remain inactive, as Lieutenant Robin Lemon of the Reconnaissance Troop quickly found out:

'Shortly after we crossed the embankment I heard that the Recce Troop commander had been killed, so I found myself in command. I had had no real role in the attacks on the ridge and just had to watch a tank battle in full swing, with the Germans holding the commanding ground. Sherman after Sherman went up in flames, but it was very good to hear the occasional claims on the radio of German tanks being knocked out. After the attack had failed Colonel Silvertop ordered me to go on foot, up the embankment and see what was happening on the other side. I crawled up the bank, over the railway line and peered gingerly down the far side. I could see all the ground from Soliers to Bourguébus. Clearly a tank battle was raging there too. It seemed quite incredible that two quite separate tank battles were going on on either side of the embankment. And then I saw four Panther tanks advancing down the slope from Bourguébus towards Soliers. It looked as though two of them were making for the bridge under the embankment, almost underneath my nose. So I rushed back and reported this and most of C Squadron trained their guns on the bridge, and waited. But nothing happened.'

Suddenly and dramatically the situation had changed. The peaceful rural scene which had greeted the regiment when they emerged west of the railway embankment at shortly after 10.00 am, was now, just a few hours later, a cauldron of burning tanks, blazing corn, dust, smoke and the stench of battle, while small groups of men, many wounded, some badly burned, tried to make their way back to the cover of the embankment. In later years Close paid full tribute to the riflemen of G Company:

'It really was a horrific scene, but I well remember the riflemen of G Company, especially David Stileman and his platoon, who, despite the constant hail of fire, motored up to our burning tanks, helped to get the crews out and then put them on their carriers and half-tracks and brought them back to the RAP. They saved many lives that day.'

If life for the tanks was grim, it was no less so for Stileman and his riflemen in their open-topped carriers and half-tracks:

'It really was very, very unpleasant, with armour-piercing shot flying around, and tanks going up in flames. With no overhead protection we were horribly exposed and wherever we moved, so a hail of high explosive fire seemed to follow us. Mercifully it died down late in the afternoon after a sergeant from the Carrier Platoon found a German OP concealed in the railway embankment. When he was despatched, the artillery fire eased a bit. But my most vivid memories of a dreadful afternoon are the ghastly sounds of gallant tank crew members unable to escape from the raging inferno of their tank, and the hideous condition of the badly burned men as we tried to get them back to safety.

'Eventually Noel Bell suggested to Colonel David Silvertop that as this was so obviously a tank battle, there was nothing constructive that the motor company could do. So, during a lull in the battle, we withdrew, thankfully, east of the embankment.'

By 2.00 pm General Roberts realised that, with 3rd Tanks having fought themselves to a standstill west of the embankment, and 2nd Fife and Forfar Yeomanry and 23rd Hussars similarly battered east of it (Chapters 12 and 13), he was running very short of tanks. The only reserves he had available were the Cromwell tanks of the divisional reconnaissance regiment, 2nd Northants Yeomanry. He therefore ordered that as soon as they could be released from the attacks on Cuverville and Démouville they were to move forward and come under command of 29th Armoured Brigade for a further attempt on Bras. At 3.30 pm 2nd Northants Yeomanry started to move forward, arriving, at 4.40 pm, in the area just north of Grentheville. The regiment was comparatively fresh, having had little serious fighting at Cuverville and Démouville, so Brigadier Harvey immediately ordered them to pass through 3rd Tanks and try to capture Bras. B Squadron crossed west of the railway embankment in the area of the Caen to Cagny road, and swung left, hoping to advance towards the ridge in a wide right hook. They were immediately confronted with the problem of the east-west Caen to Vimont railway, which proved a difficult hazard. Shortly after crossing it they came under fire from tanks or anti-tank guns from Cormelles, about half a mile further west, and lost two tanks. An inconclusive gun battle took place, but it was quite clear that further advance in that area would be impossible. Meanwhile A and C Squadrons were moving south. A Squadron passed under the embankment by way of Close's 'drainpipe' and started to advance south while C Squadron, east of the embankment, advanced on Soliers. In very quick time C Squadron had come under heavy fire, lost a number of tanks and been forced back. Prudently, A Squadron was also pulled back before it ran into serious trouble. Behind them B Squadron, following its abortive right hook, moved to the area of the 'drainpipe' through which it passed. Arriving on the east side of the embankment it became immediately caught up in C Squadron's battle in that area, and the squadron leader, Major Stancomb, was wounded. As evening drew on 2nd Northants Yeomanry was withdrawn further north, leaving 3rd Tanks still in position on the right.

There was nothing more that 11th Armoured Divisions could do, west of the railway embankment except hang on grimly to the ground they had won at such cost – not an ideal task for tanks without infantry support.

As dusk approached the vital ridge villages remained firmly in German hands.

Chapter 12

'A GRAVEYARD OF BURNING TANKS'

2nd Fife and Forfar Yeomanry crossed the second railway at the same time as 3rd Royal Tanks, with A Squadron on the right and B on the left. Hitherto speed had been essential, with tank troops moving in an almost non-tactical line abreast. Now, with the artillery barrage having run its course, tanks spread out, moving tactically by bounds, covering one another forward. Lieutenant Colonel Alec Scott had originally intended to pass C Squadron through A and B, and to advance up the slope towards Bourguébus on a single squadron axis between the villages of Four and Soliers. The final drive to the ridge would be the moment to call on the experience of Major Chris Nicholls. But Nicholls was dead and C Squadron no longer a fighting force. It was at about 10.00 am that Colonel Scott ordered Major Sir John Gilmour and B Squadron to lead the advance:

'We had no tank casualties in my squadron until we passed Le Mesnil Frémentel, although my second-in-command, Captain Raymond Traherne, was killed by a stray bullet, probably from a sniper, as we crossed the railway line. Near Cagny we lost our first tank when Sergeant Hogg was hit just beside me. I saw him and his crew bale out. I had no real idea where the fire was coming from. We were concentrating like mad on pushing on. You couldn't stop and investigate where every shot came from. Sadly they were all killed by artillery or mortar fire as they made their way north.

'The day was fine and sunny and I could see our objective not far ahead. It didn't look as though it would be too difficult to get there. We shook out into tactical formation, passed Grentheville on our right, shooting up a number of Nebelwerfers in the woods there, and pressed on. Once my leading troops had gone about 6-700 yards south of the railway line, the rest of the squadron had to come out into the open, in order to cover them forward. Initially all went well, and we reached the line of the Four to Soliers road without real trouble. Then, quite suddenly, we were hit by heavy fire, first from Soliers and then from Four. Of course while the enemy were in well concealed positions, we were completely exposed in open ground. Tanks all around started to brew and we found it almost impossible to get on. We couldn't identify targets clearly, but through the dust and smoke I could see German tanks and SP (self-propelled) guns up ahead in the Bourguébus and La Hogue area. But they were way out of range and, as we had now outrun our artillery barrage, there was nothing I could do about them. The things that really helped us most that day were the Typhoon aircraft. We should have had a RAF liaison officer at brigade HQ, who could talk direct to the pilots in flight, but he had been knocked out early in the battle. However I was able to talk on the radio to someone who could contact them and I called them down onto the Germans on the ridge. They did a marvellous job.'

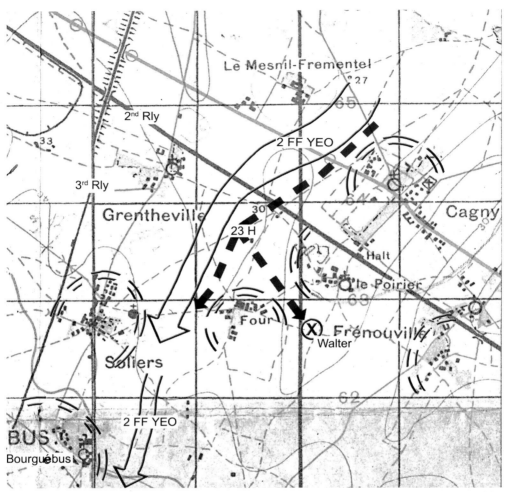

Map 8. Attempts by 2nd Fife and Forfar Yeomanry (Chap 12) ⇨ and 23rd Hussars (Chap 13)
▬ ▬➤ to reach Bourguébus. The site of Captain Walter's action is at ⊗.

For the next two hours Gilmour and B Squadron waged an intense fire fight
with the German defenders in the villages, the Engineer Battalion of 21st
Panzer Division and a variety of tanks and anti-tank guns. Doggedly they
tried to push on. Somehow the leading troop forced its way past Soliers and
Four and advanced up the slope towards Bourguébus. At 11.15 am they
managed to reach the Bourguébus to La Hogue road, where all the tanks were
quickly knocked out by fire from La Hogue. Gilmour could also see German
tanks to his left in the Frénouville area, some 2,500 yards east – doubtless von
Luck collecting reserves in the area of his HQ. Shortly after 11.30 am Colonel
Scott reported to Brigadier Harvey that his leading squadron was pinned
down by heavy fire from several villages, including Frénouville. Harvey told
him to 'Leave Frénouville to the Guards. Press on to Borguébus and Tilly la

Campagne.' But by 11.30 am Gilmour, having lost a dozen tanks, had to report that B Squadron could do no more. With his eye still on Bourguébus, Scott ordered Major John Powell and A Squadron to take over the lead.

A Squadron had already lost five tanks in the Cagny area. At about 11.45 am Powell set off, taking Lieutenant Forbes' 1 Troop, to follow up B Squadron's advance along the main axis. But he was no more successful than Gilmour and he also lost most of his tanks. It was clear that any direct tank assault across open ground between strongly held villages was destined to fail. The only alternative was to try to drive the Germans out of one of the villages, and to use that as a lever to open up the way to the ridge. Powell therefore ordered his second-in-command, Captain Douglas Hutchison, with the five remaining tanks of 3 and 4 Troops, to work his way round the north-east edge of Four, and see whether he could drive the enemy out of the village. Hutchison and his party set off from the railway line, heading south towards Four:

> 'First, I tried to get Eric Spittal and 3 Troop forward into the east side of Four, but Lance Corporal Bush's tank was quickly knocked-out, and Spittal's became badly ditched and had to be abandoned. Clearly there really wasn't much chance of getting into Four, so I was then told to remain in the area and block the left flank.
> 'We had a pretty busy time. We engaged a number of tanks and anti-tank

Sherman 17pdr 'Firefly'. Its excellent gun could penetrate all German tanks, except the Mk VII King Tiger. But its long gun barrel made it easily identifiable to German gunners.

guns. In particular we had quite a duel with a Panther to our left in Le Poirier. He was very skilfully handled. He blew a hole in the farm wall, stuck his gun through it, fired several rounds, hit one of my tanks and then withdrew. He tried it again and I was waiting for him. I remember the absolute frustration of watching my own 75mm rounds simply bouncing off his glacis plates. On the third time, we got him. Corporal Croney, who had the 17-pounder in Steel Brownlie's 4 Troop, nailed him, which was very satisfactory.

'Then I could see a number of tanks in the area of La Hogue, nearly 3,000 yards away and well out of our range. Two of them advanced straight towards us, and then stopped about 2,000 yards away, which was foolish as Corporal Croney got them both. Excellent shooting for a Sherman at that range. And I could see more advancing towards Four from La Hogue, so I warned John Gilmour on the right. By the time we withdrew we had lost another tank, destroyed a number of SP guns, and were running perilously short of ammunition.'

By 12.30 pm Colonel Scott reported that he was now down to less than twenty tanks. Brigadier Harvey ordered him to concentrate on trying to take Soliers. If this could be achieved he would bring forward 23rd Hussars and, using Soliers as a launch-pad, direct them onto Bourguébus.

The battle had now degenerated into a confused slugging match, with the Germans having the advantages of concealed positions in the villages and the greater hitting power and range of their tanks and anti-tank guns. Shortly after 12.30 pm Scott's tank was knocked out, as was that of his second-in-command, Major George Trotter. As the regimental signals officer, Lieutenant Robert Clark's battle station was as radio operator/gunner in Trotter's tank:

'We were somewhere south-west of Cagny when we were hit. The round came into the side of the tank just below the turret, passed within a few inches of my back and went into the engine compartment. George Trotter immediately ordered "Bale out", which we all did. This was quite difficult for Lance Corporal Crichton, the driver, and the co-driver because of the gun barrel above their hatches. We all took cover in some nearby trees or shrubs. The tank did not burn immediately, but about five minutes later it just exploded, with flames and smoke wooshing up into the air. Orders were to make one's way back to the echelon near the start line if KO'd, so we set off and walked about seven or eight miles north.'

For some time Major Gilmour, in the dust and grime of battle surrounded by a graveyard of burning tanks in the open ground just north of Soliers, was unaware that he was, in effect, now commanding the regiment, or what was left of it. Even when this did become apparent he had no communications with brigade HQ. With tank numbers ever dwindling, Gilmour was forced to pull the remains of the regiment back north towards Grentheville. At 2.45 pm, as he withdrew, he met Scott, on his feet and unharmed. Scott quickly commandeered Gilmour's tank and resumed command, leaving Gilmour to find whatever replacement tank he could. Gilmour ended the day in the turret of the regimental dozer tank! 2nd Fife and Forfar Yeomanry, now down to a handful of tanks, could do not more. Scott pulled the battered remains of his regiment north of the second railway.

* * * *

How General Roberts must have rued the absence of his infantry brigade at this critical moment. An infantry attack, launched from the railway line, supported by the tanks of 23rd Hussars and 2nd Northants Yeomanry, with fire support from 11th Armoured Division's two artillery regiments, would surely have taken Four and Soliers. It is easy for the armchair tactician to picture the likely plan – the artillery firing smoke to blind the German tanks and anti-tank guns on the Bourguébus ridge; a tank regiment and an infantry battalion to capture Four; next a similar grouping to take Soliers, with close range fire support from Four; then the drive on to Borguébus.

The clear identification of German tanks along the Bourguébus ridge from about midday was an ominous sign of things to come. As 29th Armoured Brigade's War Diary records:

> 1155 – 2 FF Yeo report four camouflaged enemy tks at 083605. [Just south-east of Bourguébus].

> 1200 – 2 FF Yeo report tks moving into Bourguébus.

> 1214 – 2 FF Yeo report eight tks, probably Tigers, moving into Bourguébus from SE.

Incidents recorded neatly in brigade logs, with clearly identified timings beside them, give no impression of the true situation facing the man at the front who initiated that report, and the inevitable delay in reporting it. Crouching as low as possible in his turret, his eyes just above the top of the cupola, constantly scanning to left, right and ahead. A flash from a barn on the right and another tank goes up. Less than a minute later the fuel explodes with a great 'whoomph' of flame and smoke from the turret; perhaps the horrific sight of a flaming torch as one of the crew manages to escape. Just a few minutes and then the ammunition starts to explode and the turret glows red-hot. The acrid smell of burning tank, burning corn, and perhaps burning flesh. Ahead, Bourguébus, but out of range. Are those tanks moving into the village? Must have a bloody good look, at the same time keeping eyes skinned in all directions and frequently moving position a bit. Remaining stationary for any length of time is to invite trouble. Binos – hard to see through the dust and smoke but surely they're tanks; yes, big ones. How many – looks like eight. 'Hello 4 Able for 4, eight enemy tanks, probably Tigers, entering Bourguébus from the south-east.'

* * * *

Major Gilmour has recorded how much was owed to the Typhoons which circled the GOODWOOD battlefield on 18 and 19 July 1944. One of these was

A Hawker Typhoon fighter-bomber.

flown by Flight Lieutenant Jack Frost.

The Typhoon pilot's scene was far removed from that of the tank driver in the midst of a terrifying tank battle thousands of feet below. His horizon was not bounded by the next hedgerow or village. The freedom of the skies was his and, with confidence in the Allied Air Forces' almost complete air supremacy, the bright summer morning of 18 July surely held few dangers, but gave ample opportunity to enjoy his mastery of the sky, with a little sport thrown in. Not for him the ponderous and terrifying grind of tank warfare below.

And yet that romantic-sounding picture is almost wholly misleading. For most of the time Frost's concentration was almost entirely taken up by trying to maintain his position as wing-man to his flight commander, Flight Lieutenant Eric Vernon-Jarvis. With the speed of aircraft and the tight tactical formation flying, a lapse in concentration of even a few seconds could prove fatal. The Typhoon pilot was not the individual cavalier of the sky, but, just as in the tanks below him, a member of a team.

Before D-Day the rocket-firing Typhoons operated from England in wings of thirty-six aircraft. Their targets were identified concentrations of German troops, especially tanks, and the road and railway network, in particular the choke points, such as bridges over the main rivers. Their aim was to isolate Normandy from post-invasion reinforcement and to restrict German movement inland from the beaches. 175 Squadron, of which Frost was a member, was part of 121 Wing in 83 Group. Frost's first operational sortie was flown on 4 March 1944. Throughout April the squadron had been withdrawn in order to prepare for the intensive flying programme required in the month immediately before D-Day, and to be ready to move to France at the earliest possible opportunity after the invasion.

Only a few days after D-Day the Typhoons started to operate from grass airstrips in Normandy, refuelling and rearming there, but returning to England at dusk each day. On 17 June the ground crews of 121 Wing were deployed to France. By the end of June the whole of 83 Group was based in the narrow beachhead, with 84 Group following in July. Squadron Leader

Mike Ingle-Finch commanded 175 Squadron, based at a rough grass airstrip east of Bayeux. The squadron had eighteen rocket-firing Typhoons, of which twelve must be available for operations at all times. The dust and dirt which was quickly sucked into the aircraft engines meant that the ground crews, in addition to rearming and refuelling aircraft quickly on landing, had a constant battle to keep sufficient aircraft airworthy.

At each wing headquarters there was an army/air liaison officer. The duty squadron was held at fifteen minutes notice – fifteen minutes in which to be briefed on target, geography, formation, flying conditions, locations of friendly troops, and to get airborne. The pilots of the duty squadron would hang around the 'stand-by' tent, fully dressed for flying, but with their parachutes left in the aircraft, awaiting a call on the tannoy loudspeaker. Meanwhile the ground crews would ensure that engines were kept warmed up; the Typhoon was a notoriously bad starter when cold. On receipt of the alarm call the pilots, hastily briefed, raced straight to their aircraft, as Frost described:

'Getting airborne was our first problem. With airstrips only a few miles from the front taking off south or east meant that we were over the German lines before we had gained sufficient height. Taking off to the west meant that we had to overfly the Americans, which was almost as dangerous. Heading north meant overflying the Navy, and that was the most dangerous of all!! "If in doubt, open fire" seemed to be the rule, and as aircraft recognition probably hadn't featured highly in naval training, they often were in doubt.

'The German low-level flak was very good. If you stayed below 5,000 feet for more than a few seconds you got a very hot reception. And above 9,000 feet you encountered the 88mms. So the aim was to get into that safe window between 5,000 and 9,000 feet as quickly as possible. We would try to patrol at about 8,000 feet, just below the cloud level, from where our leaders could best identify places and targets on the ground. In the early days we operated as a complete squadron, with three "finger 4" formations, the centre one leading, the up-sun one lower and the down-sun one higher. In that way we could all see one another without having to look into the sun.

'By July squadron missions were few and most missions involved flights of four to six aircraft. This involved aircraft operating in pairs, with a "finger 4" or arrowhead formation overall. Our drills were very slick and we could change direction or formation almost instinctively, without the need for radio orders. Radio silence was important because we did not want to alert the German fighters, which were the only weapons which could threaten us at our patrol height. The need to defend against enemy fighters inevitably meant that we had to abort our ground-attack mission, which might be vital to the soldiers fighting below.

' "Diving now. Target at 12 o'clock", might be the only order you received. The leader would put his nose down and dive at about sixty degrees. Behind him we would follow hot on his tail. Maximum revs – full speed – you must be below 5,000 feet for the shortest possible time. No time to search for the target.

Throttle and stick well forward, concentrating like mad on the aircraft in front. The sudden dive from patrol height to attack took just a few seconds – just time to flick up the cover of the firing button with the thumb of the right hand, while the left kept the throttle fully open. Peering ahead, almost mesmerised by the leader, you had no option but to follow and hope that at the last moment you could identify the target.

'Fire at about 4,000 feet – quite a judder as two of the eight 60-pound rockets took off. If you were a back number you really had no chance of picking out the target. The whole area would be a maelstrom of earth and debris thrown up by earlier rockets. You just fired into the general area, hoping that the leader had got it right. He often used his four Hispano cannons to observe strike before firing his rockets. As soon as you had fired, pull up, climb to a safe height and reform. The dive had probably taken you down to about 1,500 feet, where the flak and the debris thrown up by your own attack caused most of the damage which we sustained.'

Frost undertook two missions on 18 July. His log records them:

'Aircraft – Typhoon 1B. Number – MN 536. Pilot – F/Lt JW Frost. VCP patrol – attacked 5 Panthers near Vimont, SE of Caen. Duration – 45 mins. One definitely hit. Enormous tank battle going on – big push to break out of bridgehead.

'RP attack on gun positions SE of Caen. 3 guns seen but result unobserved. F/O Fred Botting missing – believed to have baled out over Hun lines.'

Next day, flying again as pair to Vernon-Jarvis who was leading six aircraft, it was Frost who identified the target, five tanks, nose-to-tail in the open. He broke radio silence to alert the leader. His log records:

'Attack successful, and although only one Panther seen to be hit the effect on the others must have been most alarming.'

To the Typhoon pilot it was an impersonal war. He could not measure the overall result of his actions. He did not see the gruesome casualties he caused, nor could he gauge the effect on those subjected to aerial attack. Doubtless the unknown pilot of 193 Squadron had no idea of the significance of his actions as, on 17 July, he attacked a lone car near St Foy de Montgomerie, and removed from the war Germany's most famous battlefield commander, Field Marshal Erwin Rommel. That is the nature of war in the air.

Chapter 13

'HULLO GUNNERS, HULLO GUNNERS!'

At midday the situation for 29th Armoured Brigade looked distinctly bleak. On the right of the embankment 3rd Royal Tanks were held up by strong and unyielding enemy positions in Bras and Hubert-Folie. On the left 2nd Fife and Forfar Yeomanry had found it impossible to break into Four or Soliers. Nevertheless, Brigadier Roscoe Harvey decided to have another concerted thrust, this time using his reserve regiment. At 12.55 pm, therefore, he ordered Lieutenant Colonel Perry Harding, commanding 23rd Hussars, to pass through the Fife and Forfar Yeomanry and take Soliers before exploiting south towards Bourguébus. Three minutes later he amended the order; 'secure Soliers, but do not try to advance further south'.

Like Scott in 2nd Fife and Forfar Yeomanry, Harding was a regular officer from 5th Royal Inniskilling Dragoon Guards. Having not served in the desert campaign, he was, at thirty-nine, rather older than most other commanding

Brigadier Roscoe Harvey DSO, commander of 29th Armoured Brigade, watching pre D-Day training with Lieutenant Colonel Perry Harding, DSO, commanding 23rd Hussars.

officers, indeed he was two years older than General Roberts. But he had already proved his ability, having been awarded a DSO during the pre-Dunkirk campaign of 1940. He would shortly win a bar to that award.

23rd Hussars were still back in the area of Le Mesnil Frémentel where they had been left to 'mask' Cagny, pending the arrival of the Guards Armoured Division. The picture confronting Colonel Harding, as 23rd Hussars moved up to take over the lead, was somewhat misleading. Radio communications were not working well. He had heard garbled reports that the Fife and Forfar Yeomanry had reached Bourguébus and that 3rd Tanks had got to Bras, but he was unaware that both attacks had been beaten back. Reaching the second railway line shortly after 1.00 pm he had his first sight of the Bourguébus ridge. A number of tanks could be seen in the open near Soliers and Four, and even some right up near Bourguébus. Harding assumed that 2nd Fife and Forfar Yeomanry had progressed much further than was in fact the case. It seemed likely that neither Soliers, nor an advance further towards Bourguébus, would prove too difficult. Unaware that most of the tanks ahead were already 'dead', he ordered Major Seymour's B Squadron to press on forward.

Lieutenant Ted Harte commanded 2 Troop in B Squadron:

'We then received orders to advance, cross the second railway and take the high ground near Bourguébus, our axis being between Four and Soliers. B Squadron was to lead, with A and C following. We advanced, 1 Troop on the right, mine on the left, and made good speed across the open ground until we were about 400 yards from the road running between Four and Soliers. Suddenly we came under very heavy fire. My two rear tanks, including my 17-pounder, were knocked out almost immediately, and I could see that 1 Troop had lost three tanks. My troop sergeant and I engaged some enemy in the north edge of Soliers, but then he was hit and killed. I was now the sole surviving tank of my troop and I expected to be hit at any minute. I was totally exposed, without any cover at all – it really was most alarming. I used local smoke to move position several times, engaging targets whenever I could see them. Eventually, after what seemed a horribly long time, Major Seymour ordered me to withdraw to join the rest of the squadron, and I was mightily relieved to do so.'

Realising, soon after 2 pm, that B Squadron's advance had stalled, Harding went forward to visit Seymour, but in the smoke and dust of battle was initially unable to locate Seymour's tank. Eventually they met, and while they were discussing the situation Major Gilmour of 2nd Fife and Forfar Yeomanry arrived. He climbed onto the back of Harding's tank and told him that his regiment was now down to about five tanks, and that the colonel and second-in-command had both been knocked out, and that as far as he was aware he was now commanding the remains of the regiment. He was in the process of pulling back the few remaining Yeomanry tanks, and he considered that further advance in the Soliers area was quite impossible.

Harding made a new plan. Seymour was to pull B Squadron back to a hedgerow about 500 yards south of the railway, which would be held as a firm base. Major Wigan's A Squadron was to secure the right flank, in particular the area between Grentheville and the railway embankment, and also make contact with 3rd Tanks west of the embankment. Meanwhile Major Shebbeare's C Squadron, which had hitherto been held back in reserve, was to move south-east between Four and Le Poirier and try to take Four from the east.

Shebbeare had been waiting for just this chance. He had only recently taken over command of C Squadron, having been left behind in England as a battle casualty replacement when the regiment crossed to France. He had therefore missed the first battle on Hill 112. A man of great charm and ability, he was destined, in the eyes of those who knew him, for a highly successful political career after the war. Like many who later graduated to the Labour Party, he was at the time an active communist, and his hatred of the Nazi regime was deep. The war against the Third Reich was something of a personal crusade for him, and it was perhaps this, coupled with his lack of battle experience, which led to actions which, in the light of subsequent events, look somewhat rash.

Responding to its commander's orders, C Squadron charged forward. No attempt at tactical movement with tanks covering one another forward, the leading troops simple raced through the gap between Four and Le Poirier and out into the open ground, looking for hull-down positions from which to shoot up the Germans in Four. But there were no hull-down positions – just a large, flat, open cornfield. Captain Peter Walter was, it will be recalled, feeling distinctly short of sleep after two days and nights as regimental harbour-master. He had hoped that his role as second-in-command of the reserve squadron of the reserve regiment would afford him ample chance to catch up with some sleep as the vast tank armada ahead rolled inevitably on to the Bourguébus ridge. He was about to be brutally disillusioned:

> 'It was when we got into the open ground that our trouble really started. We came under fire from all directions at once. The leading troops all went up in flames. I saw Bill Shebbeare's tank hit and burst into flames, and my own head-gear was blown off. The noise of battle was really quite terrifying, so I quickly put my earphones back on, crouched down lower in the turret and tried to see what I could through the periscope. As I was doing this, something came in through the right side of the turret and went out through the left, I felt a high ringing noise in my right ear, a dull thud in my left hand, and a sharp stinging all over my face. So I finally gave up all ideas of trying to catch up on my kip, told the gunner to put the gun into free elevation so as not to block the driver's hatch, and gave the order to bale out. Once on the ground I rushed around in the corn waving my arms, making frantic signals for the following tanks to withdraw. I was very relieved when they did, though a bit disappointed when I later found out that they were actually obeying a radio order from our ever-observant colonel. They hadn't even seen me.'

Captain Peter Walter – looking almost unrecognisably neat and tidy!

In the depths of Walter's tank, his driver, Trooper 'Mush' Wright, was initially concussed by the blast:

> 'I woke up to a feeling of intense heat. Everything seemed to be on fire. I opened my hatch, and remember being relieved that the gun wasn't covering it. Twice I tried to get out, but was held back by my earphones. Stupidly, instead of breaking the snatch-plug, which was there for exactly that reason, I pulled off my headset. If I hadn't done that I would probably have some ears now! Fortunately I had my driving gauntlets on, which saved my hands.'

The rest of the crew had escaped unharmed, but Walter described Wright's face as 'a black charred mass'. Together they rolled Wright on the ground to extinguish his burning clothes, and Walter set about doing what he could for the wounded:

'I was able to collect some First Aid kits from the back of tanks, and so patch
people up a bit, giving the worst ones morphine. I was even able to find one tank
which had a bent gun but was a runner, and I piled on as many of the wounded
as I could and sent it back. Then our medical officer, George Mitchell, turned up
in his half-track, quite oblivious of the shell-fire which was going on all around
us. He proceeded to redress many of the wounded, telling me exactly what I had
done wrong with them. He even dressed my own wee wound. He also gave me
some sulphamelamine tablets, for which I shall never forgive him! Together we
loaded as many of the wounded as we could onto his half-track, and he set off.'

Among those taken out by Mitchell was Trooper Wright, but not before the
medical officer had carried out an emergency tracheotomy in the middle of
the battlefield, since Wright was in dire danger of swallowing his tongue and
choking to death. Wright was later convinced that this, and the actions of
Lieutenant John Addison [later to become well-known as a composer of
Hollywood film scores], who held onto Wright's tongue to stop him
swallowing it for perhaps twenty minutes before Mitchell arrived, saved his
life. Addison had been commanding one of the leading troops, and his tank
had been one of the first to be hit:

'I felt a terrific blow in the thigh. I managed to climb out of the turret and open
the driver's hatch. He and the co-driver appeared to be dead. Flames were
everywhere and the co-driver's hair was already on fire. I tried to drag out the
driver, but couldn't. I then climbed back into the turret, found that the gunner
was also dead, but that the radio operator was conscious, although his leg was
badly smashed. Somehow I managed to drag him out and get him onto the
ground. By now the tank was a flaming mass. I wasn't properly wounded; just
a badly bruised thigh, so I set about doing what I could for those who were.'

With Major Shebbeare dead, Walter was now in something of a quandary:

'It was as the MO disappeared that I realised what a bloody fool I was.
Obviously I should have gone with him. But here I was in this wretched
cornfield, completely on my own. No map, no glasses; all I had was my pistol.
I had no idea what one was expected to do in this sort of situation. So I started
to wander back north when a tank suddenly appeared. Actually he had come to
look for me. An awfully nice sergeant stuck his head out of the turret and asked
how I was, but before I could reply his head disappeared. It had been shot off by
a passing shell. Grim, but at least it solved my immediate problem, because here
was I, a commander with no tank, and now here was a tank with no
commander.'

In the bowels of the tank, Corporal Walter Kendall, the gunner, realised that
his commander had been hit, when the body slumped down into the turret. It
was with the greatest difficulty that he and Lance Corporal Griffiths, the radio
operator, managed to get the sergeant's body out of the tank and lower it onto
the ground beside Walter. Concerned that they were in an exposed position
Kendall and Griffiths quickly remounted the tank to look for targets to
engage, while Walter wrapped the body in a groundsheet, and, since the
identity tags normally worn on a bootlace round the neck had been blown off

with the head, wrote the name on the groundsheet. While Walter struggled with this, made harder by his own 'wee wound', which was in fact a badly shattered left hand, Kendall was able to identify the high profile of a German anti-tank gun in the edge of Four, doubtless one of Major Becker's unusual constructions. He opened fire, and it exploded with a satisfying 'whoosh' of flame and smoke.

By then Walter was ready to take command of the tank. With considerable difficulty he clambered into it, intent, as he later put it, 'on rejoining the war'. The tank had now been stationary in the open for several minutes. Inexplicably it had not been hit, but it seemed prudent to find some cover as quickly as possible. Walter could, of course, withdraw, but, 'because it didn't seem the right thing to do', he declined that option. Instead, noticing a belt of trees about 200 yards further east, he ordered the driver to drive to it, while he got onto the radio and rallied the remains of C Squadron there. In due course five other tanks joined him, and together, under Walter's direction, they proceeded to engage any targets they could identify.

'Quite late in the afternoon Sergeant Smith, a splendid chap who was later to win a DCM, beckoned me over[1]. I climbed up onto his tank and he proceeded to point out a mass of Panther tanks and infantry in a gap in the woods near La Hogue. It looked like a strong counter-attack forming up, but was well out of our range, so I decided to get some help from the artillery. Now the map I was using was the one I had inherited with the tank, and in cleaning all the flesh and blood off it I had wiped out the chinagraph markings. Besides, I was feeling a bit woozy at the time, the result, I think, of those wretched tablets the MO had given me, so thinking it better to be hung for a sheep as a lamb, I got onto the blower and said, "Hullo gunners; hullo gunners. This is Peter Walter. May I have a stonk on . . .", and I gave what I hoped was a sensible grid reference. I remember Sergeant Smith burying his head in shame at this lamentable radio procedure. Anyhow, much to my surprise I was given a shoot. The first round fell short, so I upped it good and strong. The next one went over, so I halved it, and, as luck would have it, the third round fell smack in the middle of the target, so I gave the order "Gunfire". The gunners really plastered the area and whatever was there rapidly disappeared. After that we felt safe from attack for a bit.'[2]

Meanwhile, having, like 2nd Fife and Forfar Yeomanry before him, failed to break through to Bourguébus, and having lost many tanks, Colonel Harding had concentrated the battered remains of his regiment in the area of Grentheville. Ever close at hand, Major Peter Gaunt, commanding G Battery

---

1. The Distinguished Conduct Medal was the highest award for gallantry in action, short of the Victoria Cross, available to non-commissioned ranks.

2. Walter's unorthodox radio procedure story sounds almost fictitious. However, in 1976, when Anglia TV was preparing to make a programme on the Staff College, the producer attended the battlefield tour. Hearing Walter tell this extraordinary story he announced that he had been a Royal Signals officer responsible for monitoring the radio nets of forward units in July 1944. He had heard Walter's appeal for help and had acted as the link between Walter and the Gunners. Fact and coincidence are sometimes stranger than fiction!

German Mk V Panther. An excellent tank, its sloping armour meant that British tank rounds frequently bounced off.

13th Royal Horse Artillery, spent much of the rest of the day trying to locate targets and bring down artillery fire on them:

> *'To identify any hostile-looking silhouette against the dark shadows of trees and buildings, and in the dust and smoke of the battle, was well nigh impossible. The only hope was to look out for gun flashes and then fire from memory. For much of the time Colonel Harding's Tac HQ was in a hedge forward of the railway line. The enemy, too, must have been having difficulty as, although he knew where we were, he clearly couldn't identify individual tanks. AP shot seemed to be flying around in all directions. Our 25-pounders were fine against infantry, but could not knock out a tank, so the only "big stick" we had available were the 5.5s of the medium regiments still way back the other side of the Orne. I managed to get some allocated to me and concentrated them on Bourguébus. Their fire was very accurate and effective and certainly slowed down the rate of fire coming our way. And we had a tremendous fillip when a self-satisfied Panther, sitting in front of Bourguébus disintegrated under a direct hit from a 5.5.'*

Late in the afternoon Harding withdrew his group behind the low railway embankment, which provided some protection against direct, but not indirect fire. As it got dark he ordered Walter to rejoin him there:

> *'When we arrived, everyone else seemed to be asleep – everyone except the Colonel. He sent for me and wanted a detailed description of what we had been doing. When I had finished he paused for a minute and then said "Well, you seem to have found yourself a pretty good funk-hole. You'd better get back there*

Captain Peter Walter, DSO, o C Squadron, 23rd Hussars, whose actions at Four nearly won him a VC photographed in the early 1980s.

before first light". Of course there are only about four hours of darkness in mid July, and by the time we had filled up with ammo and petrol, and had a welcome cup of tea, it was time to set off back again. So I still didn't get my sleep. We got back by first light, and the second day was, as far as I can remember, pretty uneventful. To be honest I wasn't feeling great, but I think we engaged a few targets from time to time, until by late afternoon tanks from 7th Armoured appeared in the area, and we were pulled back to rejoin the rest of the regiment in the Grentheville again.'

Walter's somewhat laid-back description of the battle belies his own physical state and achievements. Sergeant Smith and Corporal Kendall were in no doubt. They later described how Walter consistently refused to be evacuated, insisting on returning 'for the second day's play', how there were times when he lapsed into unconsciousness, was kept warm by being rolled in a blanket and 'toasted' on the back of a tank when the area seemed quiet, and how his personality and leadership were all-important to the few remaining tank crews of C Squadron. A body of men, however depleted by casualties, will almost always respond to clear leadership, but where leadership is absent nothing will be achieved. But those who picture the steely eye and bulldog jaw of the screen-image leader would have been surprised by Walter. A quiet, gentle, sensitive and rather dishevelled man, who gave no obvious impression of ambition or drive, Captain Peter Walter was to be awarded an immediate Distinguished Service Order for his actions on 18 and 19 July, a highly unusual award for an officer of his junior rank. His citation ends with the words 'I consider this only very little short of being worthy of an even higher award'. There is only one higher award – the Victoria Cross. Few of those who were with him would have been surprised if he had been awarded it.

After the battle the medical officer, Captain George Mitchell insisted that Walter be evacuated. He managed eventually to catch up with his long-delayed sleep, some three days later in a small hospital outside Glasgow. Medical repairs took many months, and it was not until Spring 1945 that he rejoined 23rd Hussars, just as the war was ending.

* * * *

Mitchell was the ideal medical officer. Before training as a doctor he had served in 4th/7th Royal Dragoon Guards, now in Normandy as an armoured regiment in 8th Armoured Brigade.

'The real value of an MO in front-line units in war is almost more psychological than medical. Perhaps surprisingly wounded soldiers do not mind who treats them, but the unwounded are never keen to leave their wounded chums with other than a trained MO. In battle I travelled with the colonel's command group, so that I could quickly find out where I was needed, and get there. I had three scout cars, usually crewed by the sick, lame and lazy. I had no trained Medical Corps assistants, but I did have Corporal Preston, an outstanding psychiatrist, known to all and sundry as 'Doc'. Colonel Harding laid down that

Preston must never go into action; he was quite prepared to lose me, but not Doc Preston! Preston would analyse each exhaustion case most efficiently. If it was 75% exhaustion and 25% shock the remedy was twenty-four hours in the echelon, barbiturate, rum and sleep, then back to the squadron. If it was 25% exhaustion and 75% shock, then we had to get rid of him.'

* * * *

General Montgomery's operational directive of 15 July had decreed that VIII Corps' armoured cars should 'push far to the south, spread alarm and despondency and discover the form'. During the afternoon of 18 July, in the midst of the gruesome tank battle taking place on the northern slopes of the Bourguébus ridge, the corps armoured car regiment, the Inns of Court, had tried continuously to discover gaps in the German defences through which they could penetrate in order to carry out the deep reconnaissance for which they were trained. It is hardly surprising that they were, for the most part, unsuccessful. And yet two patrols of D Squadron did manage to slip through the German defences. At 3.30 pm one reached St Aignan de Cramesnil, some three miles south of Bourguébus, which it reported to be clear of Germans. Somehow it returned via Bourguébus and Grentheville, surprisingly intact. An hour and a half later another patrol, using much the same route, actually reached the much-desired Caen to Falaise road just west of Cramesnil, and returned reporting no serious opposition. It is doubtful whether these two daring patrols actually spread much alarm and despondency, and the 'form' they discovered was of little help to those running the battle, but, like Lieutenant Stileman at Hubert-Folie, they are examples of what can be achieved by small parties, under leaders with courage and initiative. Doubtless the speed of the armoured cars was the key factor in their success.

* * * *

While 2nd Fife and Forfar Yeomanry and 23rd Hussars had been having such a torrid time at Four and Soliers, their attached motor companies had not been idle. There was no role for them at the front of what was essentially a tank/anti-tank gun battle so, during the late morning and early afternoon, they had been left in relative safety north of the second railway line. But, just as Le Mesnil Frémentel could not be left as an island of opposition in the wake of the armoured advance, so Grentheville had now to be taken. It was clearly strongly held, with anti-tank guns which had already taken a toll of 3rd Tanks, and infantry, and it also housed the multi-barrelled *Nebelwerfers* of 14th Werfer Battalion. At 2.00 pm Colonel Harding of 23rd Hussars ordered Major John Dickenson and H Company, 8th Rifle Brigade, to capture the village. This proved to be far from easy as the German positions were well concealed in the orchards and farms. By 2.20 pm 16 Platoon had forced an entry into the village, and for the next three hours H Company made slow progress in clearing enemy from the orchards and the northern edge of the village. At 5.30 pm F Company was ordered to detach itself from 2nd Fife and Forfar Yeomanry, pass through H Company and take the main part of the village and the orchards south of it. Major Foster Cunliffe ordered Lieutenant Philip Sedgwick and 6 Platoon to lead the attack. During a short, savage but successful battle Sedgwick's men captured twelve *Nebelwerfers* and their crews. Cunliffe reinforced Sedgwick's success by pushing his other platoons on through the village. Resistance suddenly broke, and within an hour Grentheville had been taken. The bag consisted of four 88mm anti-tank guns, eighteen *Nebelwerfers* and about fifty men. Sergeant John Trasler was a platoon sergeant in F Company:

'After we had captured the village and orchards we established a defensive position. I decided to have a good look round just to be sure that there were no Germans lurking around unknown to us. It was just as well I did as in one dug-out I found nine Germans. It was quite a job getting them out. They were scared to death – too scared to give themselves up when we over-ran the orchard. They looked pathetic, just cowering there waiting to be shot. The officer, who spoke broken English, told me that many of them were not keen to carry on the war and only did so because they had to.'

Having ordered F Company to hold the village for the night, Brigadier Harvey quickly brought forward the self-propelled 75mm guns of 119 Anti-tank Battery, Royal Artillery, to join them in the orchards on the southern edge of the village, as a defence against German tank counter-attack.

* * * *

As Colonel von Luck had feared, 11th Armoured Division had punched a hole in the defences between his battle group and Colonel Rauch's 192nd Panzer-Grenadier Regiment. But the strong screen of 88mm anti-tank guns and the panzer-grenadiers of 192nd Panzer-Grenadier Regiment, well sited and concealed on the Bourguébus ridge, had been enough to hold up the leading regiments of 29th Armoured Brigade. Major Becker's 200th Assault Gun Battalion had also been in the thick of the fighting. 1 Battery had been lost at Démouville, but 2 Battery, having been driven out of Giberville by the Canadians (chapter 15), had pulled back to reinforce the defences at Bras. And, following their actions at Le Prieuré and Cagny, 4 and 5 Batteries had withdrawn from Cagny to Four and Le Poirier respectively, shortly after midday. 3 Battery, which had engaged 3rd Royal Tanks from well-concealed positions in Grentheville, had been ordered to move to Soliers in mid afternoon, when it became clear that Grentheville was isolated and must fall. Captain Nösser had festooned his guns with sheaves of corn and crept back through the fields, reaching Soliers about 3.45 pm. That this move went undetected by 2nd Fife and Forfar Yeomanry and 23rd Hussars, who were both in the area at the time, explains something about the chaos of a battlefield. Visiting the ground today it is impossible, in the scene of rural tranquillity, to imagine how a battery of up to ten self-propelled guns could cross that area unseen. But in the midst of a tank battle, with the smoke of burning tanks and corn, the constant shellfire, the all-pervasive odour of death, whether from the bloated carcases of dead cattle or burned tank crews, and the ever-present awareness that one's name may be on the next 88mm round, it is entirely understandable. With the height of the corn which, at about five feet, masked much of the vehicle chassis, the sight of what may look, at a quick glance, like tanks advancing south suggests that other squadrons are pressing forward, not that an enemy battery is making a run for it. Any junior commander who has the courage to exploit the chaos of battle has a good chance of getting away with it, if he acts boldly. Becker's batteries, superbly led by excellent officers, played a classic hand of 'mobile defence' throughout 18 July.

By now the inaccuracies of the pre-battle Intelligence picture had become all too obvious to those in 11th Armoured Division. As has already been stated, it is now clear that many of the German senior commanders, especially Rommel, actually expected an armoured-heavy attack in this area on or about the 18 July. The defence of the area had been planned accordingly, with particular emphasis given to depth. 1st SS Panzer Division, having been relieved from its ground-holding position west of Caen, had been moved to a position only three miles south of Bourguébus, astride the Caen to Falaise road near Cintheaux. In the same area were the Tiger tanks of 501st Heavy Tank Battalion, while 12th SS Panzer Division was only ten miles south near Falaise. As soon as he heard of the British advance General Eberbach, who had replaced Geyr von Schweppenberg a fortnight earlier as commander of Panzer Group West, reacted quickly. He ordered General Dietrich of I SS Panzer Corps to launch an immediate counter-attack. This was a typically German response. The tactical doctrine of all but the static divisions was always to counter-attack quickly, while the enemy might be slightly off-balance. General Wisch's 1st SS Panzer Division was to move forward to the Bourguébus area, secure it with Panzer-Grenadiers and use it as a launch-pad for a strong counter-attack north. Close at hand, it did not take the division long to react.

From midday onwards the defences along the Bourguébus ridge, already strong, were immeasurably strengthened by the arrival of 1st SS Panzer Division. Ordered to counter-attack as quickly as possible, General Wisch had despatched Colonel Peiper and his 1st SS Panzer Regiment to the area. Peiper, a formidable and ruthless armoured commander, was just the man to impose his personality on the Bourguébus ridge battlefield. He ordered Major Kuhlmann, with the forty-five Panther tanks of the 1st Battalion, to launch an immediate attack from the ridge and drive the British north of the Caen to Vimont road. There is no record of this attack being launched. Perhaps it was Captain Walter's artillery 'stonk' that so effectively disrupted Peiper's and Kuhlmann's plans. Behind the tanks, Wisch moved up his Panzer-Grenadier regiments to strengthen the defences of the ridge villages.

Chapter 14

THE OTHER PRONGS OF THE TRIDENT – GUARDS AND 7TH ARMOURED DIVISIONS

The tactical success of Operation GOODWOOD depended upon the speed with which the follow up divisions could come up into line alongside 11th Armoured. 29th Armoured Brigade had advanced quickly to the Cagny area, and then swung off south-west. But at 10.00 am, when 3rd Royal Tanks and 2nd Fife and Forfar Yeomanry were already across the second railway and advancing towards the ridge villages, 23rd Hussars had just become involved in a separate tussle with 5 Battery, 200th Assault Gun Battalion at Le Prieuré. This was most unfortunate. Brigadier Harvey had been ordered to leave a regiment to mask Cagny until the Guards Armoured arrived in the area. This was the task of 23rd Hussars. Hindsight suggests that if they could have broken loose from Le Prieuré quickly and undertaken their masking role from Le Mesnil Frémentel area, clear of the VIII Corps centre-line from about 10.00 am, the way forward for the following divisions might have been eased. In the event their presence north of Cagny and Le Prieuré until about midday only added to the log-jam of vehicles in the area. In theory 11th Armoured could hammer away at Bourguébus, Hubert-Folie and Bras throughout the rest of the day. Success in

Sherman tanks, with infantry onboard, moving forward during Operation GOODWOOD.

Cromwell tanks of 7th Armoured Division wait peacefully in their concentration area, ready to move forward on 18 June 1944. They could not have sat in the open, uncamouflaged, if the German Air Force had posed any real threat.

this would have been of almost secondary importance, so long as it allowed room for the Guards and 7th Armoured Divisions to join the action as the other two prongs of the VIII Corps trident, preferably by late morning or early afternoon. The pressure on the German defences would then have been intolerable. Hindsight is indeed a marvellous weapon!

Shortly before midday General Roberts met General Adair, commander of the Guards Armoured Division near Le Mesnil Frémentel. Roberts explained that since his division had swung off to the south-west the way was now clear for the Guards to take over the Cagny problem and head south-east. But he warned Adair that Cagny was clearly strongly held and might be a tough nut to crack. Having spoken to Adair he asked HQ VIII Corps to bring forward 7th Armoured Division, between 11th and Guards Armoured Divisions, as quickly as possible so that all three divisions could operate in line abreast.

* * * *

Major General Alan Adair, the popular and respected commander of Guards Armoured Division.

Brigadier Sir Henry Floyd, Chief of Staff at O'Connor's VIII Corps HQ, had always been aware of the need to push the follow-up divisions forward as quickly as possible, once 11th Armoured had cleared the centre-line of the advance. And well before the start of the battle he had identified the significance of Cagny. His planning notes before Operation GOODWOOD record:

BUILD UP OF ARMOUR.
(Assuming H Hr 0745 hrs.)

1. 29 Armd Bde leading regt will arrive Cagny approx 0930 hrs.

2. If two armd regts, Gds Armd Div, start to cross [Orne] brs at 0815 hrs they will be clear of brs by 0945. This being so the two ldg regts should reach Cagny approx 1030 hrs.

3. Third armd regt approx 1 hr behind.

4. If 22 Armd Bde (7 Armd Div) can cross at 0815 hrs, leading regt will be across by 0945 hrs and should reach Cagny at 1030 hrs (ie same time as two leading regts Gds Armd Div).

5. If present restriction continues this regt will be delayed one hour, ie will reach Cagny area 1130 hrs.

6. Second regt 22 Armd Bde will be clear of brs by 1330 hrs, and should reach Cagny area by 1430 hrs.

7. Third regt 22 Armd Bde will be clear of brs by 1330 hrs and should reach Cagny area by 1430 hrs.

8. This shows a continual flow of armour into the Cagny area from 0930 hrs to 1430 hrs.

There was clearly a real sense of urgency at HQ VIII Corps. Admittedly Guards and 7th Armoured Divisions were to cross the Orne and canal by different bridges, but the suggestion that three armoured regiments could move up towards Cagny almost in line abreast, where 29th Armoured

Carriers and soft-skinned vehicles crossing the River Orne into the bridgehead before advancing south.

Brigade had earlier found it barely wide enough only for one, sounds unduly hopeful.

The leading tanks of the Guards Armoured Division were scheduled to reach the Orne Bridges at 7.45 am and to start crossing at 8.15 am. Floyd decided to visit the bridges in time to watch them cross. But 7.45 am came and went, and there was no sign of them. By 8.00 am he was getting increasingly angry. 'Where are the Guards? The Guards are late! Call up the Seventh.'

This, however, proved unnecessary. A liaison officer located 5th Guards Armoured Brigade nearby and by shortly after 8.30 am they were crossing the bridges. The explanation for the delay was simple. Brigadier Norman Gwatkin, commanding the brigade, was concerned that 'to be in the area of the bridges at H Hour was a neat way of committing suicide. I decided to keep my people about a mile back and to call them forward when the bridges were clear'. The moral of the story, he would later admit, is that 'if you decide to disobey orders, (which is more honest than saying 'use your own initiative'!) you must clear it with your superiors so that there is no ambiguity whatsoever.' In fact the delay made no significant difference. By 9.45 am 2nd Armoured Battalion Grenadier Guards had caught up the rear of 23rd Hussars, in the area of the first railway line.

Gwatkin was fully aware of the need for urgency. He ordered 2nd Armoured Battalion Grenadiers Guards to take Cagny, while on their left 1st

Armoured Battalion Coldstream Guards would move east of Cagny and press on towards Vimont. Following behind, 2nd Armoured Reconnaissance Battalion Welsh Guards would protect the east flank, and in particular mask Emiéville. 1st Armoured Coldstream quickly swung off left and advanced towards the gap between Le Prieuré and the Chateau de Manneville. At 10.45 am they came under fire from the Mk IV and Tiger tanks of 22nd Panzer Regiment and 503rd Heavy Tank Battalion in the area of the chateau and Emiéville. For the next hour and a half, try as they did, it proved impossible to get through the gap, which was only about half a mile wide.

On the right 2nd Armoured Grenadiers had their eyes firmly set on Cagny. At 11.15 am Lieutenant Colonel Rodney Moore, ordered No 2 Squadron to advance on the village using the road as the axis. In the fields ahead were the smoking remains of C Squadron 2nd Fife and Forfar Yeomanry. The leading troop had not gone far when it came under fire from the village and lost two tanks. Moore went forward on foot and discussed the situation with No 2 Squadron commander, Major Sir Arthur Grant. Shortly after he left Grant's tank was hit and, although the rest of the crew were uninjured, Grant was killed. Advance on Cagny from this direction was clearly impossible.

By 12.00 pm it was clear to Brigadier Gwatkin that both his leading battalions were now firmly held up. A new plan was required – and quickly, so that Guards Armoured could leave room for 7th Armoured to come

A Sherman flail tank, of 79th Armoured Division, passing the damaged church in Escoville.

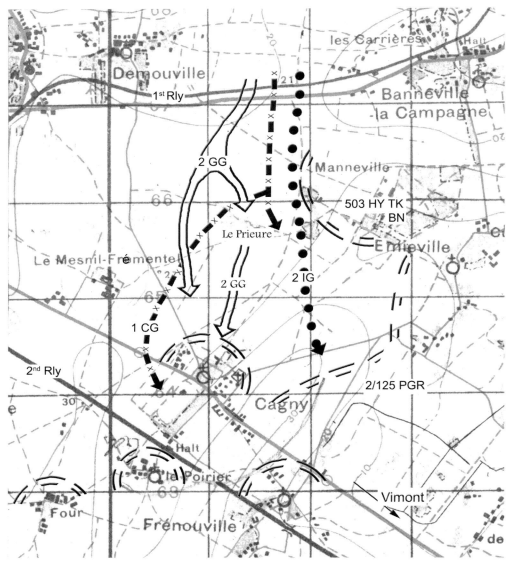

Map 9. Guards Armoured Division's attack on Cagny and attempts to press on towards Vimont.

forward. At least 23rd Hussars were now clear of the area, so the congestion was somewhat relieved. Gwatkin told 1st Armoured Coldstream Guards to break off their attempt to bypass Cagny to the east and to move down the western side of the village. Once across the Caen to Cagny road they were to swing left, moving south-east through the gap between Cagny and the railway towards Frénouville and Vimont. In the centre 2nd Armoured Grenadiers were to probe the Cagny defences. If these were found to be too strong they were not to mount a direct attack, but were to follow the

Coldstreamers down the west side of the village and try to attack from the south-west. Meanwhile 2nd Armoured Reconnaissance Welsh Guards were to try to find a way through the German anti-tank screen on the east flank.

By 2.45 pm 1st Armoured Coldstream Guards, having passed west of Cagny, had started to move south-east between Cagny and the railway. Meanwhile Colonel Moore of the Grenadiers decided to use the cover of the orchards of Le Prieuré, from which Lieutenant Schreiner's assault gun battery had withdrawn, for his probing attack. No 3 Squadron was to guard the exposed east flank, while No 1 Squadron sent a force forward towards the village. Captain Tony Heywood was second captain of the squadron:

> 'Half the squadron, under Captain Jones, worked its way forward from Le Prieuré, supported by fire from the rest of us in the area of the farm. They managed to get into the northern outskirts of Cagny, although Captain Jones' tank was brewed up and two others had turned over in bomb craters. However, they did knock out one Mk IV tank and a couple of flak guns.
>
> 'By this time Tiger tanks had engaged us from Emiéville. We lost a number of tanks and had the unpleasant experience of seeing our own 75mm rounds bouncing off the German tanks. I could see one of our 17-pounders engaging two enemy tanks, but his shots were going wide, so I moved my tank alongside to give corrections. As we got into position my operator said "I think 4 Charlie has had it". Sure enough smoke started to erupt from the turret and the crew quickly baled out. Now the Tiger turned his attention to me. We managed to get three quick shots at him, and watched in horror as they bounced off. The Tiger fired, and somehow missed us. We quickly fired smoke, and as we reversed I could see that the Tiger was also withdrawing – honours about even, I thought, with some relief!'

Shortly after 4.00 pm Moore despatched his attached motor infantry company, King's Company, 1st Battalion Grenadier Guards, to move up to the tanks of No 1 Squadron on the edge of Cagny and to try to get into the village.

Cagny – Welsh Guardsmen at the west end of the village on the road to Caen, consolidating their position after the capture of the village.

The attack went in at 6.00 pm and reported that the enemy had withdrawn, leaving behind them a number of anti-tank guns. General Adair immediately ordered Brigadier Johnson to send two infantry battalions of 32nd Guards Brigade straight into the village to secure it against counter-attack. Johnson quickly ordered 5th Coldstream and 1st Welsh Guards forward and at 7.30 pm he was able to report that Cagny had at last been taken. 2nd Armoured Grenadiers, having lost twenty-two tanks and nearly forty men, pulled back to the orchards on the northern edge of the village.

Meanwhile 1st Armoured Coldstream Guards, advancing south-east along the narrow strip between Cagny and the railway, had encountered strong opposition in Frénouville and Le Poirier. An attempt to take Le Poirier failed and the battalion was eventually halted close to the railway and due south of Cagny. Further advance proved impossible.

The third tank battalion, 2nd Armoured Irish Guards, arrived on the scene in the early afternoon and quickly joined the fray on the eastern flank. Soon after crossing the first railway they inevitably came under fire from the German tanks in the woods near the Chateau de Manneville. By 5.00 pm it was clear to Brigadier Gwatkin that 1st Armoured Coldstream Guards were firmly held up south of Cagny. Still determined to press on towards Vimont, he decided to try again east of Cagny. He ordered 2nd Armoured Irish Guards to try to force their way through the Cagny/Emiéville gap towards Frénouville. Lieutenant John Gorman was commanding one of the leading troops:

> 'This was my first time in action, and I was excited. I got across the little stream north-east of Cagny, but the rest of my troop got stuck. I pushed on alone for a bit, found plenty of targets, and was beginning to think that this war business was not too bad after all. In fact I was beginning to quite enjoy myself. This did not last long, as, glancing left I saw to my horror the unmistakable outline of a King Tiger coming through a hedge less than 200 yards away. I ordered my gunner "Traverse left – On – Fire". He did and I watched with dismay as the shot bounced off the Tiger and went sizzling up into the air. I ordered him to fire again, but a hollow voice came from the bowels of the tank "Gun jammed, sir". Glancing anxiously at the Tiger I saw with horror that his long gun was slowly swinging in my direction. Someone had once told me that when in doubt the thing to do is to advance, so I ordered my driver to advance at full speed and ram the Tiger. We lurched forward, gathered speed and hit him amidships with a terrific crash, just before he had got his sights on us. Both crews baled out and, as there was quite a lot of shelling going on in the area, we dived for cover. My operator jumped into a convenient trench and found it already occupied by the Tiger's crew. They all stayed there with their heads down, while I crawled back, brought up my 17-pounder and brewed up the Tiger. I then collected my own crew and the Tiger's and we made our way back, handed over our prisoners and got into another tank.'

Unconventional Gorman's feat may have been, but it was, perhaps, the only course of action which could save the lives of him and his crew. The Sherman's 75mm gun could penetrate only 60mm of armour; the frontal

'A terrific crash'. The King Tiger (left) and Lieutenant Gorman's Sherman (right).

Guards Armoured Division memorial on the Cagny to ...éville Road, at the scene of ...utenant John Gorman's clash ...h the Mk VII King Tiger.

armour of the King Tiger was a massive 185mm thick. Conversely the Tiger's 88mm gun, capable of penetrating 168mm of armour, would have cut like a hot knife into butter through the meagre 76mm of Sherman armour (Annex B). No military training course can teach how to respond in this sort of situation, and there is no time available for considered thought. Reactions must be instantaneous and almost instinctive. To have saved the lives of his crew and destroyed a King Tiger tank certainly justified the subsequent award of an MC to Lieutenant John Gorman.

The King Tiger was one of Captain Fromme's 503rd Heavy Tank Battalion which, sited in the orchards of the Chateau de Manneville, had taken the full force of bombing. Throughout the morning the battalion, or what was left of it, had worked feverishly to get as many tanks serviceable as possible. Some had to be dug or towed out of bomb craters, engines had to be cleaned and all weapon sights needed recalibration. By mid afternoon sufficient tanks were operable that the battalion could move to a new position. Determined to strengthen his defensive screen from Emiéville to Frénouville, von Luck had ordered the battalion to move south from the grounds of the chateau. It must have been during this move that the King Tiger from 1 Company met Gorman in his Sherman. What was particularly alarming to Lieutenant von Rosen, commanding the Tigers of 3 Company, was that during this move he lost several tanks, knocked-out having been hit head-on, from the direction of Cagny. It was well known by both sides that only the 17-pounder Firefly could penetrate a Tiger's front armour and that there were not many of them around. Later research suggested that the battery of 88mm anti-aircraft guns which von Luck had found in Cagny and 'persuaded' to join the fray, had so enjoyed their new tank-killing role that they had engaged anything that moved. The sight of some tanks moving south from the Manneville orchards was sufficient to draw their fire. Tank recognition was clearly not a high priority in German anti-aircraft batteries!

The Guards Armoured Division's Memorial stands on the site of Gorman's action, about half a mile out of Cagny on the Emiéville road. It was the high water mark of the 2nd Armoured Irish Guards' attempts to advance south-east. Clearly von Luck still held a strong defensive screen stretching from Emiéville and the orchards down to Frénouville, and round to Le Poirier.

With two infantry battalions forward in Cagny, 32nd Guards Brigade Commander, Brigadier Johnson, ordered his third battalion, 3rd Irish Guards, to take up a defensive position in the area of Le Prieuré. At shortly after 9.00 pm, as they were finishing digging their trenches, Johnson ordered Lieutenant Colonel Joe Vandaleur, to move the battalion to Frénouville, where it was reported that an armoured battalion had just captured the village. Few things are more annoying for infantrymen than to be told, when they have sweated hours digging a defensive position, to move elsewhere. Vandaleur was not best pleased, but orders are orders. By now it was getting dark so he sent his leading company off on a compass bearing direct towards Frénouville. They had just left, when he was told that they were to go via Cagny. It proved impossible to recall them, so he collected the other companies, gave out fresh orders and set off. Passing through Cagny, which he described as 'like Dante's inferno' he pushed on east along the main road, only to find that Frénouville was very definitely still strongly held by the Germans. With von Luck's regimental headquarters in the village, it was, after all, the nerve-centre of the German defence! They came under heavy fire from machine-guns, mortars and *Nebelwerfers*, and, to add insult to injury, from other guardsmen who had not been told that they were advancing in that area. Colonel Vandaleur described the scene:

> *'There I was, being shot at by Germans in front and some of our own chaps from the flanks, with one company missing, not knowing the real situation and unable to get any fresh orders. So what did I do? I tossed a coin; heads, move forward in Wellington style, bayonet to bayonet; tails, consolidate where I was. Luckily it came down tails, so, with assistance, metaphorically, from the drill-sergeant's pace stick, we hatched out some sort of defensive layout and dug like beavers.'*

* * * *

Shortly before midday General Roberts was delighted to see Brigadier Robert 'Looney' Hinde, commander of 22nd Armoured Brigade in 7th Armoured Division, arrive at his tactical headquarters:

> *'I felt sure that this heralded the early arrival of 7th Armoured to fill the gap*

Cromwell tanks of 7th Armoured Division moving forward – and looking fairly relaxed!

between us and the Guards. But Looney Hinde took one look at the mass of tanks in the area and said "There are far too many bloody tanks in the area. I'm not bringing forward my brigade yet". And he left without giving me a chance to explain that most of them had been knocked out earlier on. I'm afraid to say that at that moment I cursed my old division and my old brigade.'

By early afternoon it had become quite clear to Roberts that 11th Armoured Division had, for the moment, shot its bolt:

'At 1.50 pm I met the Corps Commander and General Erskine of 7th Armoured just behind Le Mesnil Frémentel. I explained the situation to them. I said that all these small villages, all mutually supporting, were strongly held by tanks and anti-tank guns, and that no real advance could be achieved until they were all dealt with or neutralised. I said that as my objectives were on the right, I could do no more until the gap between us and the Guards was taken over by 7th Armoured. General Erskine noted this, and said that he would get his division forward as soon as possible to fill the gap. So I had great hopes that during the afternoon we would see the arrival of 7th Armoured, and that we would then be able to resume our advance towards our objectives on the right.'

General O'Connor fully understood Roberts' parlous situation and the need for speedy action by 7th Armoured. In particular he was concerned that 11th Armoured, having lost so many tanks, could be vulnerable to counter-attack. He therefore told Erskine that 22nd Armoured Brigade was to move its units forward individually as quickly as possible, rather than accept delay by trying to bring the whole brigade forward together. This was not easy to achieve. All the difficulties of trying to move three divisions in line astern, on a single, narrow axis, were now apparent. Although the leading regiment, 5th

A column of tanks and reconnaissance vehicles of 7th Armoured Division on the road to Escoville. The narrowness of the front and the density of traffic ahead led to frequent delays.

Royal Tanks, had passed Démouville and was already in the area of the first railway line, ahead of it was a sea of tanks, with Guards Armoured deployed in a semi-circle round the obdurate Cagny.

Having spoken to O'Connor and Erskine, Roberts again went forward to visit Brigadier Harvey. Harvey's brigade major, Major Anthony Kershaw, travelled in his commander's tank:

'Our tank had been specially modified. It had a wooden gun. I sat in the Gunner's seat, with a second hole cut in the top of the turret. The brigade signals officer was in the machine-gunner's seat, responsible for ensuring that all the radios were working and helping me by monitoring the nets. Roscoe was a marvellous chap and a superb armoured commander, but he was not an easy man to work for. To start with he would not talk on the radio. I had been Pip Roberts' brigade major in North Africa. Pip was always on the brigade net while I was on the rear link to division. But with Roscoe I had to keep abreast of the battle, keep Roscoe informed and pass on his orders on the brigade net, keep division happy on the rear link and talk to the driver on the intercom. It did not make life easy.

'Furthermore, he was also utterly fearless. Most people have a stock of courage and in prolonged conflict that can run out – some run out quicker than others. Roscoe was quite different. The longer and more dangerous the battle, the braver he became. He really didn't seem to know the meaning of fear, and that is not always easy for those around. He would park his tank well forward and in the most obvious place. If I remonstrated with him he would say that he needed to be there so that he could see the whole battlefield. And of course the Germans could also see us, an obvious command group of three tanks and a protection troop, and they promptly shelled us. It happened frequently. Pip was different; very brave, but prudent. Roscoe was rash.'

At various times during the afternoon General O'Connor told 7th Armoured Division to 'push on as quickly as possible', but battle diaries suggest that the sense of urgency which he demanded never really reached the front of 22 Armoured Brigade. At 4.20 pm O'Connor personally came on the air to HQ 7th Armoured, 'What is holding things up?' The reply was 'Traffic', but he was told that a plan to overcome the congestion, agreed between Generals Adair and Erskine, would be put into effect within thirty minutes. But events continued to move frustratingly slowly and it was not until about 6.30 pm that the leading squadron of 5th Royal Tank Regiment had caught up with the rear of 29th Armoured Brigade. Behind them the rest of 22nd Armoured Brigade was strung out, with 1st Royal Tanks just east of Démouville and the third regiment, 4th County of London Yeomanry, still caught up in a traffic jam way back in the area of the Orne bridges.'

As Brigadier Hinde later pointed out, there was no easy way forward for 22 Armoured Brigade:

'After crossing the Orne I travelled with the leading tanks of the brigade. On reaching the first railway shortly after 10.00 we seemed to be in the middle of 5 Guards Armoured Brigade and could see the tanks of the rear squadron of 29th Armoured Brigade only a few hundred yards in front. Most of these seemed to be burning and there was AP fire coming from the left. I reported the situation to the divisional commander and told him that it did not appear sound to advance further. It was pretty evident that the favourable situation for which 7th Armoured Division was to wait, before passing between 11th and Guards Armoured Divisions, did not exist. It is impossible for anyone who was not present at the time to realise the state of affairs in the narrow corridor through which three armoured divisions were attempting to pass. And it was worst for 7th Armoured as we had to thread our way through the other two'.

To General Roberts the delay of 7th Armoured proved hugely frustrating. He certainly did not believe that they were only to come forward when a 'favourable situation' existed. Nor is there any record of O'Connor or Dempsey applying this restriction. Roberts expected them as early as possible, and he was clear that by late morning his own division had pulled far enough to the west to allow sufficient room for 7th Armoured to come up into line. His first attack on the Bourguébus ridge villages had taken place at shortly after 10.00 am. Having lost more than half his tanks and without his infantry brigade, he was feeling distinctly exposed. For the ensuing nine hours, as his division was progressively worn down by accurate fire from the well-concealed enemy on the ridge, he had waited in vain for 7th Armoured to come up on his left and assert pressure on the German defences. And it was during those vital hours that the majority of the German reserves, and in particular 1st SS Panzer Division, were moved up to reinforce the defences of the Bourguébus ridge.'

By 7.00 pm 5th Tanks had reached the battered remains of 2nd Fife and Forfar Yeomanry and 23rd Hussars. The leading squadron pushed on to the area of the orchards south of Grentheville. All attempts to advance further proved fruitless and after losing a few tanks 5th Royal Tanks was ordered to leaguer for the night just south of Le Mesnil Frémentel, leaving A Squadron forward near Grentheville.

For 7th Armoured Division it had been a thoroughly frustrating day. Having expected to be in contact by late morning or early afternoon, by the end of the day just one regiment had had one minor brush with the enemy, while the rest had spent the day grinding slowly forward, held up in countless traffic jams.

* * * *

From midday it had been quite clear, at least as far up the command chain as O'Connor and his staff at HQ VIII Corps, that the leading division had met quite unexpected resistance which it could not penetrate, and that the follow-up divisions were having great difficulty getting forward. For some quite inexplicable reason this message never seemed to penetrate HQ Second Army. As late as 8.00 pm a Press statement about operations up until midday was issued from Army HQ. It included these sentences:

'The armoured division moved very fast and was followed by two more. By midday strong armoured formations of VIII Corps had advanced seven miles to the south and had broken through the main German defences.'

The last phrase of this report clearly gave an entirely misleading picture of the situation. It must have been written by a staff officer who only had access to reports until about 10.30 am when the situation still looked encouraging, and who assumed, based on the pre-battle Intelligence picture, that an advance of this depth must indeed have broken through. But although the report was dealing with operations up to 12.00 pm, by the time it was issued some eight hours later the correct picture should surely have been known at HQ Second Army. This report, when read by such as Eisenhower and Tedder at Supreme Headquarters back in the UK, must have encouraged them to think that all the ambitious hopes of GOODWOOD were about to be realised. The possibility of reaching Falaise; the prospect of at last holding ground suitable for the construction of airstrips; these thoughts must surely have been hugely encouraging. When, later, reality dawned, the let-down will have been very real. The consequences of this misinformation were to be considerable.

Chapter 15

THE INFANTRY ON THE FLANKS

In military history Operation GOODWOOD has become almost synonymous with the advance of the three armoured divisions of VIII Corps. With the spotlight inevitably focussed on this, it is easy to forget the hard fighting undertaken by the infantry divisions on the flanks.

The Eastern Flank - 3rd Infantry Division.
With 6th Airborne and 51st Highland Divisions already holding the bridgehead east of the Orne, as they had since D-Day, Lieutenant General John Crocker's I Corps provided the springboard for Operation GOODWOOD. But Crocker was also ordered to launch 3rd Infantry Division in an advance south, securing the left flank of VIII Corps and clearing much of the close wooded country south along the Bois de Bavant ridge. For this operation 3rd Division, which normally consisted of three infantry brigades, 8th, 9th and 185th, was reinforced with 152nd Infantry Brigade from the 51st Highland Division and the tanks of 27th Armoured Brigade. Major General 'Bolo' Whistler had been in command of 3rd Division for less than a month. Like Roberts, Whistler was very much a fighting general, with three DSOs to prove it. He seemed to have an innate ability to read a battlefield, turning up at the vital place and time. Many who served under him testify to the effect that his arrival had on his soldiers. His presence and seemingly relaxed manner amidst the terror and chaos of battle made them feel several inches taller and several degrees braver.

jor General lo' Whistler, amander of 3rd antry Division a inspiring, hting' General.

Whistler planned to launch his brigades in series. Immediately after the bombing Brigadier Cass's 8th Infantry Brigade, supported by the tanks of 13th/18th Royal Hussars, would advance south from Escoville, capture the orchards just south of Le Pré Baron (Task One) and continue for a mile and a half to destroy some German positions on a slight spur about 500 yards west of Touffréville (Task Two). Next they were to take Touffréville (Task Two (a)), Sannerville and the area of the main Caen to Troarn road at Banneville-la-Campagne (Task Three). Meanwhile Brigadier Cassels' 152nd Brigade would capture the road triangle a mile east of Escoville. If enemy resistance had been slight, the brigade would then exploit south-east along the road towards Troarn. For support 152nd Brigade was given the flame-thrower tanks of 141st Regiment, Royal Armoured Corps.

8th Brigade's capture of Sannerville and Banneville would be the key to the next phase of operations. Brigadier Smith's 185th Brigade would then despatch an infantry battalion, carried on the tanks of the Staffordshire Yeomanry, to take Lirose, south-west of Sannerville. Lirose would then be the firm base for an attack by the rest of the brigade on Le Quai and Cuillerville (Task Four). Finally, when 185th Brigade was firmly established protecting the

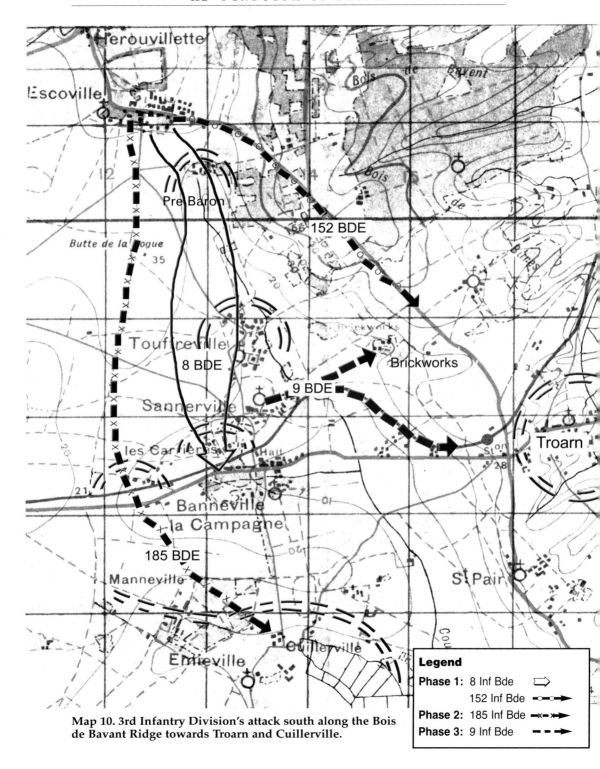

Map 10. 3rd Infantry Division's attack south along the Bois de Bavant Ridge towards Troarn and Cuillerville.

Hérouvillette

Escoville

Pre Baron

Bois de Bavent

Butte de la Hogue
35

152 BDE

Toufreville

8 BDE

Brickworks

9 BDE

Sannerville

les Carrières

Troarn

Banneville
la Campagne

185 BDE

Manneville

St Pair

Emieville

Cuillerville

Legend

Phase 1: 8 Inf Bde ⇨
152 Inf Bde ●─●─●→

Phase 2: 185 Inf Bde ×─×─×→

Phase 3: 9 Inf Bde ▪ ▪ ▪→

southern flank, Brigadier Orr's 9th Infantry Brigade, with the tanks of the East Riding Yeomanry, would pass through 8 Brigade at Sannerville, swing east and attack Troarn (Task Five). Having taken Troarn Orr would press on and seize the Dives bridge and to carry out vigorous patrolling north and south along the river to ensure that the Germans could not launch an attack into the flank of the British advance.

* * * *

At 7.45 am, as the bombing ended and the guns opened up, 13th/18th Hussars crossed the start line ahead of the infantry of 8th Brigade. They rapidly bypassed Le Pré Baron and moved swiftly on towards Task Two, reaching the spur west of Touffréville at about 8.45 am. On their left, 1st Battalion, The South Lancashire Regiment, advancing on foot, progressed well until held up by heavy machine-gun and mortar fire in the area of some sandpits on the edge of Le Pré Baron. The area was more thickly wooded than it is today, and against an enemy who was hard to locate, the leading companies became separated and the attack lost cohesion. At 11.00 am, however, D Company reported that it had reached its final objective and order was quickly restored. As there was considerable mopping up to be done, it was 2.20 pm before Task One, the capture of the Le Pré Baron orchards, was complete.

Advancing on the right of the Lancashires, and in the wake of the 13th/18th Hussars, 2nd Battalion The East Yorkshire Regiment made good progress across relatively open ground until they too came up against a line of well-concealed weapon pits. But the defenders, still shaken by the air and artillery bombardment, put up only brief resistance and were soon overcome. The leading companies continued to press forward, only to be delayed again, this time by an anti-personnel minefield north of Touffréville. Flail tanks were quickly called forward and cleared a path through the mines so that by 11.00 am 2nd East Yorkshires were fighting in the northern outskirts of Touffréville.

At 9.30 am, hearing that 13th/18th Hussars had secured Task Two without difficulty, Brigadier Cass ordered his reserve battalion, 1st Battalion The Suffolk Regiment to move up quickly and attack Sannerville. Having covered the two and a half miles from their assembly area rapidly, the Suffolk's commanding officer, Lieutenant Colonel Dick Goodwin, made a quick battle plan with 13th/18th Hussars, and, at 11.40 am, launched his attack on Sannerville, which was captured by 12.30 pm. Goodwin, keen to maintain the momentum, immediately ordered his leading companies to send strong patrols to the main road at Banneville. They reported the area clear, and by 2.00 pm he was able to report that 1st Suffolk had secured all Task Three objectives. The battalion settled down to consolidate its position in the Sannerville/Banneville area. This proved to be more difficult than expected. The ground was so pitted with huge craters that even walking through the rubble became extremely difficult. Battered beyond description, Sannerville and Banneville were quite impassable to vehicles, and the Suffolks knew that

Soldiers of 1st Suffolk digging a defensive position among the bomb craters, near the remains of the railway line at Sannerville.

9th Brigade and the tanks of East Riding Yeomanry must shortly pass through them to attack Troarn. Bulldozers were quickly called up to ease movement in the area.

Further north Touffréville was still proving a difficult nut to crack. For some reason it seemed to have escaped the worst of the heavy bombs, and the spirit of the defenders was in consequence tougher. Many houses had been wrecked by artillery fire. Well concealed in the ruins and supported by mortar fire, German snipers and tanks made life very difficult for the men of 2nd East Yorkshires. Relentlessly they fought their way through the village until by 6.00 pm they were able to report that resistance had ceased. Task Two (a) had been successfully completed. Yet further north 1st South Lancashires were still fighting in woods south of Le Pré Baron, which were not cleared until 8.00 pm.

* * * *

In a subsidiary operation the highlanders of Brigadier Cassels' 152nd Infantry Brigade launched their attack on the road triangle south-east of Escoville. With 5th Battalion Seaforth Highlanders in the lead, the advance quickly encountered strong opposition in the area of the two northern angles of the triangle. Fighting was intense and at close range, and the 'crocodile' flame-thrower tanks of 141st Regiment, Royal Armoured Corps proved invaluable in dealing with the enemy in their deep and well prepared dug outs. By 9.00 am the Seaforths had reached the southern point of the triangle, though the enemy continued to hold out in several places and mortar fire was considerable. By midday, however, the position was sufficiently firm for the next phase to be launched.

This called for 5th Battalion Cameron Highlanders to pass through the Seaforths, advance down the road towards Troarn, secure the Manoir du Bois on the left of the road and continue to the road/track junction about 1,000 yards south-east. The Camerons crossed their Start Line at 1.30 pm and made steady progress until, at about 2.35 pm, the leading troops were within fifty yards of the Manoir. But the ruins of the buildings provided excellent cover for the enemy, who held out stubbornly. Unfortunately the crocodile tanks had been withdrawn to rearm with flame-thrower fuel and were not available. The battle for the Manoir lasted several hours, and it was not until 7.15 pm that it was finally secured. Thereafter, despite continued German mortar fire in the area, 152nd Infantry Brigade sent patrols forward along the Troarn road, where contact was made with 13th/18th Hussars, who, having secured Task 2 and supported the Suffolks into Sannerville, had bypassed Touffréville to the north, struck east, and reached the Escoville-Troarn road at the junction north-east of the Le Maizeret brickworks at 1.45 pm. Here they had remained throughout the afternoon, guarding the east flank against possible counter-attack.

* * * *

General Whistler was keen to launch Task Four, the capture of Lirose, Le Quai and Cuillerville, as quickly as possible. As soon as he heard that 13th/18th Hussars had taken the spur at Task Two, he ordered Brigadier Smith to bring 185th Brigade forward. The Staffordshire Yeomanry set off, with the infantrymen of 2nd Battalion The King's Shropshire Light Infantry on the backs of their Sherman tanks. The remainder of the brigade followed on foot, making best possible speed. At 9.45 am the Staffordshire Yeomanry passed through 13th/18th Hussars and continued south, only to come under fire just north of Lirose. 2nd KSLI quickly dismounted and launched an attack on the hamlet. At 12.35 pm, having taken Lirose, they pressed on, crossed the railway and road, heading for the orchards north-west of Le Quai and Cuillerville. This area, much of it enclosed within the grounds of the Chateau de Manneville, was, it may be remembered, the location of the Tiger tanks of Captain Fromme's 503rd Heavy Tank Battalion. Although these had been badly battered by the bombing, they were hardly easy meat for an infantry battalion. Reaching the area at 5.50 pm, and realising the presence of German tanks, the KSLI prudently held back, awaiting the arrival of the rest of the brigade.

Behind, the remaining battalions of 185th Brigade were struggling forward on foot as fast as they could, through the dust of a hot July day, to be ready to launch a brigade attack on the orchards, Le Quai and Cuillerville as soon as they reached the area. This attack, supported by the Staffordshire Yeomanry and an artillery barrage, went in at 9.00 pm. By last light the brigade was still 200 yards short of its objective, which had therefore to be cleared in the dark. At 11.55 pm, however, Brigadier Smith was able to report to General Whistler that the Germans had withdrawn, all opposition had ceased, and that the orchards, Cuillerville and Le Quai had been taken. Task Four was complete.

* * * *

Task Five was to be Brigadier Orr's 9th Infantry Brigade attacking east from Sannerville, now held by the Suffolks, towards Troarn. During the morning and early afternoon the Brigade moved to a forming-up place about a mile and a half west of Sannerville. The advance began at 4.00 pm, with two battalions up, on the left 2nd Battalion The Royal Ulster Rifles, on the right 1st Battalion The Kings Own Scottish Borderers, both supported by the tanks of East Riding Yeomanry. Despite the efforts of the Suffolks, both tanks and infantry had considerable difficulty getting through the rubble of Sannerville.

Just east of the village, a small stream, the Cours de Janneville, crossed the route. All bridges had been blown by the Germans and the approaches were covered by fire. After several attempts the Ulster Rifles eventually managed to force a crossing a few hundred yards north-east of Sannerville, along a small track [now a road] to the brickworks at Le Maizeret. As soon as they had secured the far bank, a bridgelayer tank was brought up to enable the East Riding Yeomanry to cross the Cours. Having achieved this, the Ulster Rifles continued east and by 8.00 pm had secured their objective, the Le Maizeret brickworks. The Borderers had been less fortunate and, despite many attempts, had failed to cross the Cours. Eventually Brigadier Orr ordered them to break contact in the south, move north, cross by the Ulster Rifles' bridge, and then drop down to resume their advance. By 9.30 pm the Borderers had taken La Croix de Pierre, a small clutch of buildings beside the main road, about half way between Sannerville and Troarn.

By nightfall on 18 July, therefore, 3rd Division had secured all its objectives except Troarn. Much of the advance had been made through wooded country against ever stiffening opposition. Only in the Sannerville/Banneville area had the heavy bombardment so demoralised the enemy that they put up little resistance. Elsewhere they had fought back robustly, and this, combined with the debris, craters, dust and heat had made it a difficult and exhausting day for the division. With 8th Brigade holding the Touffréville/ Sannerville/Banneville area, 9th Brigade about a mile west and north-west of Troarn, 185th Brigade at Le Quai, and 152nd Brigade holding the west flank

Sherman tank operating in support of 3rd Infantry Division at Banneville.

at the Manoir du Bois, General Whistler had every right to be well pleased
with his division's achievements, as he planned the next day's operations.

* * * *

The Western Flank - 3rd Canadian Infantry Division.

3rd Canadian Infantry Division, under Major General Bob Keller, was to
mount a similar attack down the west flank of the armoured corridor.
Launched from the area of Le Bas de Ranville, they would move south along
the east bank of the Orne, destroy the German positions in the Colombelles
steelworks, and then fan out to take Giberville, Mondeville and Fauberg de
Vaucelles (Caen south of the river). The axis of the advance being less than a
mile wide for the first two miles of the advance, Keller ordered Brigadier
Blackader's 8th Canadian Infantry Brigade to lead, advancing behind an
artillery barrage fired by four field regiments and supported by the tanks of
the divisional reconnaissance regiment, the Royal Canadian Hussars, until it
reached a line where the River Orne swings west into Caen. Having cleared

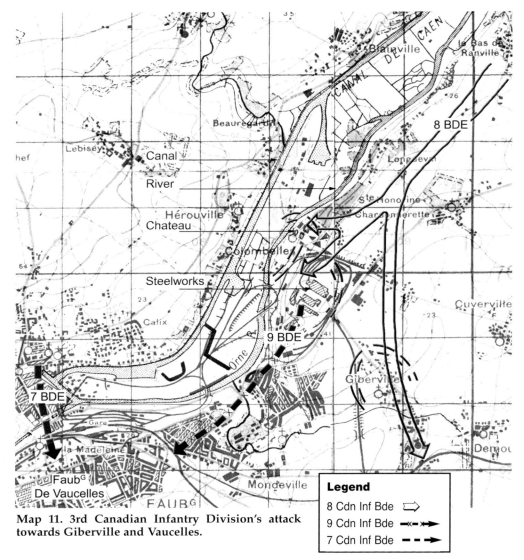

Map 11. 3rd Canadian Infantry Division's attack towards Giberville and Vaucelles.

Legend
8 Cdn Inf Bde ⟹
9 Cdn Inf Bde ⟼
7 Cdn Inf Bde - - ➤

the Colombelles area, 8th Brigade would continue south and south-east, to secure Mondeville and Giberville, while Brigadier Cunningham's 9th Brigade would then pass on the right, follow the bend of the river west and clear Vaucelles. Brigadier Foster's 7th Brigade would be in reserve.

At 7.45 am on 18 July 8th Brigade crossed their start line, with The Queen's Own Rifles of Canada leading on the left and Le Régiment de la Chaudière on the right. By 8.30 am the leading battalions had crossed the Longueval to Ste Honorine road and were heading south into uncleared country, led by tanks of Royal Canadian Hussars. Initially they met with little opposition. On the left the Queen's Own Rifles pushed on, their eyes set firmly on Giberville. At 9.40 am they brushed aside light opposition in the area of the Colombelles to

Cuverville road, and by 11.05 am had reached the outskirts of Giberville, having taken many prisoners.

On the right, however, the situation was far less satisfactory. For a mile the Chaudières advanced south almost unopposed, between the river and the parallel road. But when they reached the area of the chateau and village, snipers and machine-gunners came to life. In the face of heavy resistance the Chaudières' attack stalled. Behind them The North Shore Regiment caught up, and both were then joined by the leading battalion of 9th Brigade, The Stormont, Dundas and Glengarry Highlanders, keen to pass on by and break into Vaucelles. The presence of three battalions from two different brigades in such a small area led to chaos, with no-one quite clear who was who and trying to do what. In the words of the post-war Canadian Military Operations Report 'a scene of indescribable confusion followed . . . By noon the woods and orchards in the neighbourhood were full of a mêlée of soldiers entangled with one another and with the enemy.' This was compounded when an artillery bombardment was called for, but fell upon the unfortunate Stormont Highlanders.

It took several hours to sort out this confusion, and by 3.45 pm it became clear that the Chaudières, whose orders had been to press on through the village and take the steelworks, still had a hard fight ahead of them in the area of the chateau and village. So at 4.10 pm Brigadier Blackader ordered the North Shores to bypass the Chaudières and move on towards the steelworks. This they managed to do and the advance made steady, but slow, progress. By now General Keller was concerned that things were falling behind schedule. He needed to regenerate the momentum of the advance. At 4.45 pm he ordered 8th Brigade to concentrate on the capture of the chateau, steelworks and Giberville, while 9th Brigade was to pass by and push on to Mondeville and Vaucelles.

At last the pendulum of battle began to swing in the area of the chateau, which, by now in flames, was becoming an increasingly unhealthy spot for the German defenders. Resistance crumbled, and by 5.30 pm the Chaudières had captured it and were mopping up in the village. Meanwhile the North Shores were having a hard time in the steelworks, where, once again, the Germans were in no mood to concede easily. This was not a battle of the higher commander with the well-honed tactical plan. Rather it was the gutter-fighting of small teams of infantrymen, where the leadership that counted was that of the platoon and section commander. Small parties of men hunted one another down, snipers proliferated, and much raw courage was shown by both sides. Throughout the evening and most of the night the fight continued, in the ghostly light of burning buildings, the chaos of rubble, around mounds of bomb craters and the shattered remains of the wrecked factory. It was not until dawn on 19 July that the enemy was finally subdued.

On the left the Queen's Own Rifles, for whom the first part of the advance had been relatively easy, encountered their first serious opposition at Giberville. In 1944 Giberville was just a straggling line of houses stretching for nearly one mile astride the road south-east from Colombelles as far as the Caen to Troarn road. The village had suffered heavily in the bombardment.

The resulting ruins and the surrounding orchards gave the defenders admirably concealed defensive positions, and the Canadians were made to fight for every yard of the way. With the tank support of the B Squadron, Royal Canadian Hussars, they fought their way through the village, eventually reaching the main road and railway line by 3.00 pm. By 3.45 pm all resistance had ceased and they dug in, ready for the inevitable counter-attack. At 9.00 pm this duly arrived. With admirable support from the tanks, it was repulsed, and by 9.30 pm over 500 prisoners, mostly from 192nd Panzer-Grenadier Regiment, had been taken.

Meanwhile Brigadier Cunningham decided to leave the Stormont, Dundas and Glengarry Highlanders to sort themselves out after the confusion of Colombelles, while he ordered The North Nova Scotia Highlanders and The Highland Light Infantry of Canada to move east of the steelworks and advance on Mondeville and Vaucelles. By midnight they had cleared Mondeville and reached the first railway line, but had not yet entered Vaucelles. Behind, the Stormont Highlanders had started to move forward again and, keeping close to the river bank, advanced, despite mines, sniping and spasmodic mortar fire, to a position just south-west of the steelworks.

* * * *

By late in the morning it had become clear to Lieutenant General Guy Simonds, commanding II Canadian Corps, that 9th Brigade would not be able to clear Vaucelles by last light. Caen [in 1944 just the area north of the Orne] had fallen on 9 July. Simmonds now ordered Keller to send a patrol from his 7th Brigade, which had been held in reserve, to try to cross the river in the middle of Caen, direct into Vaucelles. If this was successful then a full battalion was to cross as soon as artillery support could be spared from other operations. At 2.00 pm a patrol from The Regina Rifles Regiment, guided by a member of the French resistance, managed to cross the Orne by one of the partially destroyed bridges. Encountering little more than a few machine-guns, it reported favourably. Simmonds immediately ordered the rest of the battalion to cross and advance as far as the main lateral road, La Rue Royale. The aim would be to drive back the enemy machine guns which had hitherto made work on bridging sites impossible. At 4.30 pm the battalion started to cross, covered by machine-guns, mortar fire and the corps artillery. Some struggled over the damaged bridges, but the majority either waded or swam. Heavy fighting ensued, and by midnight the Regina Rifles had cleared the area half a mile back from the river, as far as La Rue Royale.

3rd Canadian Division had had a bruising day. By its close, a somewhat battered 8th Brigade had secured Giberville and Colombelles, though fighting continued throughout the night in the steelworks area. Meanwhile 7th Brigade had one battalion across the river in Vaucelles, but had not yet made contact with 9th Brigade which had reached the eastern edge of Vaucelles, but had not yet crossed the Caen to Vimont railway.

* * * *

2nd Canadian Infantry Division.

On the extreme right flank Major General Foulkes' 2nd Canadian Infantry Division was also in action, west of Caen. [Strictly speaking this was Operation ATLANTIC, but it cannot be divorced from GOODWOOD.] They were ordered to cross the Orne, take the villages of Fleury-sur-Orne, Ifs and St André-sur-Orne and advance a further three miles east, to capture Verrières, just west of the Caen to Falaise road, if VIII Corps had not already achieved this.

Brigadier Letts' 4th Canadian Infantry Brigade, with a squadron of tanks, was to capture Louvigny, on the north bank of the Orne about two miles south-west of Caen. This should attract German attention away from, and provide flank protection for, the activities of Brigadier Megill's 5th Brigade,

Map 12.

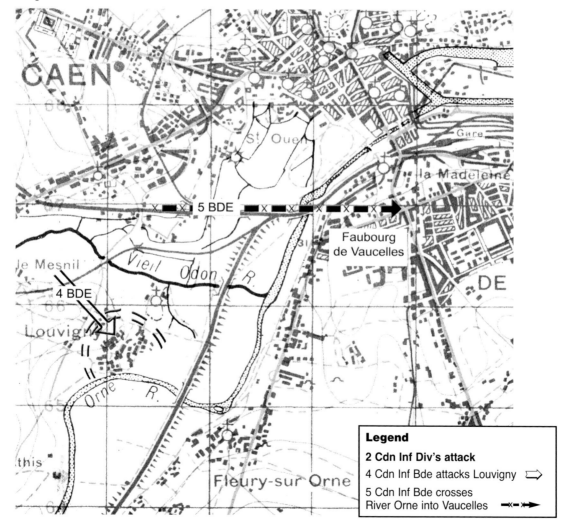

Legend
2 Cdn Inf Div's attack
4 Cdn Inf Bde attacks Louvigny ⇨
5 Cdn Inf Bde crosses River Orne into Vaucelles ➤

which was to cross the Orne into the western end of Vaucelles, and secure bridging sites prior to exploiting south.

On the night of 17/18 July, in a preliminary operation, 8th Canadian Reconnaissance Regiment sent patrols forward from Le Mesnil to find out whether Louvigny was held by the Germans. It was. Brigadier Letts therefore ordered The Royal Regiment of Canada to capture it on the evening of 18 July, with the support of a tank squadron from 10th Canadian Armoured Regiment. At 7.00 pm the Royal Regiment crossed its start line, the road running through Le Mesnil, while the divisional artillery and mortars plastered the objective. Three companies advanced one behind the other down the road towards the orchards on the north-west corner of Louvigny, while the fourth, with battalion headquarters, occupied the high ground west of the village, from where the tank squadron provided fire support onto the village. Initially the advance went well and the attackers drove the enemy from the orchards. But as they advanced further into the village they came under increasingly heavy fire. Casualties mounted, and these included the brigade commander, Brigadier Letts, who had come forward to watch the attack. The leading companies managed to clear half of the village, but could do no more. As dusk approached they pulled back to the area of the orchards, planning to renew the attack on the morning of 19 July.

Satisfied that the Germans' attention had been firmly captured by the attack on Louvigny, Brigadier Megill launched his main attack at 10.15 pm. The Black Watch of Canada managed to capture intact the railway bridge at the west end of Vaucelles and, despite machine-gun and mortar fire, pushed on east until by 3.00 am next morning they had made contact with the Regina Rifles of 7th Brigade just west of the Caen to Falaise road.

By midnight on 18 July the 2nd Canadian Infantry Division had not reached any of its planned objectives, but it had crossed the river into Vaucelles. With good fortune progress might speed up next day.

* * * *

On the eastern flank 3rd Infantry Division, after a largely successful day, had only one objective, Troarn, not taken. Further west it had been a difficult and frustrating day for II Canadian Corps, not unlike that of the armoured divisions of VIII Corps, to which the story now returns.

Chapter 16

'The Worst Night I Ever Remember'

Shortly after 6.00 pm 159th Infantry Brigade started to move forward to join 29th Armoured Brigade, reaching Le Mesnil Frémentel at 7.45 pm. At last General Roberts would have his entire division available. But it was too late for the infantrymen to affect the battle for the Bourguébus ridge that day. Roberts did consider launching them in a night attack on the ridge, but quickly dismissed the idea on the grounds that there were too few hours of darkness in July to make this a sensible option. Besides, the area was illuminated by burning tanks.

Throughout the afternoon the Germans had continued to reinforce their defences along the Bourguébus ridge. They were to be further strengthened during the night. With 11th Armoured Division now held on the slopes below Bourguébus, Hubert-Folie and Bras, with Guards Armoured unable to penetrate the strong defensive screen built up by von Luck further east from Le Poirier and Frénouville to Emiéville, and with 7th Armoured Division not yet having entered the fray, there was no need for the Germans to spread their newly-arriving reinforcements thinly along the entire ridge. They could be concentrated against 11th Armoured Division and used offensively. And attack the German tanks certainly did.

At around 8.20 pm Germans tanks could be seen entering Soliers, doubtless prior to launching a strong counter-attack. All available British

German Mk VI Tiger. Weighing fifty-six tons, armed with an 88mm gun and with 100mm of frontal armour protection – a truly formidable tank.

artillery guns were ordered to fire on the village. Nevertheless, only half an hour later six Tiger and five Panther tanks advanced north along the west side of the railway embankment. Intense fire from 3rd Tanks and the artillery knocked out one Tiger and one Panther, and the rest withdrew. By now 3rd Tanks were running perilously short of ammunition, but their position was far too exposed for resupply vehicles to be able to reach them until after dark. They had no option but to hang on and hope that the Germans would not try again too often.

At 9.30 pm the Germans did indeed try again, this time east of the embankment. Led by a Sherman tank which had been captured some weeks earlier in fighting west of the Orne, six Tigers and six Panthers advanced out of Soliers towards Grentheville. In the orchards south of the village the riflemen of F Company 8th Rifle Brigade and the gunners of 119 Anti-tank Battery watched them coming and were not taken in by the Sherman. In short time the gunners had knocked out it and two Panthers before the rest scuttled back to the protection of Soliers. Even as late as 10.40 pm, as visibility faded, the Germans made yet another attempt to drive 3rd Tanks from their position. Down almost to their last rounds, Silvertop's men held grimly on.

As darkness approached on 18 July Brigadier Harvey took stock. He had lost 128 of the 219 tanks that had crossed the start-line that morning. And those which were still operating desperately needed a resupply of ammunition and fuel. With only a short night and with a vast number of units from three armoured divisions crammed into a small area, it was important to make resupply simple. He decided, therefore, to harbour his brigade as tightly as possible for the night. On the right 3rd Tanks, still holding onto their exposed position near the Soliers to Cormelles road and still under intermittent fire, had lost forty-one tanks. He ordered them to pull back about 500 yards north-east, to the area of a quarry. On the left 23rd Hussars, with losses of twenty-six tanks, had already leaguered just north of the second railway line, about half a mile east of Grentheville, with the exception of Captain Walter's small group still in its hedgerow near Le Poirier. 2nd Fife and Forfar Yeomanry, now down to only eleven tanks, was ordered to pull back north of the Caen to Cagny road and to leaguer near Harvey's own tactical headquarters just west of Le Mesnil Frémentel. Harvey also made it clear to Colonel Scott that his few tanks were the brigade reserve. It is a vital military principle that, however reduced a force may be by heavy fighting, commanders at every level should always constitute a nominated reserve, ready to react quickly to any sudden threat.

Sergeant Buck Kite, of A Squadron 3rd Royal Tanks, had been in the thick of the fighting all day.

'My engine had been cutting out for most of the day and was getting worse. The light was fading when we were ordered to move back. I zig-zagged my way, hoping that the engine would not let us down. Suddenly, as we were on a rise in the ground, there was a terrific thud at the back and the engine stopped. We had been hit a glancing blow. For a few terrifying moments we sat sky-lined,

while the driver tried to get the engine going - in vain. So I decided that we had no option other than to abandon the tank. I ordered the crew to bale out. At that moment a stick of mortar bombs landed nearby, so we all took cover and waited for the bombardment to stop. It was now quite dark and somehow my operator, Lance Corporal Pete Elstob, became separated from us. When we did get back to the leaguer I was given a new tank. Next morning I heard that my tank had been recovered, but that story belongs to Pete Elstob.'

Elstob had taken cover in a convenient trench. So exhausted was he by the day's activities that he immediately fell asleep, despite the bombardment. He woke to find that the others had gone and that he was now alone. Feeling distinctly cold he returned to the tank to collect his 'bale-out' kit. As he approached he heard voices. He stopped to listen and realized that they came from Sergeant Kite's earphones which were hanging over the side of the tank. He put them on and asked if he should destroy the tank. In reply he was asked whether it was still 'a runner'. He climbed into the driver's seat and tried to start the engine. To his surprise it started at once. On reporting this on the radio he was asked whether he could hear the engine of a tank racing a few hundred yards south. He could, and was told to drive over to it and help bring in a badly wounded man.

The noise of his activities had alerted another soldier who was also taking cover in the area. He proved to be a driver whose tank had been knocked-out earlier and who was waiting to withdraw under cover of darkness. He agreed to drive the tank while Elstob climbed into the turret. They headed towards the noise of the roaring engine. On reaching the tank they found a member of the crew who told them that the driver was trapped inside, conscious but seriously wounded. Taking a torch, Elstob looked at the driver's legs. They were hideously smashed - a mass of blood, splinters and torn flesh. Together the three soldiers scooped up the legs, bound them in a blanket and, with great difficulty, managed to extract the driver from the tank and carry him to Elstob's tank. As gently as they could they lowered him onto the back of the tank. The driver and Elstob then climbed into the tank while the other crewman hung onto the wounded man, and they set off north again. Finding it impossible to see his way in the dark, Elstob dismounted and walked in front of the tank, shining a torch. Somehow they managed to find the regimental leaguer, where they passed the wounded man on to the medical officer. By now it was 2.30 am, and all Elstob wanted to do was to sleep. But he was summoned before Colonel Silvertop, warmly congratulated on his achievement and told that he was promoted to corporal with immediate effect and was to take over as a tank commander.

* * * *

Not all were to have the luxury of even brief sleep. Captain Peter Walter of 23rd Hussars, as has been recounted, spent his night withdrawing from and then returning to his hidey-hole near Le Poirier. And if Lieutenant David

Stileman of G Company 8th Rifle Brigade felt that, with his mad rush through Hubert-Folie and his involvement with casualties and prisoners, he had done a full day's work, he was to be disappointed:

> 'Quite honestly, I thought that I had earned my 15 shillings a day, but my betters clearly thought otherwise. I was told to report to Colonel Tony Hunter at Battalion HQ. He told me to take out a section-strength patrol under cover of darkness and lay a necklace of Hawkins anti-tank mines across the Bras to Hubert-Folie road. I had the feeling that the colonel was not over-keen on this little outing but had been told to do it from above, because he particularly told me not to get involved in any fighting and not to have any casualties. He could see that I was so dead tired that he was even good enough to set my compass for me.
>
> 'We duly set off, but, the whole area was floodlit by burning tanks, which cast long ghostly shadows across the ground. Movement was therefore very slow. There are not many hours of darkness in mid July, so we never even reached the road. We got close enough to hear the Teutonic tongue on the ridge before we ran out of time and had to pull back. Perhaps if I'd been allowed to take just two men, not a full section, I might have made it, but it seemed at the time a pretty crazy outing – and it still does!'

F Company, in the orchards south of Grentheville, spent a night which none would ever forget. With the arrival of darkness the threat of another German tank attack evaporated. As it got dark 119 Anti-Tank Battery was therefore withdrawn north of the railway, leaving the riflemen with the distinct feeling of being out on a limb, armed only with their rifles and machine-guns. The risk of a German infantry counter-attack under cover of darkness and the frequent shelling and mortaring made for a dangerous and disturbed night. Major Foster Cunliffe commanded F Company:

> 'It was a quite the worst night I ever remember throughout the entire campaign. Although we had dug shallow trenches the shelling was so accurate and frequent that we had many casualties. I called for more stretcher bearers but they were already overstretched and the casualty clearing station was a long way back. All we could do was give morphine to relieve pain and apply what little first aid we knew. My signals NCO, Corporal Maskens, had his arm completely severed. We did what we could but I'm afraid that he died a few days later. When we moved on next day we were relieved by 1st Rifle Brigade, from 7th Armoured. I remember their CO, Colonel Victor Paley, an excellent, calm and friendly man, arriving. He took over and looked after the casualties we had to leave behind, for which I will always be grateful.'

July nights may be short, but for those in F Company this one seemed interminable. In this sort of situation the imagination can run riot. Lance Corporal Farmer was ordered by Cunliffe to take out a small reconnaissance patrol, to 'ensure that the front door-step was clear'.

> 'We had only gone about 200 yards when I could see some Germans digging beside a bank. Having been told not to get involved in a battle I bypassed them

and carried on. When I got back I reported what I had seen. Next morning I got permission to investigate. We found the spot and the bank, but no Germans! Just the seat of an old plough stuck into the bank, which, beside some grass which had been waving in the breeze, had given the impression of Germans digging. To a section of highly apprehensive young riflemen on patrol during a dreadful night it seemed totally real. Next morning it seemed almost laughable.'

* * * *

After a day of intense fighting all three armoured regiments were in dire need of resupply. Under cover of darkness rations, petrol and ammunition trucks came forward from the regimental administration echelons back near Ranville, and the surviving tanks were restocked for the next day's battle. There are only about five hours of darkness in mid July. All this essential administration had to be carried out with the utmost speed and efficiency so that tank crews should at least have a hot meal and a few hours sleep before facing the problems that the next day would certainly present.

Staff Sergeant Tom Willmott was a squadron quartermaster sergeant in 2nd Fife and Forfar Yeomanry.

'As SQMS it was my job to bring forward supplies to the Fighting Echelon. The principle was that after a day's fighting RHQ would send back an estimate of requirements - fuel, ammunition, food, water, above all mail and cigarettes, and a map reference of where they would leaguer for the night. We would set off from A1 Echelon as it got dark. In theory it all sounds quite easy, but in reality it was anything but. You knew the start and finish points, but the route in between was up to you - in the dark, unreconnoitred, using minimum lights. It would have been easy to get lost, or find that you arrived with fewer trucks than you started. I am glad to say that throughout the entire campaign we never did. It needed good map reading skills, experience and a good deal of luck! I would use the brigade centre-line, which might or might not be marked by periodic dim torches beside the road. Once in the forward area I would head off to whichever flank the regiment was on and hope for the best.

'On 18 July, when the tanks set off after the bombing, the echelons were left way back in the glider fields near Ranville. So we were a long way back, and the area in between had been plastered by bombing and gunfire. Nearing last light I set off with a small column of vehicles and moved up the west flank, past the Colombelles factory area, where the Canadians were clearly still fighting, and followed the railway line south until I met the MO, Captain Beamish. He had many of the casualties and brewed-up crews there. I had actually brought up the cook's 3-tonner, which I didn't usually do, and so was able to give hot soup and drinks to many of them, before the de-horsed crews made their own way back to the echelon area. We then gave supplies to the tank crews, who had only a few hours to refuel, rearm and try to get some sleep. Eventually I got back to the echelon area at about first light, only to find that there had been a big air-raid in the area and that we had had many more casualties.'

Meanwhile regimental fitters worked like beavers to see that as many knocked-out tanks as possible were brought in, and, where possible, prepared for battle again. Second Army had already established a reserve of over 500 tanks in Normandy, and the Forward Delivery Squadron managed to get forward during the night to reinforce all three armoured regiments. By dawn the brigade, having ended the previous day with only ninety-one tanks still operational, was able to muster 124.

* * * *

That night the Luftwaffe launched a heavy bombing raid on the area of the Orne bridges. Whether this was because they were aware of the particular build up of forces in the area, or whether it was just a chance raid on an obviously important target, is uncertain. Just east of the bridges were the administrative units of 11th Armoured Division. Many casualties were caused among tank crews who, having survived being knocked out earlier in the day, had made their way north to the administrative area. Caught in the open, with neither tanks nor trenches to protect them, they were very vulnerable to the bombs which rained down upon them. Among them was Lieutenant Robert Clark of 2nd Fife and Forfar Yeomanry.

'At about 11pm German aircraft appeared overhead - the first we had seen. They dropped flares to illuminate the area, and then came the bombs. I crawled under a nearby vehicle, and that was when I was hit. A bomb must have landed just beside me and a large piece of shrapnel hit me in the stomach. Realizing that it was pretty serious I thought that if I didn't do something quickly I would die. Fortunately I remembered where the medical tent was, so I set off to get there. I found an abandoned Jeep and somehow managed to drive it. Flares still lit up the area, so I could see where I was going, although bombs were still dropping all around. Eventually I reached darkness, drove into a bomb crater and was thrown out of the jeep. When I had recovered a bit I crawled on till I reached the medical tent. There was no-one there - I suppose they had taken cover. I found a stretcher and just lay there until the bombing ended and someone came. He asked me what I was doing, so I told him that I'd been hit. He took a look and clearly didn't like what he saw. He patched me up a bit and then sent me quickly back by truck to the Field Hospital near Bayeux, where I was operated on immediately. About a week later I was sent back to England, where I spent six months in Liverpool Royal Infirmary.'

Meanwhile the Germans were using the cover of darkness further to strengthen the defences along the ridge. General Wisch brought forward his two panzer grenadier regiments. Colonel Frey's 1st SS Panzer-Grenadier Regiment took over Bras, Hubert-Folie and Bourguébus, while Colonel Sandig's 2nd Regiment moved into Le Poirier, Four, Soliers and La Hogue. Further back, 12th SS Panzer Division, the infamous Hitler-Youth, was ordered to move up from Falaise and replace von Luck's battle group in its defensive screen between Frenouville and Emiéville on the morning of 19 July. Any idea of using the panzer divisions for co-ordinated offensive operations had to be given up. Once again they were sucked into ground-holding on the east flank, which was exactly what Montgomery wanted.

* * * *

In the early hours of 19 July HQ Second Army issued the following report to cover operations between 12.00 pm and midnight on 18 July:

> 'During the afternoon our rapid advance of the morning was slowed up by stiffening enemy opposition and the need for moving forward of infantry units to assist the armour. Infantry had got a small bridgehead over the River Orne in Fauberg de Vaucelles, were attacking Louvigny and were clearing the factory area. A heavy counter-attack on Giberville was driven off and approximately 500 prisoners captured. Enemy counter-attacks with tanks developed against our own armour, which had been forced to take up positions in the area of Bras/Bourguébus/Grentheville. A strong anti-tank screen between Frénouville and Emiéville halted the armoured thrust in the area of Vimont. The infantry on the left were established as far south as Cuillerville. The drive towards Troarn continues.'

Although more accurate than the earlier report, this was still somewhat misleading. The impression given is that both Bras and Bourguébus had been taken, when in fact both were still firmly in German hands and being strongly reinforced. Nor did it give any indication of the tank losses sustained by VIII Corps, which would have a marked effect upon what could be achieved next day.

Military history is full of examples of incomplete, misleading or plainly incorrect reports leading to higher commanders forming an inaccurate picture of the battlefield and either expecting too much or fearing failure in the next phase of operations. From Shakespeare's Henry IV to the trenches of the First World War it is clear that the front-line soldier often has a sceptical disregard for those on the staff of higher headquarters, who are doubtless living a more comfortable and less dangerous life. 'We will tell them just enough to keep them happy and off our backs' sounds fine, but it does not serve the interests of the front-line soldier if those behind are left to expect more from future operations than can in fact be delivered. Quite why the staff of HQ Second Army were not told, or chose to ignore, the true picture is unknown. But, as events next day would prove, there was much blood still to be spilt before GOODWOOD had run its course, and even then the tactical achievements would fall far short of those expected by Eisenhower and his staff.

During 18 July General Montgomery sent a message to the Field Marshal Brooke in London:

> 'Operations this morning have been a complete success. The effect of the air bombardment was decisive and the spectacle terrific. VIII Corps advanced at 0730. The present situation is as follows:

11 Armd Div - reached Tilly-la-Campagne (0760) and Bras (0663).

7 Armd Div - passed Démouville (1067) and moving on to la Hogue (0960).

Gds Armd Div - passed Cagny and now in Vimont.

3 Div - moving on Troarn.

'I have ordered the armd car regts of each div, supported by armd recce regts, to recce towards and secure crossings over the Dives between Mezidon and Falaise. Canadians are fighting hard in Vaucelles.

'Have issued a brief statement for tonight's 9pm BBC News and am stopping all further reports today. The situation is very promising and it is difficult to see what the enemy can do at present. Few enemy tanks have been met so far, and no mines.'

This was a wildly inaccurate reading of the situation. At Bras and Troarn the Germans had repelled the British attacks. Tilly, and La Hogue had not even been reached. Falaise and Mezidon were more than ten miles away from the action; indeed the latter, far off to the east, had featured in no-one's plans as an objective. From the start there had been two battalions of German tanks confronting the advance, and from midday onwards 1st SS Panzer Division had been rushed into the area, to be followed next day by 12th SS Panzer Division. There were, however, no mines! There was plenty that the enemy could do, and he was already doing it. It is hardly surprising that anyone reading this, or similar reports that Montgomery sent to Eisenhower at SHAEF, should have been completely misled about the likely achievements of GOODWOOD. And this unsatisfactory situation was further compounded by the most unfortunate press conference which General Montgomery held that evening. In it he exuded confidence and his satisfaction at the progress of GOODWOOD Day One. He spoke about 'having broken through' and 'operating in open country', neither of which was true. Doubtless those who attended left in an atmosphere of misplaced optimism. General de Guingand, his loyal chief of staff, was very critical of this conference which he considered should never have been held. When reality dawned at the end of GOODWOOD vitriol descended on Montgomery's head from far and wide, contributing to a real crisis of confidence in his command, which is discussed further in chapter 22.

Chapter 17

THE RIDGE AT LAST – BRAS AND HUBERT-FOLIE

Any chance of a speedy break-through had of course evaporated by nightfall on 18 July. 19 July was to be a very different sort of day. Gone was the air of excitement and expectation. There would be no vast tank armada surging confidently forward behind a devastating aerial and artillery bombardment. It was to be a day of regrouping, replanning and then a hard slog to secure the vital villages on the Bourguébus ridge. At 6.45 am General Roberts informed General Erskine of 7th Armoured Division that, in view of the reorganization necessary following the heavy tank losses of the previous day, 11th Armoured Division would not be able to undertake concerted offensive action for several hours. This did not mean, however, that the division remained inactive.

As dawn broke the Germans increased the intensity of the artillery fire which had continued spasmodically throughout the night. Artillery fire has often been used to conceal a withdrawal; it was important for General Roberts to find out quickly whether the Germans had pulled back or were still holding the ridge villages in strength. This was an obvious task for the divisional reconnaissance regiment. Accordingly, at 6.00 am, C Squadron 2nd Northants Yeomanry were sent to reconnoitre south along the line of the railway embankment. The question was quickly answered when they came under anti-tank fire from Bras and were forced to withdraw having taken a few casualties. The Germans were clearly still there in force.

Nor did they intend to sit passively awaiting the next British attack. At 7.00 am they launched a strong attack from the area of Bras and Hubert-Folie, on 3rd Royal Tanks, who had moved forward shortly after first light from their overnight quarry to the position that had held the day before near the Cormelles to Soliers road. Although this was beaten off, Brigadier Harvey was concerned that, being in open ground west of the railway embankment and some way forward of other units, 3rd Tanks was unduly exposed. At 7.30 am he ordered them to withdraw a mile to the north. Once there Colonel Silvertop reorganized his regiment into two small squadrons each of about ten tanks.

At 8.00 am it was reported that large numbers of German infantry could be seen at Four, doubtless Colonel Sandig's 2nd SS Panzer-Grenadier Regiment. And at 9.00 am, following a report from A Squadron 2nd Northants Yeomanry, artillery fire was brought down on tanks and infantry, seen digging positions on the north-east edges of Bras and Hubert-Folie. The infantry were Colonel Frey's 1st SS Panzer-Grenadier Regiment which had moved up during the night. It is impossible accurately to site infantry weapons in the dark, so the first few hours of daylight were important to the defenders as they prepared their positions, only too aware that they were likely to be attacked shortly.

* * * *

At 9.30 am Second Army Commander, General Dempsey, visited General O'Connor at HQ VIII Corps to review the situation. Following their discussions he wrote a personal note of his instructions:

VIII Corps - 19 July.

11 Armd.	a. NE of BRAS.
	b. Get BRAS.
	c. Get on line IFS - HUBERT-FOLIE.
	d. Get on line BEAUVOIR - VERRIERES.
7 Armd.	a. SOLIERS - FOUR.
	b. TILLY - LA HOGUE.
	c. CRAMESNIL spur.
Gds Armd.	a. CAGNY - FRENOUVILLE towards VIMONT.

Following Dempsey's visit O'Connor told Generals Roberts and Erskine to meet him at Roberts' tactical headquarters near Le Mesnil Frémentel at 12.00 pm. However, Roberts, so often a step ahead of the game, had already invited Erskine and Adair to join him and discuss future operations. By the time O'Connor arrived the three divisional commanders had worked out a joint plan which they put to the corps commander. With a few modifications, it was accepted by O'Connor.

1. At 4.00 pm 11th Armoured to attack Bras and then Hubert-Folie.
2. At 5.00 pm 7th Armoured to attack Bourguébus and Four.
3. At 5.00 pm Guards Armoured to attack Le Poirier, and then move on to Frénouville.
4. All attacks would have full artillery support.

General Roberts then went forward to see Brigadier Harvey:

'At about two o'clock I went forward to find Roscoe Harvey to discuss the next phase of operations. As usual he had sited his Tac HQ in a most bloody awful place, so it wasn't surprising, with a collection of tanks milling around, that we quickly came under heavy artillery fire. We crawled under the tanks or got into nearby trenches, all except the unfortunate brigade major, Anthony Kershaw, who got a large splinter in his bottom.'

Roberts and Harvey agreed that since 2nd Northants Yeomanry had lost fewer tanks than the other regiments, they should come under command of 29th Armoured Brigade and lead the attack on Bras. With artillery support from 13th RHA, they would advance at 4.00pm, closely followed by the motor

Major General Roberts (right), who was so often one step ahead of the game, visiting Brigadier Harvey at the latter's tactical headquarters

companies of 8th Rifle Brigade who would then clear the village. The Yeomanry would then provide covering fire from the south-east corner of Bras, for an attack on Hubert-Folie by 3rd Tanks with G Company 8th Rifle Brigade.

Shortly before 4.00 pm 2nd Northants Yeomanry started their advance on Bras, while a heavy artillery barrage plastered the village. Still holding the right flank was Major Close, whose A Squadron 3rd Tanks had been reinforced that morning to number eleven tanks:

'At our regimental O Group at 3.00 pm I was told that we would be attacking Hubert-Folie with G Company, after the Northants Yeomanry and the rest of 8th Rifle Brigade had taken Bras. The Northants Yeomanry were to pass through my position on the right, so I was told to contact their CO and point out the danger areas. When they arrived I got out of my tank and ran over to his. I showed him where my tanks had been knocked out the day before and I said "For goodness sake don't go too far over to the west. Ifs is strongly held with 88s, and you'll get into real trouble." '

The attack set off, but although the leading elements almost reached the outskirts of Bras, the regiment had indeed gone too far round to the right and come under heavy fire from Ifs. Close could see the all too familiar spirals of

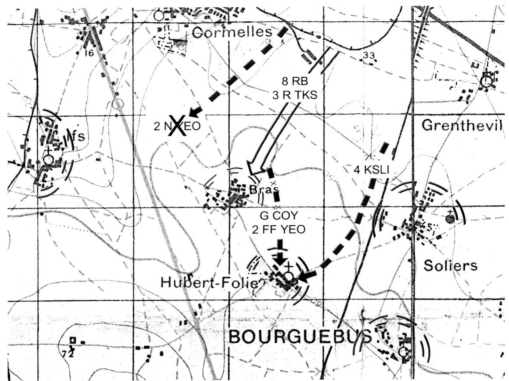

Map 13. 11th Armoured Division captures the ridge villages, showing 2nd Northants Yeomanry's attack, and 3rd Royal Tanks and 8th Rifle Brigade's successful attack on Bras. Also showing the attack by 2nd Fife and Forfar Yeomanry and G Coy 8th Rifle Brigade on Hubert-Folie, and the route taken by 4th King's Shropshire Light Infantry when they moved up to the village.

smoke as the attack ground to a halt:

> 'In a matter of minutes they seemed to have lost a complete squadron, and I could see the remainder of the regiment starting to withdraw down the slope towards my position. Colonel David Silvertop also saw what had happened and he quickly got on the radio to the brigadier and suggested that we should take over the attack and lead the companies of 8 RB, who were just coming up to our position, into Bras. This was agreed and we set off.
>
> 'I hadn't gone more than a dozen yards when there was a hell of a crack. The tank stopped and I baled out. The front had been practically blown off. The driver was dead, but I did manage to get the co-driver out, though he was in a terrible state. The rest of us were unharmed. I told the gunner to give the co-driver morphine, but unfortunately he died very soon after. I then tore across to the nearest tank, which happened to be Sergeant Freddie Dale's, told him to get out, which he was very reluctant to do, and I climbed in and set off for Bras again. We got right up to the village and were able to give very good covering fire to F and H Companies of 8 RB as they stormed the village.'

HUBERT-FOLIE   BRAS   IFS

3RD ROYAL TANKS AND 8TH
RIFLE BRIGADE'S ATTACK

297

A modern photograph taken from the top of the railway embankment, above Major Close's 'Drainpipe', looking towards the ridge villages. Disregard the new factory buildings in the middle distance and this is almost exactly the peaceful view which greeted 3rd Royal Tanks on the morning of 18 July. Imagine thirty hours later as 3rd Royal Tanks and 8th Rifle Brigade mount their assaults on Bras, through a sea of knocked out tanks.

Lieutenant Johnny Langdon was again in the thick of the action on the left flank of A Squadron:

'I had received a fresh tank and crew, none of whom had been in action before. As we advanced up the slope I ordered my new gunner to spray the corn in front with machine-gun fire, as we had reached the enemy trenches. He proceeded to press the wrong button and fired a 75mm HE round which, with the gun fully depressed, exploded just a few yards in front of us. I did not have time to dwell on the trials of an untrained crew, as Bill Close ordered me to move further left, with a view to entering Bras from the east. I was now heading directly towards the blackened but still smouldering hulk of my tank of the day before - a most unpleasant feeling. Travelling at top speed we passed more enemy positions, but, just as we reached the edge of the corn, we were hit. Fortunately no-one was wounded this time, but the tank had had it, so we baled out and started to move back down the slope, crouching down in the corn because we had to move through the German positions that we had just overrun.

'I stuck my head above the corn periodically and was delighted to see the half-tracks and carriers of 8th Rifle Brigade. Initially they thought we were Germans

and it was uncomfortable to be gazing down the barrels of British rifles, but a few quick shouts convinced them that we were a baled-out tank crew. They asked us to look after the twenty prisoners they had already taken, so we escorted these back down the slope. Near the embankment we all had to take cover when a 'moaning minnie' stonk landed beside us. We handed over our prisoners at brigade HQ, and I rejoined A Squadron when they pulled back after the battle was over.'

There can be little doubt that Silvertop's decisive action and leadership saved, indeed won the day. Major Anthony Kershaw, Harvey's brigade major, recorded it clearly:

'I had found it almost impossible to get the commanding officer of the Northants Yeomanry to speak on the radio. As a result they were rather stiff and unresponsive to command. The extraordinary flexibility of David Silvertop in 3rd Tanks, however, was in marked contrast. When he saw that the Yeomanry were stuck he immediately switched the line of attack, gave a few quick orders over the air and simply charged the village. One tank commander later told me that he went through the outer wall of the village at 25 mph! David Silvertop was without doubt the most fearless and marvellous regimental commander that I met throughout the entire war.'

Silvertop had already attacked Bras on two occasions, losing virtually a regiment's worth of tanks and many men, and he had seen what had just happened to the Northants Yeomanry. As Colonel von Luck at Cagny had turned a most unpromising situation into a clear success by seizing the pendulum of battle at a vital moment, so Colonel Silvertop provided the crucial drive which was to lead, at last, to the break-in to the Bourguébus ridge. It is actions like these that are the measure of true leadership. If the attack on Bras had failed, that on Hubert-Folie could not have been mounted, and the Germans would still have been masters of the Bourguébus ridge at nightfall.

Lieutenant Colonel David Silvertop, DSC MC – the outstanding commanding officer of 3rd Royal Tanks.

It was at 4.40 pm that the leading tanks entered Bras. Hot on their heels was Colonel Tony Hunter, with F and H Companies of 8th Rifle Brigade:

'I gave out my orders from the railway embankment, where it crosses the Caen to Cagny road. We formed up just west of the embankment and moved forward at 4.00 pm. We had a certain amount of difficulty crossing the second railway, but by 4.25 pm we had crossed our start line, the Cormelles to Soliers road. We could see the Northants Yeomanry burning on our right, but David Silvertop's regiment was already moving on the village. We tucked in close behind them and headed for Bras. On the way up the slope we overran quite a number of enemy infantry in the corn. They were quickly rounded up by the carrier platoons. F and H Companies debussed as they approached the outskirts of the village and pressed on into it. I sent Support Company to take up a position facing west, to protect that vulnerable flank from attack.'

Commanding F Company was Major Foster Cunliffe:

'From our point of view it was a classic infantry/armour attack. We came in

from due north hot on the tails of the tanks. We had to travel flat out to keep up with them, which made for a very rough ride as we bucketed in and out of shell holes hidden in the cornfield, and dodged round the burnt-out shells of tanks. H Company was to take the orchard to the north-east of the village, while we took the village itself. We debussed on the edge of the village. No time for reorganizing and sorting out straight lines, etc, we just rushed straight in. We had to make the most of the shock action of 3rd Tanks who just drove straight through the village. My leading platoon, 6 Platoon under Philip Sedgewick, went so fast that they took the Germans completely by surprise. Initially they put up quite a fight, and we had some pretty exciting moments - not surprising as they were SS panzer-grenadiers. But then co-ordinated resistance suddenly seemed to collapse - I suppose we looked as though we meant business. Philip's platoon reached the far side of the village so quickly that they had a marvellous shoot at about fifty fleeing Germans who tried to escape south - not many of them made it. Then we started to clear all the remaining German positions and round up the prisoners. Some put up brief resistance, but we managed to sort them out. I remember being amazed when it emerged that the battalion had taken nearly 300 prisoners. Conversley, I doubt whether our two companies numbered more than about 100 riflemen. A motor company is not like a normal infantry company. By the time you have left drivers, gunners and signallers with the half-tracks, there are not many riflemen on the ground. And we had already had casualties at Grentheville the night before. We managed to capture quite a lot of weapons and equipment, including a Volkswagen command car, which joined F Company and served valiantly as far as Antwerp!'

Corporal Jones was in 7 Platoon:

'It had been a horrible night at Grentheville. We'd been heavily mortared, and had three more casualties, one of whom was the platoon sergeant. So I was acting in his place. When we dismounted I think the platoon only numbered about nine or ten men. I grabbed a Bren gun and decided to try my hand at firing from the hip as we charged the village. It was a reassuring, almost exhilarating experience, until I suddenly realised that the figure I had been firing at was an old woman in black, reluctant, as old folk are, to leave her home whatever the circumstances. Fortunately I missed! Once in the village we had quite a tussle with some pretty determined SS men and took a large number of prisoners.'

Perhaps the defenders thought, when they saw the Northants Yeomanry's attack founder, that they had won. After all, it was the third tank attack that had been beaten off in thirty hours. But the speed of Silvertop's reaction and the dash of Hunter's riflemen following closely behind the tanks, clearly surprised them. Crack troops that they were, they did not yield lightly. Some emerged from their slit trenches, armed with grenades, and were quickly cut down. A few machine-gun posts held out initially, but by 5.15 pm most of the village had been cleared, though the riflemen spent some time hunting down a few gallant snipers among the shattered ruins. However, by 5.40 pm, just one hour after the tanks entered the village, Hunter was able to report that resistance had ceased, mopping up was complete and that 300 prisoners had been taken, virtually the whole of 3rd Battalion, 1st SS Panzer-Grenadier Regiment:

> *'I met David Silvertop by a Dutch barn at the north-west corner of the village, and we made a joint plan for holding the village. Then soon after 6 pm the leading elements of 3rd Monmouths arrived to relieve us. For us, the next stage was to be G Company's attack on Hubert-Folie.'*

Bras was a vital acquisition. It was the first toe-hold on the Bourguébus Ridge. Having given such clear orders on the priority of targets for attack by VIII Corps, General Dempsey had naturally kept in close touch with events. At 5.45 pm he heard of the seizure of Bras and immediately ordered that it was to be firmly held by 159th Infantry Brigade, until he could arrange for II Canadian Corps to move forward, when they had finished clearing Vaucelles, and relieve 11th Armoured Division. But General Roberts had needed no such encouragement. He had earlier warned Brigadier Churcher to be ready to bring forward his 159th Brigade as soon as 29th Armoured Brigade had broken through to the ridge. 3rd Monmouths quickly moved up to Bras.

With 3rd Tanks having led the charge on Bras, Brigadier Harvey now had to change his plans for the attack on Hubert-Folie. Speed was essential in order to capitalise on the capture of Bras. Despite its recent battering, he felt that 2nd Northants Yeomanry were still strong enough to take on Hubert-Folie. And they were nearby, while 2nd Fife and Forfar Yeomanry and 23rd Hussars were both well back, still east of the embankment and north of Grentheville. He ordered Colonel Cooke, commanding the Northants Yeomanry, to lead the attack. By 6.10 pm they were on the move, but then came a radio report that 22nd Armoured Brigade from 7th Armoured Division had already taken the village. Although this seemed highly unlikely it had, of course, to be checked, so the attack was halted. It was during this halt, while Cooke was giving orders to his squadron leaders, that they came under heavy artillery fire. There were several casualties, including Major Peck, C Squadron commander, who was killed. Once again the regiment seemed to be in some disarray.

One of the marks of a good commander is that having given out his orders he does not waste time dwelling on the present but immediately starts to think ahead. Harvey had earlier warned Colonel Scott that 2nd Fife and Forfar, as the nominated reserve, were to be ready to move up quickly if required. When, at 6.40 pm, he realised that the Northants Yeomanry had stalled, Harvey was therefore able quickly to order Scott to bring forward his regiment and lead the attack on Hubert-Folie. Although they had not been involved in any offensive operations that day, the Fife and Forfar Yeomanry had its taste of misfortune. Lieutenant Steel Brownlie commanded 4 Troop in Major John Powell's A Squadron. His contemporary diary records:

> *'Just as he was about to give out orders JP was killed when shells landed amongst us. I had a very narrow escape, being almost run over by Cpl Croney's tank. And had I not moved I would have been blown to bits by a shell which*

smashed my map board to pieces. I got into my tank just in time as another shell landed a yard or two in front throwing splinters everywhere - the radio aerial was clipped off.'

Inevitably it took time for Scott to bring his regiment forward from their position near Grentheville. Having crossed to the west side of the railway embankment they had to move forward nearly two miles to join 3rd Tanks and 8th Rifle Brigade at Bras. The delay proved to be an uncomfortable time for those at Bras. G Company, waiting on its start line on the edge of the village, was subjected to periodic shelling, the most unpleasant being a ten minute period when four regiments of British guns mistook Bras for Hubert-Folie. On arrival, and following a brief discussion with Silvertop and Hunter, Scott quickly linked up with Major Noel Bell and G Company and made an artillery fire plan for the attack. By 8.00 pm Scott was ready and the attack went in. Major Sir John Gilmour:

'We had remained in reserve all morning. We had received some reinforcements during the night and Colonel Alec Scott reorganized us into two squadrons of eleven tanks each, with two in RHQ, his and mine, as I was now acting as second-in-command. Earlier in the day a stray shot had come over and killed Major John Powell of A Squadron. This was a real blow to me personally. John was a long-term friend of mine - we had been at school together. Indeed I had persuaded him to join the Yeomanry and he had married a cousin of mine. And of course Chris Nicholls had been killed the day before, so one squadron was commanded by a captain and the other by a troop leader.

'Having crossed under the embankment we made our way over the open country and came under a very heavy bombardment, which we motored through as quickly as possible, fortunately without taking casualties. The attack was a joint affair with G Company 8th Rifle Brigade, and went in at 8.00 pm behind an artillery barrage. We got into the village without trouble, one squadron going in with G Company and the other moving round to the south-west to protect against counter-attack.'

G Company followed closely behind the tanks. Lieutenant David Stileman's 11 Platoon was right assault platoon:

'Having seen the success of F and H Companies at Bras, "Shiny" G was champing at the bit to deal with Hubert-Folie. We made our way to our start line on the north-west corner of Bras, where Noel Bell met up with Colonel Scott and made a quick joint plan for the attack. We could see the artillery barrage coming down on the village, but of course it had to lift as we approached. Tanks could motor right up to an artillery barrage, but in our open-top half-tracks we were much more vulnerable. When the artillery lifted our own 3-inch mortars really came into their own, providing an effective smoke screen to cover us in. We debussed about 100 yards short of the village and went straight into the village, two platoons up. Mine was on the right.

'Noel Bell became almost epileptic with rage with the Fife and Forfar when we started to take casualties from a nearby Sherman tank. This was equally hotly denied by the squadron leader. It then transpired that it came from an

extremely gallant German who had climbed into one of Bill Close's tanks which had been knocked out the day before and was manning the machine-gun. He was quickly despatched. The village clearing went very well and within an hour we were able to report that the position was secure. We had killed quite a number of enemy and taken over eighty prisoners.

'During the attack I had occasion to fire my absurd .38 revolver into a foxhole in the orchard. To my astonishment a miniature Red Cross flag emerged from the bowels of the earth. Attached to it was a small man who introduced himself, in impeccable English, as Herr Doctor Schmidt. He was a real charmer and readily agreed to help with the casualties of both sides.'

* * * *

General Roberts quickly ordered Brigadier Churcher to bring forward his other battalions. Churcher told 4th King's Shropshire Light Infantry to take over Hubert-Folie, which, with 3rd Monmouths in Bras and 1st Herefords in depth down the slope between the two villages, meant that 159th Brigade would hold a firm position on the dominating ground of the Bourguébus ridge.

Moving a battalion forward to take over an already captured village sounds a simple and relatively safe operation. It was to prove anything but that for 4th KSLI. During the night of 18/19 July Lieutenant Colonel Ivor Reeves had arrived to assume command of the battalion, and Major Max Robinson had reverted to second-in-command.

Speed was obviously important, and the distance nearly three miles. Perhaps that is why Reeves decided not to follow the longer, flanking route of the armoured attack, but to take a more direct, and hopefully quicker, but uncleared, route, close to the railway embankment. The battalion would advance with two companies up, B on the left, A on the right, with C close behind and D held well back in reserve.

Initially things went well, and it was not until they were within 500 yards of the village that they came under fire. Captain Jack Clayton was commanding B Company:

'Without warning we were enfiladed by machine-gun fire from the high embankment on our left. In a matter of seconds this had accounted for almost a third of my already weakened company. Beside me my wireless operator, Lance Corporal Whelan, was shot in the head, but miraculously survived. I shouted for 2-inch mortarmen, and Prosser answered. I think we were both rather glad to find that someone else was still alive. He put down smoke on our left, and then I ran forward to a hedge to see what I could. I managed to pin-point the enemy positions, dug into the embankment. I placed three Bren-guns to give continuous covering fire, while I organised the men we had left into two platoons, one to provide fire support while the other attacked the position.

'This was successful for only about 100 yards before we were pinned down again. Colonel Reeves then came forward. Despite my warning he stuck his

head round the hedge to see for himself what was happening. We hooked him back in time to save his head from being blown off by a machine-gun burst. Meanwhile, George Edwards, who was behind us with C Company, and who had read the battle well, thickened up our smoke screen and put in a left hook attack. But that, too, was pinned down.'

A few minutes later they were subjected to heavy artillery or mortar fire and Colonel Reeves was severely wounded. Major Robinson, who had remained back near the start line, was quickly called forward to re-assume a command which he had only handed over a few hours earlier:

'When I got to the line of the hedge I found the CO looking slightly green, having been hit in the back. The attack had clearly stopped and all the men were lying down taking part in what I suppose one calls a fire fight. It was very hard to find out where the fire was coming from, but it seemed to be the area of the embankment. I got hold of "Hank" Henry, an attached officer from the Canadian Army who commanded the carrier platoon, and sent two sections charging round to the right at top speed, firing like mad from their Vickers and LMGs. They did excellent work and had considerable effect. I also got the mortars into action. The enemy fire then eased and the companies were able to get on their feet and get to the village. We then reorganized for the night.

'It was a very unpleasant night indeed. We were continually shelled, mortared and rocketed. At about 5.00 am we were counter-attacked from the Bourguébus area. This was actually the direction I was expecting. Our divisional left flank was very much in the air, as the enemy still held Bourguébus, which should of course have been taken by 7th Armoured at the same time as Hubert-Folie was taken.'

The battalion had sustained thirty casualties in what had sounded like a simple 'relief' operation. As Private Ted Jones, who fought throughout the entire war with 4th KSLI, later remarked.

'I think it was the most frightening two days of my life. Having returned to Hubert-Folie in recent years I am still amazed that any of us survived that second day's attack on the village.'

At last, and after more than thirty hours of intense fighting, 11th Armoured Division had captured the crest of the Bourguébus ridge. As the infantrymen of 159th Brigade consolidated their positions, the tanks and riflemen of 29th Armoured Brigade were pulled back into reserve in the general area of Grentheville and Le Mesnil Frémentel. At least for them Operation GOODWOOD was over.

Chapter 18

PARTIAL SUCCESS – GUARDS AND 7TH ARMOURED DIVISIONS

Guards Armoured Division.

As with 11th Armoured, the first task of Guards Armoured Division, as dawn broke on the morning of 19 July, was to confirm whether the Germans were still holding the same positions in strength. It did not take long to find out. Early reconnaissance patrols reported that the defences were just as strong and still based upon a screen of anti-tank guns and tanks from Emiéville to Frénouville.

At 7.00 am 2nd Armoured Irish Guards, who had spent the night in the fields half a mile east of Cagny, tried to advance on Emiéville, but a very abrupt exchange of fire with well-concealed tanks and anti-tank guns in the woods made it quite clear that any attempt in that direction would be extremely costly. By 8.00 am the attack had been called off. Perhaps surprisingly the Germans made no attempt to counter-attack west into the flank of the Guards. A state of watchful stalemate persisted in that area throughout the rest of the day.

At the same time 1st Armoured Coldstream Guards, after a very uncomfortable night hemmed into the narrow strip between Cagny and the railway line, were ordered to resume their advance towards Vimont. But they, too, met heavy resistance, from well-prepared positions in Frénouville and the orchards on the Cagny to Vimont road. Following this failure it was decided not to launch any new offensives until after the corps commander's midday meeting. Consequently, the only actions carried out by Guards

Map 14. Guards Armoured Division's attacks on Le Poirier and Frénouville.

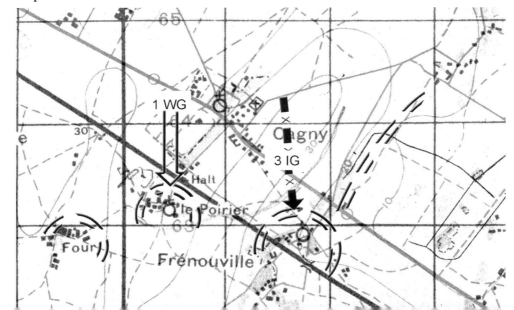

Armoured during the rest of the morning and early afternoon were low-level patrols, designed to ensure that the Germans did not spring any surprises, but that they were kept on their toes.

As a result of General O'Connor's meeting with his divisional commanders, Guards Armoured Division was given the comparatively small tasks of capturing Le Poirier and then Frénouville that evening. At 5.00 pm 1st Battalion Welsh Guards duly attacked Le Poirier on foot, behind an impressive artillery barrage. With 2 and 4 Companies leading they quickly broke into the small village, only to find that the Germans had already pulled out. By 5.30 pm they reported that the village was secure. Patrols then went out to see whether the Germans had also evacuated Frénouville, only to find that they very definitely had not. It was therefore decided that a formal infantry battalion attack, with air and artillery support, should be mounted at 5.45 am on the morning of 20 July by 5th Coldstream Guards. In preparation for this 3rd Irish Guards managed to advance down the main road from Cagny and eject the enemy from the orchards north of Frénouville.

By dusk 32nd Guards Infantry Brigade was holding an arc facing south and south-east, with its battalions in Le Poirier (1st Welsh Guards) and the orchards north of Frénouville (3rd Irish Guards), while 5th Coldstream

Cagny. Troops of Guards Armoured Division in the village after the battle. Cagny today.

Guards held Cagny. The three tank battalions of 5th Guards Armoured Brigade had, in effect, moved anti-clockwise, with 1st Armoured Coldstream Guards having replaced 2nd Armoured Irish Guards on the open ground north-east of Cagny, the Irish having moved half a mile north, while 2nd Armoured Grenadier Guards were between Le Poirier and Cagny, where 1st Armoured Coldstream Guards had been twenty-four hours earlier. All in all it had been a day of little action, but ever-present shell fire.

7th Armoured Division.

Following its previous day of frustrating traffic jams and no real sight of the enemy, 7th Armoured Division had a certain amount of catching-up to do. During the night of 18/19 July the battalions of 131st Lorried Infantry Brigade at last managed to cross the Orne bridges, but were still many miles short of the action.

Shortly after dawn Lieutenant Colonel Victor Paley's 1st Rifle Brigade, the motor infantry battalion in 22nd Armoured Brigade, relieved the companies of 29nd Armoured's 8th Rifle Brigade in Grentheville. Paley quickly sent forward patrols which reported that Four was still held by German tanks and infantry in considerable strength. It was clear that, as elsewhere, the enemy had not pulled out during the night. The accuracy and value of the Rifle Brigade report quickly became clear when the Germans launched a sharp tank counter-attack from Four towards Grentheville. 1st Rifle Brigade and 5th Royal Tanks were waiting for them, and the attack was swiftly beaten back. At about 7.00 am General Erskine summoned his two brigade commanders. Now up in line between the other two divisions 7th Armoured would operate east of the railway embankment and capture the villages leading up to and including Bourguébus. He told Brigadier Hinde to press on south with his 22nd Armoured Brigade, while Brigadier Pepper was to bring 131st Lorried Infantry Brigade forward as quickly as possible.

By mid morning Lieutenant Colonel Holliman's 5th Royal Tanks, with I Company 1st Rifle Brigade had launched an attack south. At 11.20 am they reported that a squadron of tanks had managed to break into Soliers, and that the platoons of I Company were mopping up, but that the enemy in Four were offering strong resistance. General Erskine therefore returned from his midday conference with Generals O'Connor, Roberts and Adair to find that one of his nominated objectives had already been taken. He ordered 5th Royal Tanks to break off its attempt to take Four and to use Soliers as a base for an attack on Bourguébus, while 1st Royal Tanks took over the problem of Four. Meanwhile 131st Brigade was to send an infantry battalion forward quickly to garrison Grentheville. 1st/5th Battalion The Queen's Royal Regiment was nominated for this task.

In accordance with O'Connor's Corps Plan, the attacks by 1st and 5th Tanks on Four and Bourguébus were to be launched at 5.00 pm. Erskine also ordered Hinde to be ready to push though his third armoured regiment, 4th County of London Yeomanry (Sharpshooters), to Verrières and Tilly-La-Campagne as soon as Bourguébus had been taken, and 11th Armoured

Major General Bobbie Erskine. Much liked and admired, he had commanded 7th Armoured Division since the desert campaign.

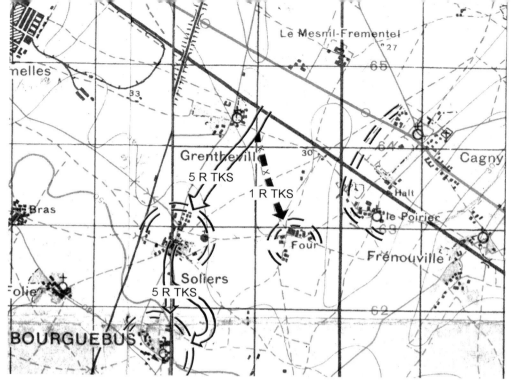

Map 15. 7th Armoured Divisions' attacks on Soliers, Four and Bourguébus.

Division had reported that it had taken Bras and Hubert-Folie.

The attacks began on time, one hour after 11th Armoured had launched its successful attack on Bras. B Squadron 1st Tanks initially made good progress towards Four against only moderate opposition, but as they got closer to the village the German resistance increased. It proved to be a hard slogging match, with the tanks of B Squadron and riflemen of C Company 1st Rifle Brigade doggedly fighting their way through the village. It was not until about 8.30 pm that Lieutenant Colonel Gibbon, commanding 1st Royal Tanks, reported that they had at last managed to subdue the village. Meanwhile 5th Tanks, with B Squadron leading, managed to reach the outskirts of Bourguébus by 6.40 pm, where they were held up by tanks and infantry in the village and also by fire from La Hogue and the woods south. During the next two hours 5th Tanks managed to work round the sides of Bourguébus, and to knock out two of the Tigers and a Panther, but they were unable to break into the village. Their position was somewhat exposed as although 11th Armoured had already taken Bras, the attack on Hubert-Folie, only a mile west of Bourguébus was not launched until 8.00 pm. An air strike called down on La Hogue duly came in at 9.55 pm and was highly successful, as a result of which 1st Tanks were able to push forward on that flank to within 200 yards of the Bourguébus to La Hogue road, half way between the two villages.

As dusk fell 7th Armoured Division had at last got into the act, albeit it twenty-four hours later than had originally been hoped. They ended the day firmly in possession of Grentheville, Four and Soliers, with the squadrons of 5th Tanks pulled back, from their positions on the east, north and west sides of Bourguébus, to leaguer for the night near Soliers.

Chapter 19

THE FLANKS

The Eastern Flank - 3rd Infantry Division.

At the end of operations on 18 July only one of 3rd Division's objectives had not been captured, the small town of Troarn. In the thick country west of the town 9th Infantry Brigade found it impossible to make much progress during the night. By 7.00 am on the morning of 19 July 1st Battalion The King's Own Scottish Borderers had managed to close up to within a few hundred yards of the railway station just west of the town, where they were held up by strong resistance. On their left 2nd Battalion The Royal Ulster Rifles reached the line of the Troarn to Escoville road. During the morning the Ulster Rifles became increasingly entangled with German infantry using the cover of the orchards, woods and the hamlet of Haras du Bois. Indeed the hamlet was to change hands frequently over the next few days.

At 11.00 am 1st KOSB, supported by tanks of the East Riding Yeomanry, launched an attack on Troarn railway station and the main cross roads 200

Map 16. 3rd Infantry Division. 9th Infantry Brigade's attack on Troarn.

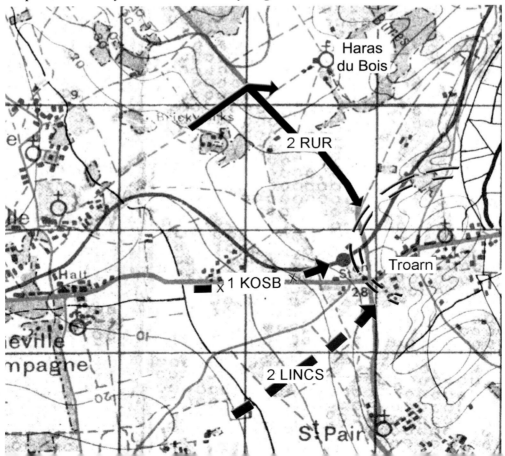

yards south-east of it. They met heavy opposition, but, after a considerable battle, managed to capture the station. However, the Germans held a number of well-sited positions, with interlocking arcs of machine-gun fire, and all attempts by the Borderers to push on to the crossroads were strongly resisted. Further progress proved impossible. General Whistler ordered Brigadier Orr to concentrate all 9th Brigade's efforts on capturing Troarn. Orr accordingly ordered 1st KOSB to hold the ground they had captured at the station while the Ulster Rifles attacked Troarn from the north. At the same time 2nd Battalion The Lincolnshire Regiment, who had hitherto been held in reserve, were to come up on the right of the KOSB and attack from the south-west.

Having been relieved in the area of Haras du Bois by 1st Battalion The South Lancashire Regiment, from 8th Brigade, the Ulster Rifles, supported by the tanks of C Squadron East Riding Yeomanry, started their advance south along the line of the Escoville to Troarn road. Their aim was to pass over the railway and press on for 300 yards to capture the main road junction on the western edge of Troarn. But the area was so densely wooded that the tanks were unable to give much helpful support. The battalion managed to advance less than one mile before encountering a strong enemy position in the area of the railway bridge. This proved impossible to overcome, and by nightfall they were ordered to consolidate in the area of the road junction 400 yards north of the bridge. On the right 2nd Lincolns, also supported by tanks, launched two attacks, one in the afternoon and the other in the evening, attempting to work their way forward into Troarn from the south-west. But they too were held up by heavy machine-gun, mortar and artillery fire and their attack, too, was held. Meanwhile 1st KOSB, having been subjected to continuous artillery fire throughout most of the day, which had cost them 150 casualties, had been forced to evacuate the station area, and pull back some 300 yards west.

By 8.30 pm it was clear that 9th Brigade's attack on Troarn had failed. Brigadier Orr accordingly ordered the KOSB and Ulster Rifles to hold their positions west and north of the town, while the Lincolns were withdrawn into reserve behind the Borderers. In close country, against a robust enemy, it had been an frustrating day with gains of not more than a few hundred yards.

The rest of 3rd Division's area showed little change. 8th Brigade remained firmly established in the Touffréville/Sannerville area, until 2nd East Yorkshires were moved to relieve the Ulster Rifles. Further south 185th Brigade continued to hold the Manneville/Le Quai/Cuillerville area. But the Germans still held the area of Emiéville and at 7.00 pm 2nd Royal Warwicks and the Staffordshire Yeomanry reported that a strong counter-attack was developing from that area. This attack, of infantry supported by tanks, was successfully beaten off.

* * * *

The Western Flank - II Canadian Corps.
At 2.00 am on 19 July General Simonds laid down that the boundary between 2nd and 3rd Canadian Infantry Divisions for all future operations was to be the Caen to Falaise road running south from Vaucelles with 2nd

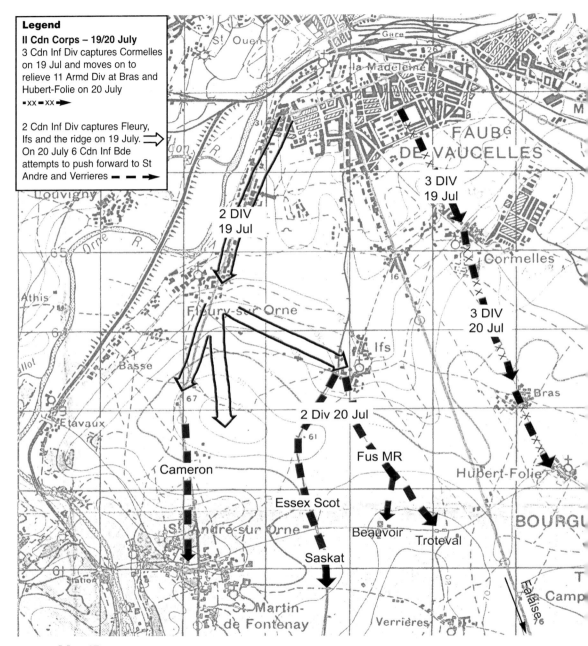

Legend

II Cdn Corps – 19/20 July

3 Cdn Inf Div captures Cormelles on 19 Jul and moves on to relieve 11 Armd Div at Bras and Hubert-Folie on 20 July

■xx■xx➤

2 Cdn Inf Div captures Fleury, Ifs and the ridge on 19 July. On 20 July 6 Cdn Inf Bde attempts to push forward to St Andre and Verrieres ▬ ▬ ➤

Map 17.

Division west and 3rd Division east.

In the 3rd Division sector 8th Canadian Infantry Brigade remained throughout 19 July in their overnight positions in the Giberville and Colombelles areas. Shortly after first light 9th Canadian Infantry Brigade set about clearing the remainder of Vaucelles east of the inter-divisional boundary, and made early contact with the Regina Rifles from 7th Brigade, who had crossed the Orne the previous evening. Once the link between 7th and 9th Brigades had been established 7th Brigade was ordered to bring its remaining battalions over the river, ready for further exploitation.

At 11.30 am 9th Brigade was ordered to send a patrol south to Cormelles to see whether it was occupied. At 12.00 pm, following a quick reconnaissance, the patrol reported that Cormelles was clear, so The Highland Light Infantry of Canada was ordered to occupy it. By 5.00 pm two companies had managed to secure the north-east corner of the factory area just east of the village, but it was clear that the earlier report was incorrect and that the enemy was still in the village and the rest of the factory area in some strength. With both the other battalions of 9th Brigade still fully occupied clearing mines and booby-traps in Vaucelles, General Keller had to call on 7th Brigade, now with its other battalions over the river, to complete the capture of Cormelles. A two-pronged attack was launched - the Royal Winnepeg Rifles from the north-west and the 1st Canadian Scottish Regiment from the north. The attack was successful and by 7.00 pm Cormelles had been taken. Keller then ordered 7th Brigade to secure the southern flank based on Cormelles, while 9th Brigade looked after Vaucelles.

* * * *

While 3rd Canadian Infantry Division was occupied at the east end of Vaucelles, 2nd Canadian Infantry Division had managed to capture intact the railway bridge further west, and was exploiting its success. The Black Watch of Canada, who had made the crossing and contacted the Regina Rifles from 3rd Division in the area of the Caen to Falaise road, were quickly followed by the remainder of 5th Brigade. By midday Brigadier Megill was preparing for an attack south towards Fleury-sur-Orne and then on to St André-sur-Orne and Ifs. The Army Commander, General Dempsey, keenly supported this plan in the hope that its success would mean that 2nd Canadian Division could link up with 11th Armoured Division at the west end of the Bourguébus ridge.

As the Canadians expanded their positions in Vaucelles their engineers started building bridges. The necessary stores had already been pre-positioned north of the river, so work began shortly after midnight. It had to be carried out under intermittent shelling and mortar fire, but by 11.00 am on 19th July two tank and two light vehicle bridges had been completed.

5th Brigade's attack on Fleury-sur-Orne was launched at 1.00 pm and by 2.30 pm the Black Watch had managed to break into the village. They encountered considerable resistance and it took some time to fight their way through, but by 4.00 pm the village was clear. Fleury was then to be the launch-pad for the next phase, and attack south by the other two battalions of 5th Brigade onto hill feature Point 67 at the bend in the road about a mile south of the village. This proved to be unoccupied, and by 6.30 pm both battalions were in position, the Régiment de Maisonneuve astride the bend in the road and the Calgary Highlanders about half a mile east along the ridge. The Germans inevitably reacted strongly launching an armoured counter-attack along the ridge as it was getting dark. Following heavy fighting the Calgary Highlanders were driven back and the Germans regained most of the position. They were not allowed to remain there for long. With the Maisonneuve holding the western end of the ridge, the Calgary Highlanders launched an immediate attack and, by 11.45 pm, following stiff close-quarter fighting in the dark, they had driven the Germans from the ridge. Shortly after midnight 19/20 July the Black Watch of Canada moved forward and attacked Ifs (which had proved such a thorn in the side of 2nd Northants Yeomanry of 11th Armoured Division earlier on). The attack came in from the north-west and found that the Germans, following the earlier losses of Bras and Hubert-Folie nearby, had already pulled out. By 1.30 am on 20 July the Black Watch reported that Ifs was secure. Contact was quickly made with 11th Armoured Division near Bras. This was the link-up which General Dempsey so earnestly sought.

West of the Orne 4th Canadian Infantry Brigade had a relatively peaceful day. The Royal Regiment of Canada, which had spent the evening of 18 July in a partially successful attack on Louvigny, managed to clear most of the village by midday, although a strong enemy position around the chateau took several hours and some hard fighting to subdue. The rest of 4th Brigade was held back in reserve and not committed to battle.

Based on the news of 2nd Canadian Division's success, at 10.00 pm General Dempsey warned General Simonds that once Ifs had been secured, the link-up with 11th Armoured Division made and the whole position consolidated, he planned to order II Canadian Corps to relieve VIII Corps on the morning of 20 July. Leaving 2nd Canadian Division to hold the ground they had just won, Simonds therefore gave orders that 3rd Canadian Division should be ready to move forward to relieve 11th Armoured Division at Bras and Hubert-Folie next morning.

Chapter 20

THE END OF GOODWOOD

On the morning of 20 July General Dempsey's plans for withdrawing the armoured divisions of VIII Corps started to be put into effect. Having secured Ifs and the important ridge south-west of it, II Canadian Corps was well-placed to relieve 11th Armoured Division. General Simonds ordered 3rd Canadian Division to undertake this while, west of the Caen to Falaise road, 2nd Canadian Division launched a further attack south towards Verrières. Accordingly, at 10.00 am, 9th Canadian Infantry Brigade (3rd Canadian Division) started to take over from 159th Infantry Brigade at Bras and Hubert-Folie. The hand-over was completed by midday, and 159th Brigade withdrew to a position some miles back, between Grentheville and Le Mesnil Frémentel. Behind them 29th Armoured Brigade, which had been licking its wounds overnight in that area, withdrew further north to the Giberville/Démouville area. And so 11th Armoured Division, which had born the brunt of Operation GOODWOOD, was now out of the line after two and a half days, which those who experienced it described as the heaviest fighting in which they were involved throughout the entire war.

Further east 7th and Guards Armoured Divisions had a certain amount of tidying-up to do. 7th Armoured was to take Bourguébus and Guards Armoured, Frénouville. Once these were secure the Canadians would expand further east to relieve 7th Armoured, while units of I Corps would move forward from the Orne bridgehead to take over from Guards Armoured.

Following their frustratingly slow start on 18 July, units of 7th Armoured Division's 22nd Armoured Brigade were on the move early on 20 July. Shortly after first light 5th Royal Tanks had, after a brief skirmish with German tanks, managed to enter Bourguébus, only to find that the German defenders had slipped away quietly during the night. General Erskine immediately ordered Brigadier Pepper to send forward an infantry battalion of 131st Infantry Brigade to secure the village. This was quickly done.

A certain amount of confusion arose because in addition to taking Bourguébus 7th Armoured had, on the previous evening, been ordered to attack south-west, cross the Caen to Falaise road, and take Verrières. This had not been amended, or if it had the news had not reached the forward units. Verrières was now to be an objective of 2nd Canadian Division. However, unaware of the change of plan and moving earlier than the Canadians, the tanks of 4th County of London Yeomanry (Sharpshooters), with its motor infantry company, A Company 1st Rifle Brigade, passed between Bras and Hubert-Folie and crossed the main Caen to Falaise road. By 10.30 am they had taken Beauvoir farm on the St André-sur-Orne to Hubert-Folie road after a brief struggle. Attempts to push on to Verrières, however, met strong resistance, so they moved back and took up a defensive position at Beauvoir. Once it became clear that 2nd Canadian Infantry Division had also been ordered to take Verrières, clarification was sought from HQ Second Army. The situation was resolved when the Sharpshooters group was ordered to withdraw from Beauvoir and move east of the Caen to Falaise road, allowing the Canadians freedom of action to the west. By 1.40 pm the Sharpshooters/Rifle Brigade group had moved back east of the road, leaving Beauvoir farm unoccupied. As events turned out it was a pity that they were not ordered to stay there until a Canadian unit was moved forward to relieve them. The farm could then have become a firm launch-pad for the attack on Verrières. But, no sooner had the Sharpshooters withdrawn, than the Germans moved back into the farm in some strength.

At the same time that 7th Armoured Division was replacing its tanks with infantry in the Bourguébus/Soliers/Four area, Guards Armoured Division was also on the move. The attack on Frénouville, planned by 32nd Guards Brigade the previous evening, duly went in at 5.45 am, behind an aerial and artillery bombardment. But von Luck and his battle group had gone and by 7.45 am the village was secure. The defensive shield which von Luck had built up between Emiéville and Frénouville on the afternoon of 18 July, with the two tank battalions and his own battalion of panzer-grenadiers, had done its job. It had bought time for General Dietrich to order 12th SS Panzer Division forward from the Falaise area, to take up a defensive position behind von Luck's Battle Group, in the area of Vimont. By nightfall 19/20 July this had been done and von Luck had therefore pulled out during the night. But 1st and 12th SS Panzer Divisions were both now back in their familiar defensive ground-holding roles. Excellent mobile anti-tank guns they might be in this role, but they were once again not available for the co-ordinated offensive action which the Germans so desperately sought. Nor were they available to oppose Operation COBRA.

At 10.00 am General Dempsey issued orders that VIII Corps should not try to advance further, but should use its infantry to consolidate the ground taken over the last two days, prior to handing over to the 3rd Canadian and 51st Highland Divisions. Once this hand-over was complete 51st Division would come under command of II Canadian Corps, giving General Simonds overall responsibility for the entire sector. Meanwhile the armoured brigades were to withdraw, in order to be built-up again for future operations. In mid-afternoon, as if to mark the end of armoured operations, the heavens opened, and the ground, so torn by bombs and shell-fire, quickly degenerated into a muddy quagmire.

On 21 July General Montgomery issued instructions that, 'since the position on the eastern flank has been so greatly improved and the enemy has been dealt a severe blow', the time had come to switch the main point of battle west, with First US Army attacking south, securing Brittany with its useful ports, and striking east into central France. Operation GOODWOOD was over; Operation COBRA was about to begin.

* * * *

Although the attack on Verrières by 2nd Canadian Division strictly falls under the heading of Operation ATLANTIC, rather than GOODWOOD, as the final episode in the events which had begun on the morning of 18 July, it is worth recording briefly here (see Map 17, page 168). H Hour, originally set for 12.00 pm on 20 July, was delayed until 3.00 pm to ensure that the Sharpshooters' battlegroup was clear of the area. The attack was to be undertaken by the three battalions of Brigadier Young's 6th Brigade, with an extra battalion, Essex Scottish, attached from 4th Brigade at the last minute. By 11.00 am the battalions were formed up, ready to go, but the delay of H Hour meant that they had to remain in their forming-up places for four hours. For many this was to be their first taste of battle. Waiting to go into battle is a nervous time for all soldiers, especially for those about to taste action for the first time. The long delay on the start line can only have made things worse. Stationary for too long, they inevitably came under shell and mortar fire and took casualties. The long wait, the hot sun and the close attention of the German gunners did not augur well for the subsequent operation. Furthermore it seems that the machinery of staff work was not yet functioning smoothly, as the post-battle War Diary of Essex Scottish records:

'It is not a pleasant picture to realize that so many of the battalion have been lost, especially as many could have been avoided by better planning and the observance of the procedure that our training had led us to expect before going into battle. All the rules of man-management were either violated or ignored, by the sudden move after midnight, the loss of sleep by all ranks, a poor breakfast and little or no noon meal. And the detailed plan, if known, was not given to junior officers or troops.'

This contrasts starkly with Lieutenant David Stileman's description of the briefing and preparation within G Company 8th Rifle Brigade at the start of GOODWOOD (chapter 6).

Eventually, following a Typhoon strike and artillery barrage, three battalions advanced in line abreast. On the right The Queen's Own Cameron Highlanders of Canada made for their objective, St André-sur-Orne. On the left Les Fusiliers Mont Royal had been ordered to take Beauvoir and Troteval farms and press on to Verrières. In between them The South Saskatchewan Regiment, following a disused railway line (now the Ifs to Fontenoy-le-Marmion road), headed for the railway/track crossing west of Verrières. In reserve, Essex Scottish, ordered to follow behind the Saskatchewans, was to secure the track/road junction west of Beauvoir farm.

Initially the advance went well. By 5.00 pm the Saskatchewans reported that they had taken their track crossing and were starting to dig in. Shortly afterwards the Camerons were in St André. On the left the Fusiliers, however, encountered stiff opposition in the area of Beauvoir and Troteval farms, and were unable to capture either. Subsequent events might have turned out very differently if the Fusiliers had found the Sharpshooters still firmly in control of Beauvoir farm. Behind the leading battalions Essex Scottish moved quickly forward towards their objective.

The Germans, as always, reacted vigorously. Tanks, supported by infantry, heavy machine-gun and shell fire, attacked the Saskatchewans from the direction of Verrières. They quickly broke into the Canadian position, causing considerable confusion. The Saskatchewan's anti-tank guns, which were just arriving on the position and had not yet been sited, were quickly knocked out, and the German tanks ruled supreme. By 6.00 pm communications with the battalion were lost. 27th Canadian Armoured Regiment was ordered forward to give support, but the Germans held the commanding ground and the attempt failed. At 7.00 pm an officer managed to contact 6th Brigade headquarters. He reported that the Saskatchewan commanding officer had been killed, that much of the battalion had been scattered and control lost. He was told to try to stabilize the situation as best he could – hardly an inviting order for a junior officer on his own! By now the heavy rain, which had started some hours earlier, had saturated everyone and everything. Vehicle movement was almost impossible and poor visibility in the rain and mist, which had descended on the ridge, made it very hard to identify targets. Some of the Saskatchewans took cover in the tall corn; others withdrew in disarray to the area of the Essex Scottish, about half a mile north. Of course the Germans followed up.

By 9.30 pm it became clear that the Essex, too, were in trouble and that two companies had pulled back to Ifs. The threat to the centre had become very serious indeed. In the area of Ifs, officers of 6th Brigade headquarters rounded up the two Essex Scottish companies and as many of the Saskatchewans as they could, and sent them back up to the Essex position, with orders to take and hold it at all costs.

On the left the Fusiliers Mont Royal were also having a difficult time. At 9.00 pm the commanding officer reported that in the face of the German resistance, and with the atrocious rain and mist making it impossible for tanks to help him, his battalion had been forced back onto the reverse slope north of Beauvoir farm. Although the enemy remained in the farm, he was confident that he could hold his position. In this he was entirely successful; indeed later on he managed to get two companies round to the left, across the road and into Troteval farm. On the right the Camerons were also subjected to several counter-attacks, all of which they beat off successfully. An uneasy calm descended on the battlefield during the short night of 20/21 July.

Shortly after dawn next morning it became clear that the two companies of the Fusiliers which had infiltrated into Troteval farm had become cut off and, to a man, eliminated. For the remainder of the day the remaining companies stubbornly held their position just north of Beauvoir farm. On the right the Camerons were yet again subjected to frequent counter-attacks, and they, too, held on. But all was not going well in the centre. By 11.45 am on 21 July it became clear that although some of the Essex Scottish were still holding their position, others had again pulled back to Ifs, one mile north.

During the early afternoon the divisional commander, General Foulkes decided that the position must be retaken and then held. Accordingly he ordered the Black Watch of Canada, from 5th Brigade, supported by the tanks of 6th and 27th Canadian Armoured Regiments to regain the cross-roads at the heart of the Essex Scottish objective. This attack went in at 6.00 pm and was successful. A most dangerous situation had been restored. Thereafter the Canadians consolidated their positions, but made no further attempts to press on south towards Verrières.

Chapter 21

RECRIMINATIONS AND BREAKOUT

After GOODWOOD there was a genuine crisis in command, with many questions asked about Montgomery's conduct of the campaign. The press, particularly the American press, which failed completely to understand that wars were won by defeating the enemy's army, not just by liberating real estate, had for some weeks been suggesting that the Americans were doing the bulk of the fighting, while the British remained largely passive and immobile. Like others, they expected much from GOODWOOD and, following only limited achievements, their criticism increased. As Chester Wilmot explained in *The Struggle for Europe*:

> *'The press interpreted the battle as a deliberate attempt to break out, and one that had failed. Their misappreciation followed the views taken at various higher headquarters, and by the air forces and Americans.'*

In the weeks leading up to GOODWOOD, relationships between Montgomery and Supreme Headquarters, Allied Expeditionary Force, had become somewhat strained. Following GOODWOOD , which was seen by SHAEF as extremely disappointing, they threatened to explode. Air Marshal Tedder, Eisenhower's Deputy Supreme Commander and no friend of Montgomery, let it be known that if Eisenhower sought a change in command of Twenty-first Army Group, he would support the move. He would be quite happy to suggest to the Chief of the Air Staff, Marshal of the RAF Sir Charles Portal, that he advise Churchill that General Montgomery should be replaced. The ground might be fertile for this because, in the run-up to GOODWOOD, Montgomery had seriously upset the Prime Minister.

With the Normandy campaign reaching its climax in the twin battles of GOODWOOD and COBRA, Montgomery had decreed that he would accept no visitors. He was far too busy masterminding the campaign at a very tricky moment to have time to waste on unnecessary spectators. News of this edict reached Churchill's ears just as he was planning another trip to the front.

Churchill's leadership of the country, from its worst moment at the time of Dunkirk in June 1940, can never be overstated. But his frequent urge to meddle in the detail of battles, and his hasty judgement of the capabilities of commanders in the field, were a perpetual source of trouble for Field Marshal Sir Alan Brooke, who, as Chief of the Imperial General Staff and Chairman of the Chiefs of Staff, was his principal military adviser. They were, after all, based on no personal experience of the responsibilities of high command and the handling of armies in battle, and only superficial knowledge of the detail of the events taking place. The strength of his position as Prime Minister and Minister of Defence, and the power of his personality, made life very difficult

urchill.

for the Chiefs of Staff. His lack of understanding of operational command was already well proved. Gallipoli, in 1915, based on a flawed concept forced through by Churchill, had been a real disaster, which had cost many lives and also his position as First Lord of the Admiralty. Even as recently as January 1944 he had reflected his frustration that the Anzio landing south of Rome, which he had enthusiastically supported, had not been followed by an immediate drive inland; 'Instead of hurling a wild cat onto the shore, all we got was a stranded whale.' He preferred to overlook the speed with which the Germans massed six divisions in the Anzio/Rome area. It is reported to have been said that they might indeed have reached the Alban Hills, or even Rome, which would have meant 'a few days of glory followed by fifteen months as prisoners of war'.

Controlling the wilder enthusiasms of Churchill was perhaps Brooke's hardest and one of his finest achievements. These are well reflected in his War Diaries 1939-1945 published in 2001. He clearly found it hugely frustrating when Churchill criticised his generals, frequently telling the Prime Minister that they deserved his support not his criticism.

On the morning of 19 July, Day Two of GOODWOOD, Brooke found Churchill in a towering rage. His dissatisfaction with Montgomery stemmed in part from the failure to capture Caen on D-Day, or soon after. Now he had just been told of Montgomery's 'no visitors' edict. He had immediately jumped to the conclusion that it was intended personally for him. He had a right, even a duty, to visit any front he wished whenever he wished. How dare Montgomery refuse him! Despite all of Brooke's protestations that of course Montgomery did not intend the ruling to apply to Churchill, the Prime Minister refused to be mollified. Fortunately Brooke was flying to Normandy that afternoon. On arrival he told Montgomery to write a personal letter to Churchill, explaining that the edict was for lesser folk and certainly did not apply to him, and that he would welcome a visit any time the Prime Minister wished to come. Brooke delivered that letter on return, and Churchill was delighted by it. Montgomery also quickly invited Eisenhower, probably at Brooke's suggestion, to visit him next day. Eisenhower arrived on the 20 July smouldering with frustration, only to find Montgomery, who could lay on the charm when required to do so, entirely confident and welcoming. Eisenhower left, just a couple of hours later, happy and relaxed. And Churchill's visit, which duly took place on 21/22 July, was also a resounding success. This was neither the first nor last time that Brooke was forced to protect Montgomery, but how fortunately timed was Brooke's visit! The storm blew over, but things might have been very different if Tedder had found Eisenhower and Churchill both dissatisfied with Montgomery. And if Brooke, having been set up to expect much by Montgomery's greatly over-optimistic report of 18 July (chapter 16), had then learned, in the next few days, of the disappointing tactical achievements of GOODWOOD, he too might have been asking some pretty searching questions. His visit to Normandy on 19 July was indeed most fortunate for Montgomery.

Montgomery always acknowledged how much he owed to Brooke, who

was the one senior officer he totally respected, both militarily and personally. If Brooke shouted 'jump', Montgomery quickly jumped. Brooke was an officer of powerful intellect, the ability to see through to the root of each problem almost before it had arisen, and the steely resolve never to waver from what he saw as the best path to victory. And his judgement was remarkable. In most of the really big strategic decisions of the war, whether they were national or international, Brooke fought his case, often against almost overwhelming opposition, until he won it. History suggests that he was almost invariably right. Never one to suffer fools gladly, if at all, he had a fearsome reputation, and it seems likely that Montgomery was, as others, genuinely frightened of him. As Commander-in-Chief Home Forces in 1941 he had visited a corps exercise in northern England. On asking the corps commander how he was employing the armoured division that had been placed under his command, he was not pleased by the reply, 'I am using it across the entire corps front, with pin-pricks here and pin-pricks there'. Witheringly Brooke replied, 'You have been given the most powerful formation in modern warfare, not a bloody pin-cushion'. Within a few days a new corps commander had taken over! Brooke's Military Assistant in the War Office kept a bottle of brandy close at hand 'to revive generals who had come to be sacked!'

ld Marshal Alan Brooke ιe architect of much success, I the one man o could make ιntgomery np'!

* * * *

Throughout early July Bradley who, following the capture of Cherbourg could now turn his attentions south, had sought to capture the St Lô to Périers road as the start-line for his attack. It had been a grim, slow and unspectacular battle in the depths of the dense *bocage* country. St Lô was finally taken on 18 July, as GOODWOOD began, and COBRA was therefore planned for 21 July. But the rain which converted the GOODWOOD area to a mud-bath had similarly affected Bradley's attack. Had COBRA been launched on 21 July no-one could have dismissed the argument that GOODWOOD and COBRA were two phases of the same Twenty-first Army Group battle. Eventually on 24 July the skies cleared and the US Air Force was able to launch its preliminary bombing raid. Unfortunately, and expressly against Bradley's instructions, the aircraft flew north to south, rather than west to east. Some bombers bombed short and the leading elements of VII US Corps were hit. Many casualties ensued, among them Lieutenant General Leslie McNair, who had gone forward to watch the attack begin. Bradley was furious and the attack was delayed for twenty-four hours.

With all the criticism which surrounded GOODWOOD and the eventual speed of the American breakout, it is easy to forget that in the early stages Bradley's COBRA proved to be even slower than Dempsey's GOODWOOD. On 25 July COBRA was launched, and by the end of the day had achieved just two miles. Late on 28 July, after four days of fighting, General Lawton Collins' VII Corps captured Coutances, some eight miles south of the start line, about the same distance as the two-day GOODWOOD advance. But unlike

American troops move through a congested village during Operation COBRA.

GOODWOOD there was no real depth to the German defence. 2nd SS Panzer and Panzer Lehr Divisions, already depleted by many weeks of fighting, could muster only about 100 tanks between them, and once they had been broken there was nothing behind. The bulk of the German armour was firmly pinned down in front of Second British Army in the east. The Americans were underway, and with General Patton's HQ Third Army taking over control of the southern flank, achievements thereafter were spectacular.

Chapter 22

SUCCESS OR FAILURE? – THE ADVANTAGE OF HINDSIGHT

Two momentous events frame Operation GOODWOOD. On 17 July, as the men of 29th Armoured Brigade were enjoying a day of rest concealed in the orchards west of the Orne, Field Marshal Rommel, having visited his commanders in the Caen area and warned them to expect an attack, was driving back to his headquarters at La Roche Guyon. On a stretch of road near Vimoutiers his car was seen by two Typhoon pilots. In the ensuing attack Rommel was so seriously injured that he was never to regain field command. And just three days later, as GOODWOOD was drawing to a somewhat frustrating and soggy close, Colonel von Stauffenberg detonated a bomb under the conference table at Hitler's headquarters at Rastenberg in East Prussia. Hitler was not seriously injured, but the shock-waves of this event ran deep throughout the German Army, costing the lives of many, including those of Rommel and von Kluge.

* * * *

Operation GOODWOOD was to become perhaps the most widely studied and argued-about battle involving British troops in the Second World War. This is hardly surprising since it was, and is likely to remain, the largest tank battle which the British Army has ever fought. [Furthermore it is close enough for parties to visit the battlefield relatively cheaply, with the knowledge of an excellent French meal to follow!] After four days of intense fighting and for the loss of more than 400 tanks, all that had been achieved, geographically, was an advance of some eight miles, from the Orne bridgehead to the Bourguébus ridge. Superficially this sounds a disappointing return, but judging the success or failure of any operation by statistics alone is unwise.

Only the most biased critic, who refuses to accept the weight of evidence which shows clearly that GOODWOOD was never intended as a breakout battle in its own right, can seriously suggest that it was a failure. But it must surely have been a real disappointment to General Dempsey, who would have hoped for far more from an operation of this size, particularly as he wished to silence the ill-informed critics of Second British Army's achievements. But go down a few levels to that, for example, of Lieutenant Colonel Tony Hunter, commanding 8th Rifle Brigade, ordered to capture Le Mesnil Frémentel with a distinctly ad hoc force on the morning of 18 July, and then Bras and Hubert Folie on the late afternoon of 19 July. Both of these attacks were entirely successful, netting over 500 prisoners from 1st SS and 21st Panzer Divisions as well as numerous anti-tank guns and *Nebelwerfers*. At

The last Staff College Goodwood Dinner – 1979. *Left to Right:* **Captain Peter Walter, DSO (C Squadron 23rd Hussars); Major General Richard von Rosen (3 Company, 503rd Heavy Tank Battalion); Ted Harte (B Squadron, 23rd Hussars); Brigadier David Stileman, OBE (G Company, 8th Rifle Brigade); Colonel Hans von Luck (125th Panzer Grenadier Regiment); Major Foster Cunliffe, MC (F Company 8th Rifle Brigade) (behind); Major General Pip Roberts, CB, DSO, MC (11th Armoured Division); Major Bill Close, MC (A Squadron 3rd Royal Tanks); Major Noel Bell, MC (G Company, 8th Rifle Brigade).**

that level the words 'failure' or 'disappointment' are clearly nonsense.

To make a fair judgement of GOODWOOD it must be seen at the level at which it was conceived. Its origins lie with Montgomery, and so it should be from his level of command that a proper assessment must be made. Montgomery's aim, as Commander-in-Chief Twenty-first Army Group, was quite clear. As his Chief of Staff, General de Guingand, explained, GOODWOOD was Phase One of the breakout battle. In Phase Two General Bradley's First US Army, in the west, was to advance south, clear Brittany and swing east towards central France. Although there is no evidence to suggest that it was Montgomery's pre D-Day plan to lure the bulk of the German armour to confront Second British Army in the east, in order to ease Bradley's breakout, he certainly adopted it once the shape of the campaign began to unfold in Normandy. Historians would have been far kinder to Montgomery if, instead of suggesting this had always been his plan, he had said something on the lines of, 'It quickly became clear that the Germans expected a breakout to be launched in the Caen area, with a thrust on Paris [there is plenty of evidence of this from German documents of June and July 1944]. In consequence each newly-arriving panzer division was immediately sucked into the defensive battle in that area. Having identified this I was able to use it to advantage by launching frequent offensives around Caen, thereby pinning the vast majority of the German tanks in the east and easing Bradley's subsequent breakout in the west.'

GOODWOOD was the final piece in the positional jigsaw, and when the Americans launched their breakout, Operation COBRA, on 25 July, they were confronted by just one and a half panzer divisions, about 100 tanks, while six and a half panzer divisions and several independent battalions of Tiger Tanks, about 600 tanks, still faced the British in the east (map 18). Both 1st and 12th SS Panzer Divisions, which had been withdrawn from the line in early July for offensive action against the Americans, were now back in the front line side by side directly confronting the Second British Army south and south-east of Caen. If GOODWOOD did not significantly 'write down' German tank numbers, it certainly pinned them down. It is interesting to speculate on what might have happened if they had been available to oppose Operation COBRA, possibly by driving into the flank of the advance, as was tried later, but too late, in the Mortain offensive. Furthermore 2nd and 116th Panzer Divisions, which were just arriving in Normandy, were also thrown into the Caen battleground. If GOODWOOD did not significantly 'write down' German tank numbers, it certainly pinned them down at a vital moment. In counting the cost of British tank losses it is worth remembering that many of the tanks knocked out during GOODWOOD were quickly repaired and that the 500 spares, already held in in-theatre stores, more than compensated for losses. Within a few days all three armoured divisions were up to fighting strength and in action again. Seen at the operational level, therefore, GOODWOOD must be rated a clear, if costly, success.

That said, it is worth considering why GOODWOOD, which started with such high hopes, did not achieve more. Part of the blame for this must lie with the faulty Intelligence picture which misled British battlefield commanders about the strength and depth of the German defences. There is no obvious explanation for this error. From early in the war British radio intercept, based at Bletchley Park, had broken the German codes. Once discussion of Ultra became open in 1974, it emerged that the code-breakers had indeed identified the strong German anti-tank belt which confronted GOODWOOD. There were cells providing Ultra information at both Montgomery's and Dempsey's headquarters, but knowledge of it was very tightly controlled. It was, perhaps, the best kept secret of the Second World War and was greeted with amazement by the public when details were released in 1974. The fact of Ultra's existence would only have been known by Dempsey and one or two others at Headquarters Second Army, while corps, division and lower levels would have been quite unaware of its existence.

Whether knowledge of what really confronted them would have led to a different plan can only be a matter of conjecture, though it is hard to imagine

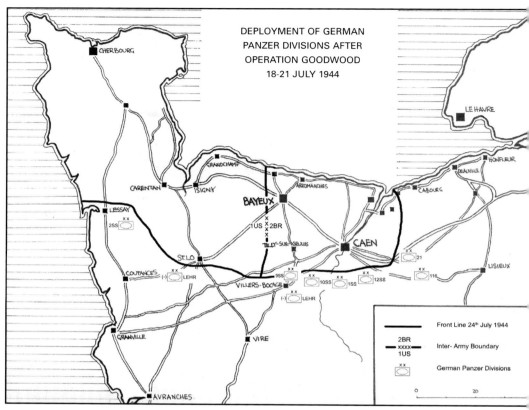

Map 18. Following Operation GOODWOOD the Germans had six and a half panzer divisions confronting the British in the East. The American breakout (Operation COBRA), launched on 25 July, was confronted by just one and a half panzer divisions.

what alternatives existed, given that it was to be an armoured attack launched from the Orne bridgehead. Knowledge of the presence of two battalions of German tanks, including Tigers, on the east flank of the advance, of the plethora of 88mm guns along the distant ridge, or of the closeness of 1st SS Panzer Division just over the horizon, would hardly have encouraged the morale of the leading regiments of 29th Armoured Brigade. Perhaps those commanders with access to Ultra information did indeed find out, in the last forty-eight hours before H Hour, that the Germans were expecting an armoured attack in that area and had greatly reinforced their defences. Perhaps they felt that the wheels were already in motion, with the bombing planned and those two night moves underway, and that for operational reasons the attack must still go ahead. They may also have felt that, in the interests of maintaining the security of Ultra, it was prudent to keep the knowledge to themselves. These thoughts, again, can only be conjecture. Seen from Montgomery's level there was a clear operational need for GOODWOOD, to keep the German tanks occupied in the east and so set the stage for the American breakout, Operation COBRA.

Against defences such as those painted by Intelligence GOODWOOD would undoubtedly have achieved more. If, by early afternoon on 18 July, 3rd Royal Tanks and 2nd Fife and Forfar Yeomanry had secured the vital ridge villages, 1st SS Panzer Division would not have had the advantage of well-concealed positions on the dominating ground, from which to make the greater range and hitting power of its tanks and anti-tank guns really pay dividends. And with Guards and 7th Armoured Divisions up in line and advancing south and south-east by late afternoon, the German reserves, rushed quickly into the area, would have been very thinly spread along a much wider front. As AA Milne's dairymaid so aptly told the Queen, 'Marmalade is tasty, if it's very thickly spread'. Confronted only by an already battered 11th Armoured Division on a narrow front, 1st SS Panzer Division was, by mid afternoon 18 July, 'very thickly spread' along the western end of the ridge.

It is intriguing to speculate, from the comfort of an arm-chair, on whether GOODWOOD could have been more successful tactically. Perhaps a preliminary attack by infantry divisions, supported by independent armoured brigades, could have expanded the Orne bridgehead to the line of, say, Cagny and the second railway. It might then have been possible to launch the armoured divisions of VIII Corps almost in parallel, rather than series. It would certainly have reduced the bottleneck which prevented 7th Armoured Division from joining the fray on 18 July. Superficially this looks attractive, but in fact it was quite impractical. Moving the infantry divisions from west of the Orne could only have weakened the centre of the entire Allied position. A lull of several days in, for example, the Tilly-sur-Seulles area, might have given the Germans just the opportunity they sought, to launch a co-ordinated attack with their panzer divisions. To keep the Germans off-balance pressure had to be maintained right across the front. Besides, the presence of the Tigers and King Tigers of 503rd Heavy Tank Battalion in the Manneville-Emiéville area would have made life for the infantry divisions exceedingly uncomfortable. Furthermore, as Montgomery's letter to Brooke made clear, Second British Army was already running short of infantry while there was an ample supply of tanks.

It is hard not to conclude that, with all its obvious faults, GOODWOOD as carried out was the only option, and, being complementary to COBRA, was a necessary battle.

But perhaps, with one or two relatively minor changes, GOODWOOD might have achieved more, even in the face of the existing defence. The first draft of the plan included halting the armoured advance along the line of the second railway line, south of Cagny. Before it resumed, the next line of villages and the Bourguébus ridge would be subjected to a second heavy bombing raid. If the Germans in Four, Soliers, Bourguébus, Hubert-Folie and Bras had received treatment similar to that so graphically described by Lieutenants von Rosen and Bandomir (chapters 7 and 10), the resistance offered to 29th Armoured Brigade's first drive for the ridge would almost certainly have been greatly reduced.

The second, and perhaps more obvious point, is that if General Roberts had not been required to detach 159th Infantry Brigade to capture Cuverville and Démouville, but had it available to support 29th Armoured Brigade's advance, his scope for overcoming opposition would have been far greater. General Roberts made clear (chapter 4) that he felt that things might have been very different if he had lost the argument over these two villages but won it over Cagny. It is not difficult to picture the situation. A quick attack by a battalion of 159th Brigade, probably supported by the tanks of 2nd Northants Yeomanry, during the late morning of 18 July, would probably have taken Cagny. Guards Armoured Division would doubtless still have run into trouble from the Tigers and King Tigers on the east flank near Emiéville, and the push towards Vimont might not have progressed far, but, with Cagny clear the way would then have been open for 7th Armoured Division to come up into line in the early afternoon. And Roberts would still have had two infantry battalions to help his drive towards the ridge. Again, joint infantry/armoured attacks on Four and Soliers, at the foot of the slope, would probably have succeeded, and if the ridge defenders had been battered by a second bombing raid, even the open, uphill approach to Bras and Hubert-Folie might have been achieved. Armchair tactics after the event are so easy!

But for all its tactical shortcomings there were clear lessons from GOODWOOD which would bring immediate benefit to future operations. The need for infantry and tanks to work more closely together in a balanced grouping was quickly appreciated by General Roberts who, following GOODWOOD, restructured 11th Armoured Division into two square brigades, each of two tank regiments and two infantry battalions. Within these brigades tanks and infantry were then informally paired. In 29th Armoured Brigade, for example, 23rd Hussars and 8th Rifle Brigade frequently worked together. Command of this group was exercised by whichever arm would predominate in the next battle. In the mobile tank battle Colonel Harding of 23rd Hussars would command, but when a more deliberate infantry attack was required Colonel Hunter of 8th Rifle Brigade took over. At squadron/company level command would frequently pass from squadron to company commander in the middle of the action, usually when the infantry dismounted to clear an objective, supported by fire from the tanks. Later generations serving in peacetime Germany saw something of a problem in this; those who practiced it in war never did.

Following GOODWOOD II Canadian Corps, having taken over the area captured by 11th Armoured Division, used it as the launch-pad for further attacks towards Falaise. For ten days from 25 July, the day the Americans launched COBRA, the Canadians tried in vain to secure the next line of villages. By 1 August it had become clear to Lieutenant General Guy Simonds, the young and highly impressive commander of II Canadian Corps, that, if he was to break through the stubborn German defence and advance on Falaise, a new approach was required. A shrewd observer, he must surely have studied GOODWOOD because many of his innovations and the tactics he employed seem to have sprung from the lessons of GOODWOOD. First he

concluded that, as at GOODWOOD, the ground favoured defence, with the Germans able to make maximum use of their superior weapons from well concealed positions sited in depth. Conversely, the attacker, in open ground, was exposed and vulnerable. Next he accepted that, after ten days battering unsuccessfully at villages such as Tilly la Campagne, the direction and objectives of his next attack must be obvious to the Germans. Tactical surprise could only be achieved, therefore, by coming up with an entirely new and unexpected method. He concluded that the best way to gain surprise and negate the German weapon superiority was to attack by night, with tanks. This suggestion was greeted with widespread disbelief. Surely everyone knew that tanks, possessing no night viewing equipment, were blind at night. Besides, they required the cover of darkness for replenishment and rest before the next day's battle. Simonds was unmoved. Daylight attacks had failed; reinforcing that failure would be pointless. But a night tank attack would certainly provide the surprise he sought. Tactics for conducting it must therefore be devised. Furthermore, his plan must ensure that he broke through the deeper defensive echelons, not just the crust. He argued that if his night tank attack, having achieved tactical surprise, could secure objectives about three miles deep into the German position by dawn, he could perhaps use massive air support prior to launching a daylight second phase - shades of the still-born second bombing raid of GOODWOOD.

But the assaulting tanks must have strong infantry support immediately at hand. To achieve this, the assault infantry must be given a vehicle which offered the mobility and protection of a tank. The thin-skinned, open-topped half-tracks of the motor battalions, offered neither. Something better must be found. Simonds knew that some of the tracked artillery 75mm Priests were currently being replaced. He therefore commandeered some of them and, from 1 to 7 August, the mechanical engineers of II Canadian Corps worked like beavers removing the turrets and covering the openings with sandwiches of thin steel plates with sandbag fillings. How General O'Connor, who had advocated exactly this before GOODWOOD, in vain, must have appreciated, indeed envied this.

Night navigation of tanks would be the main problem, but with the German anti-tank weapons blinded by the darkness, Simonds argued that tanks could move closely packed together. He therefore laid down that the advance would be conducted in tight boxes. Each box would consist of four columns of tanks, travelling nose-to-tail with only about five yards between columns. Behind the leading tank squadron would be a company of infantry in their 'defrocked Priests', or Kangaroos. The remaining squadrons and companies would follow behind, still part of the same tight box. At the front, and with the most difficult job of all, was the navigating officer. His tank would be fitted with a sophisticated compass and a radio direction device which emitted a series of dots and dashes to keep him on course. In addition tracer rounds would be fired overhead to give him the line of the advance.

II Canadian Corps by now consisted of three divisions, following the recent arrival of 4th Canadian Armoured Division. Simonds required, asked for and obtained two additional divisions, one armoured and one infantry, and two independent armoured brigades, to carry out this attack. Phase One, the night tank attack, would be carried out by two infantry divisions, each with an independent armoured brigade under command. The inter-divisional boundary would be the Caen to Falaise road. Within each division the break-in force, under command of the armoured brigade commander, would consist of the armoured brigade and a Kangaroo-mounted infantry brigade. It would move inexorably forward, in its tight box formation, by-passing all opposition, until it reached its objective, which the infantry would immediately secure. The remaining two infantry brigades of these divisions would follow up on foot, eliminating all by-passed opposition. With the Phase One objectives secure by dawn, a heavy bombing raid would precede Phase Two, the launch of two armoured divisions to burst through the second line of defence in a drive on Falaise. In reserve, to cater for the unexpected or exploit success, was another infantry division.

This is not the place to discuss the detail of Operation TOTALISE, which has been covered in Ken Tout's two splendid books *A Fine Night for Tanks* and *The Bloody Battle for Tilly*. Suffice to say that this novel tactic worked. By dawn in the case of one division, and shortly after dawn in the case of the other, the Phase One objectives, three miles deep into the German defences, had been taken. Some of the key GOODWOOD lessons had indeed been learned. That the Phase Two attacks were frustrated by the splendidly-handled defence of Panzer Meyer and his 12th SS Panzer Division is another story.

* * * *

On 9 September 1944 General O'Connor commented in detail on Operation GOODWOOD. He summarised the results as follows:

'At the end of two days fighting VIII Corps had advanced some 10,000 yards, thereby enabling II Canadian Corps to capture Vaucelles and exploit south to Fleury and Ifs. Two thousand prisoners had been taken and the enemy had suffered a severe setback in the area in which he was most sensitive, as his whole defensive position hinged on Caen. In view of the general difficulties in mounting this attack, I consider that these very material results were achieved with comparatively light casualties in personnel, although the loss of tanks was considerable.

'Moreover, the additional objective of the operation, namely to draw the maximum amount of enemy armour into the Caen sector was also achieved. He was forced to concentrate his armour in the corps sector, which in turn prevented him from mounting any large-scale operation in any other sector.

'The fact that VIII Corps did not succeed in achieving an even greater penetration was mainly due to the following reasons. First the smallness of the bridgehead which limited the number of troops which could be brought across before the operation commenced, and forced divisions to enter the battle one after the other instead of simultaneously. Next, the narrowness of the gap

through which the armour had to pass, which affected the formation adopted, and the fact that the corps had to advance out of a deep re-entrant in the enemy defences. Finally the difficulty experienced by the infantry in keeping up with the tanks, which was due to the lack of a suitable armoured vehicle in which they could be carried forward. The introduction of some such vehicle is, I feel, of the utmost importance.'

On 8 March 1951 General Dempsey spoke about GOODWOOD. He stated that the strategy employed in Normandy was never understood by anyone outside Twenty-first Army Group. Realising this Montgomery had issued to him a personal written directive for GOODWOOD, the only time he ever did this, and that Dempsey had done likewise to his corps commanders. This was to ensure that no-one taking part failed to understand the true aim of the operation. [These directives were covered in chapter 3.] He outlined the aims of mounting a limited but powerful operation, hoping to draw the German armour away from the Americans and deceive them into thinking that GOODWOOD was intended as the allied breakout and an advance on Paris. Dempsey concluded by saying that he considered that GOODWOOD was highly successful and was well carried out by VIII Corps, though he was critical of 7th Armoured Division which he 'regarded as lacking in drive on this occasion and largely responsible for the fact that the geographical objectives were not entirely gained'.

By the end of 18 July, when the armoured onrush had ground to a halt and it was clear that only hard fighting by infantry and tanks together would enable the advance to continue, he had decided to end the operation, winding up GOODWOOD as quickly as possible. Indeed, he stated, he had already started to concentrate on the next attack - Operation BLUECOAT.

Both generals concealed any tactical disappointments, preferring to concentrate on the operational achievements of GOODWOOD. But it must be highly likely that as 3rd Royal Tanks crossed the start line at 7.45 am on the morning of 18 July, both hoped for, indeed expected, richer pickings than were actually achieved. Asked about the operation many years later, General O'Connor said, quietly and with dignity, 'It is all a long time ago. I am now a very old man. I do not look upon GOODWOOD as one of my more successful battles, and I would like to leave it at that.' A man of great charm, integrity and a peerless fighting record in two world wars, as a junior and senior officer, O'Connor was hugely respected and admired by all who knew him, or even knew of him. That he had the humility to suggest that with hindsight he might have done things differently comes as no surprise.

But perhaps the final quote on GOODWOOD should come from the other side of the hill, from a letter written by the Commander-in-Chief West, Field Marshal von Kluge. On 15 July he had received from Field Marshal Rommel a very gloomy report in which the latter recorded that the fighting strengths of divisions were sinking very rapidly, that reinforcements were both far too few and inexperienced, that Allied air and artillery dominated the battlefield

utenant
heral Sir
es Dempsey,
B, DSO, MC,
nmander,
ond British
ny in
rmandy.

and that, 'We must reckon with the fact that the enemy, within a measurable time, will succeed in breaking through our thinly-held front and in thrusting deep into France'. GOODWOOD must have persuaded von Kluge of the accuracy of this report, which he forwarded to Hitler on 21 July, under a covering letter:

'My discussions yesterday with the commanders of the formations near Caen, held immediately after the recent heavy fighting, have afforded regrettable evidence that in our present position there is no way by which, in the face of the enemy air force's complete command, we can find a strategy which will counterbalance its annihilating effect without giving up the field of battle.

'I came here with the fixed determination of making effective your order to stand fast at any price. But when one has to see by experience that this price must be paid by the slow but sure annihilation of the force, anxiety about the immediate future of this front is only too well justified. In spite of intense efforts the moment has drawn near when this front, already so heavily strained, will break. And once the enemy is in open country an orderly command will hardly be practicable. I consider it my duty, as the responsible commander of this front, to bring these conclusions to your notice, my Führer, in good time. My last word at the conference of commanders south of Caen was: "We shall hold out, and if no way out improves our position fundamentally, we must die, honourably, on the battlefield." '

It is hard to rate GOODWOOD a failure after reading that.

But what if GOODWOOD had broken through onto the ridge? It is very doubtful whether this would immediately have produced the ground suitable for airstrips, for which Tedder and the other senior airmen pressed so hard. As Flight Lieutenant Frost made clear, aircraft are very vulnerable when landing or taking off, if they are within enemy artillery range or have to overfly enemy held ground before reaching a safe height. Airstrips cannot be created on the front line. There needed to be much more depth before there was room safely to construct airstrips on the Bourguébus ridge. If the advance had managed to break through as far as Falaise, which was beyond anyone's wildest dreams, then sufficient space would have become available. But even after GOODWOOD the Germans disputed every mile of the road south. The operations of II Canadian Corps at the end of July and early August (Operation TOTALISE) to advance south and secure the high ground overlooking Falaise, were hotly disputed and only achieved a further ten miles.

Operation GOODWOOD took place six weeks after D-Day. Six weeks after GOODWOOD 11th Armoured Division entered Antwerp. Behind were the American break-out, the dreadful slaughter at Falaise, the crossing of the Seine, the liberation of Paris, and the rapid advance across northern France. It is in that context that GOODWOOD should be viewed.

Field Marshal von Kluge, Commander-i[...] Chief West. GOODWOO[...] was to convin[...] him that the Battle of Normandy co[...] not be won.

* * * *

No soldier of the Twenty-first Century would seek to study GOODWOOD in order to obtain relevant tactical lessons to apply. The passage of time and technological advances are far too great. After all, one would not have expected, in the late 1930s, to find many useful tactical lessons in the American Civil War. But there are, nevertheless, clear and relevant lessons to be learned from GOODWOOD.

First and most obvious is the huge advantage given by air superiority over a battlefield. In Normandy the Allies really had air supremacy. Von Kluge's letter to Hitler makes this point very clearly and it confirms Rommel's views before D-Day. Second is the need to ensure that one's army does not embark upon any contest with markedly inferior equipment to that of the opposition. The Normandy campaign was won because the Germans were worn down and eventually swamped by the numbers of men and equipment which the Allies could feed into the bridgehead. That should not hide the fact that much of the Allied equipment was inferior to German. To send soldiers into an attack with tanks that are outranged and out-gunned by the enemy borders on a crime. It speaks volumes for those who undertook attacks like GOODWOOD knowing that their Sherman tank could not knock out a Panther or Tiger, both of which could destroy them with ease. Many years of peace have meant that Governments demand more and more of servicemen but are often not prepared to provide them with the necessary equipment. In peace the Exchequer will always win against Defence, but those responsible for equipment procurement must never cease vociferously to demand the right equipment. To give one current example, at the time of writing it is unforgivable that the British Army, which so often achieves what others can not, is one of the few sophisticated armies to lack secure and reliable battlefield communications at all levels.

Next is the need to stand and fight. From the time that the Normandy landings had succeeded there could only be one end, the defeat of Germany. Senior German commanders, such as von Runstedt, Rommel and von Kluge all realised this, as, doubtless, did many if not most junior ranks, except, perhaps, the fanatical SS. And yet most Germans consistently fought like tigers in an almost hopeless cause. There can be a tendency for neatly-minded staff officers to like to see straight lines on maps and to be unduly concerned by that inlet which shows an enemy penetration or that protrusion which suggests that part of our own forces are vulnerable to being cut off. The classic example of this mentality during the Normandy campaign was the abortive attack on Villers-Bocage on 13 June. 7th Armoured Division achieved a deep penetration ten miles behind the German lines, but when the leading squadron/company group was destroyed, largely due to the remarkable actions of Lieutenant Michael Wittmann in a single Tiger tank, higher commanders lost their nerves and withdrew the entire division, lest it become isolated and cut off. Had 7th Armoured Division been reinforced, rather than extracted, it might have made the position of at least one panzer division almost untenable, and perhaps even loosened the German grip on Caen. At GOODWOOD, apart from those who had been recently under the devastating bombing, the Germans did not lay down their arms once they had been penetrated or outflanked. Realising that their position allowed them to threaten the later echelons of the attack, they were prepared to fight on long after the point of the attack had passed them by. One has only to remember the gallant German who manned a knocked-out Sherman tank and engaged G Company 8th Rifle Brigade's attack on Hubert-Folie. He could doubtless have found many good reasons for doing something different. The German determination to stand and fight was the reason that Cuverville, Démouville, Le Mesnil Frémentel and Grentheville could not be allowed to remain as islands of opposition in the wake of the armoured advance. There is surely a lesson here for twenty-first century soldiers.

The final, and perhaps the most important lesson, is the significance of personalities in war. The pendulum of the battle may sometimes look predictable, but it only requires one resolute man, at a critical moment, to impose his personality on the battle, to seize that pendulum and pull it firmly his way, for the whole balance of the battle to change dramatically. There are countless example of this in military history, and even a few in this small book. Technological advances in recent years mean that night can almost be turned into day. In theory the twenty-four hour battlefield already exists. But all those who have told me their stories have emphasized that war is an utterly exhausting business. Lieutenant David Stileman, a supremely fit, athletic twenty-year old, was so exhausted by the end of the first day of GOODWOOD that he could hardly set his compass for his night patrol. However much technology advances it will always be the capability of the human being and the personality of the man at the front, which dictates the pattern of warfare.

'A supremely fit and athletic twenty year-old' in 1944, Brigadier David Stileman, on a GOODWOOD battlefield tour with the Danish Staff College in 2002.

ANNEX A

OPERATION GOODWOOD
ALLIED ORDER OF BATTLE

SUPREME HEADQUARTERS ALLIED EXPEDITIONARY FORCE
Supreme Commander - General Dwight D Eisenhower.
Deputy Commander - Air Chief Marshal Sir Arthur Tedder.
Chief of Staff - Lieutenant General Walter Bedell Smith.

TWENTY-FIRST ARMY GROUP
Commander-in-Chief - General Sir Bernard Montgomery.
Chief of Staff - Major General FW de Guingand.

SECOND BRITISH ARMY
General Officer Commanding-in-Chief - Lieutenant General Sir Miles Dempsey.

I CORPS
Lieutenant General JT Crocker.

3RD INFANTRY DIVISION
Major General LG Whistler.

27th Armoured Brigade
13th/18th Royal Hussars.
1st East Riding Yeomanry.
The Staffordshire Yeomanry.

8th Infantry Brigade	**9th Infantry Brigade**
1st Battalion The Suffolk Regiment.	2nd Battalion The Lincolnshire Regiment.
2nd Battalion The East Yorkshire Regiment.	1st Battalion The King's Own Scottish Borderers.
1st Battalion The South Lancashire Regiment.	2nd Battalion The Royal Ulster Rifles.

185th Infantry Brigade
2nd Battalion The Royal Warwickshire Regiment.
1st Battalion The Royal Norfolk Regiment.
2nd Battalion The King's Shropshire Light Infantry.

Divisional Reconnaissance Regiment - 3rd Reconnaissance Regiment RAC.
Divisional Artillery - 7th, 33rd and 76th Field Regiments RA.
20th Anti-Tank and 92nd Light Anti-Aircraft Regiments RA.

6TH AIRBORNE DIVISION
Major General RN Gale.

3th Parachute Brigade
8th and 9th Battalions The Parachute Regiment.
1st Canadian Parachute Battalion.

5th Parachute Brigade
7th, 12th and 13th Battalions The Parachute Regime

6th Airlanding Brigade
12th Battalion The Devonshire Regiment.
2nd Battalion The Oxfordshire and Buckinghamshire Light Infantry.
1st Battalion The Royal Ulster Rifles.

Divisional Reconnaissance Regiment - 6th Airborne Reconnaissance Regiment RAC.
Divisional Artillery - 53rd Airlanding Light Regiment RA.

51ST (HIGHLAND) INFANTRY DIVISION
Major General DC Bullen-Smith.

152th Infantry Brigade
2nd and 5th Battalions The Seaforth Highlanders.
5th Battalion The Queen's Own Cameron Highlanders.

153th Infantry Brigade
5th Battalion The Black Watch.
1st and 5th/7th Battalions
The Gordon Highlanders.

154th Infantry Brigade
1st and 7th Battalions The Black Watch.
7th Battalion The Argyll and Sutherland Highlanders.

Divisional Reconnaissance Regiment - 2nd Derbyshire Yeomanry.
Divisional Artillery - 126th, 127th and 128th Field Regiments RA.
61st Anti-Tank and 40th Light Anti-Aircraft Regiments RA.

VIII CORPS
Lieutenant General Sir Richard O'Connor.

GUARDS ARMOURED DIVISION.
Major General AHS Adair.

5th Guards Armoured Brigade
2nd (Armoured) Battalion Grenadier Guards.
1st (Armoured) Battalion Coldstream Guards.
2nd (Armoured) Battalion Irish Guards.
1st (Motor) Battalion Grenadier Guards

32th Guards Brigade
5th Battalion Coldstream Guards
3rd Battalion Irish Guards
1st Battalion Welsh Guards

Divisional Reconnaissance Regiment - 2nd Armoured Reconnaissance Battalion Welsh Guards.
Divisional Artillery - 55th and 153rd Field Regiments RA.
21st Anti-Tank and 94th Light Anti-Aircraft Regiments RA.

7TH ARMOURED DIVISION
Major General GWEJ Erskine.

22nd Armoured Brigade
4th County of London Yeomanry (Sharpshooters).
1st and 5th Battalions The Royal Tank Regiment.
1st (Motor) Battalion The Rifle Brigade.

131st Infantry Brigade
1st/5th, 1st/6th and 1st/7th Battalions The
Queen's Regiment.

Divisional Reconnaissance Regiment - 8th King's Royal Irish Hussars.
Divisional Artillery - 3rd and 5th Regiments RHA.
65th Anti-Tank and 15th Light Anti-Aircraft Regiments, RA.

11TH ARMOURED DIVISION
Major General GPB Roberts.

29th Armoured Brigade
3rd Battalion The Royal Tank Regiment.
2nd Fife and Forfar Yeomanry.
23rd Hussars.
8th (Motor) Battalion The Rifle Brigade.

159th Infantry Brigade
3rd Battalion The Monmouthshire Regiment.
4th Battalion The King's Shropshire
Light Infantry.
1st Battalion The Herefordshire Regiment.

Divisional Reconnaissance Regiment - 2nd Northamptonshire Yeomanry.
Divisional Artillery - 13th Regiment RHA.
151st Field Regiment RA.
75th Anti-Tank and 58th Light Anti-Aircraft Regiments RA.

II CANADIAN CORPS
Lieutenant General GG Simonds.

2ND CANADIAN INFANTRY DIVISION
Major General C Foulkes.

4th Canadian Infantry Brigade
The Royal Regiment of Canada.
The Royal Hamilton Light Infantry.
The Essex Scottish Regiment.

5th Canadian Infantry Brigade
The Black Watch of Canada.
Le Régiment de Maisonneuve.
The Calgary Highlanders.

6th Canadian Infantry Brigade
Les Fusiliers Mont-Royal.
The Queen's Own Cameron Highlanders of Canada.
The South Saskatchewan Regiment.

Divisional Reconnaissance Regiment - 8th Reconnaissance Regiment (14th Canadian Hussars).
Divisional Artillery - 4th, 5th and 6th Field Regiments RCA.
2nd Anti-Tank and 3rd Light Anti-Aircraft Regiments RCA.

3RD CANADIAN INFANTRY DIVISION
Major General RFL Keller.

7th Canadian Infantry Brigade
The Royal Winnipeg Rifles.
The Regina Rifle Regiment.
1st Battalion The Canadian Scottish Regiment.

8th Canadian Infantry Brigade
The Queen's Own Rifles of Canada.
Le Régiment de la Chaudière.
The North Shore (New Brunswick) Regiment.

9th Canadian Infantry Brigade
The Highland Light Infantry of Canada.
The Stormont, Dundas and Glengarry Highlanders.
The North Nova Scotia Highlanders.

Divisional Reconnaissance Regiment - 7th Reconnaissance Regiment (17th Duke of Yorks's Royal Canadian Hussars).
Divisional Artillery - 12th, 13th and 14th Field Regiments RCA.
3rd Anti-Tank and 4th Light Anti-Aircraft Regiments RCA.

ANNEX B

Type	Crew	Weight	Frontal Armour	Speed	Main Armament	Penetration
Cromwell	5	28t	101mm	32mph	75mm	60mm
Sherman	5	32t	76mm	25mph	75mm	60mm
Firefly	5	30t	76mm	24mph	17pr	130mm
Mk IV Pz	5	23t	50mm	25mph	75mm	84mm
Panther	5	45t	110mm	34mph	75mm	100mm
Tiger	5	56t	100mm	23mph	88mm	102mm
King Tiger	5	69t	185mm	26mph	88mm	168mm
88mm Towed	-	-	-	-	88mm	168mm

ANNEX C
ROUTE DIRECTIONS

These directions follow the route taken by the armoured divisions of VIII Corps, and in particular 11th Armoured Division. It is not difficult to follow the course of 3rd Infantry Division's attack, using a map, though there are few obvious viewpoints. The Bois de Bavant is still densely wooded. Troarn has expanded greatly since 1944, when most of the houses were grouped along the main Caen road, and in a triangle of roads with its apex just south of the railway bridge. The railway line and the station have gone. On the western flank, it is almost impossible to follow the course of 3rd Canadian Infantry Division's advance on the ground today. So much of the area has been built over. What were, in 1944, small, separate villages have now been subsumed into the vast complex of Caen. In particular, the Colombelles steelworks, whose chimneys were such a feature of the landscape in 1944, and which proved to be a most difficult battleground, has been completely redeveloped.

Perhaps the best start-point for these directions is the D514 which runs from the ferry terminal at Ouistreham to Caen. About half way along, just east of the road, is the village of Benouville.

Major Bill Close and Major General Pip Roberts – two very distinguished Royal Tank Regiment officers – on a battlefield tour in 1975.

To Viewpoint 1.

Follow D514 from Benouville east towards Cabourg. Cross Pegasus Bridge and the Orne river bridge. Go straight ahead at the roundabout; the road climbs uphill with a left bend. About 500 yards after reaching the top of the hill look out for a small turning right, 'Rue du Bac du Port' towards Amfréville. Turn right. The cornfields through which you are driving were the Landing Zone for many of the parachutists and gliders of 6th Airborne Division on D-Day. On 18 July 1944, nearly six weeks later, the area was still littered with the remains of gliders. After about 500 yards a small farm track leads off right, through the cornfields, approximately 100 yards before a road junction. If you are minded to walk a bit, park the car by the roadside and walk down this track for 400 yards until the ground starts to drop away in front of you. You will then be standing near the northern edge of the concentration area into which 29th Armoured

Brigade moved on the night of 17/18 July 1944, after its second night move.

Look straight down the track in front. Slightly right, about a mile away, is the village of Ranville, easily identified by its unusual church, the tower being separate from the nave. Beyond and slightly right are the silos of the Longueval cement factory, an unattractive post-war addition to the scenery on the east bank of the Orne, halfway between the sea and Caen. Follow the line of the horizon to the left (east), past the obvious tall water tower and just left of the track extension in front of you. A clump of tall trees on slightly higher ground about two miles away marks the location of Ste Honorine La Chardonnerette, a small village which changed hands several times during the first few days of intense fighting after D-Day. Just left of Ste Honorine, on a clear day, it is possible to make out the Bourguébus ridge, some ten miles south. This was the GOODWOOD objective. The forward edge of the British bridgehead, with its protective minefields, is about two miles in front of you, just left of Ste Honorine, hidden from view in the low ground. The start line for 11th Armoured Division's advance is also just left of Ste Honorine, beyond the minefields.

Follow along the horizon to the left and in the middle distance, about three miles away, is an obvious large barn, a triangle of red on a white base, should be clearly visible. This is the area of Viewpoint 2, about half a mile beyond the start line. On your left is the wooded ridge of the Bois de Bavant, which runs south and along which 3rd Infantry Division attacked on 18 July 1944. Take note in particular of the obvious tall water tower about half a mile on your left, just south of the village of Bréville. It is an excellent reference point and can be clearly seen from most places on the GOODWOOD battlefield, including from the Bourguébus ridge on a clear day.

Imagine, if possible in today's peaceful rural scene, the sight that would have confronted you, a member of 11th Armoured Division, as dawn broke on 18 July 1944. The fields in front of you, littered with broken gliders, are crammed full of tanks, half-tracks, lorries and guns, all ready for the advance to begin, as the massive air bombardment erupts in front, throwing up plumes of smoke and dust. Although tired after a wretched second night move, you wonder how the leading elements are getting on down on the start line, waiting to go, and whether any Germans can survive under that intense bombardment.

To Viewpoint 2.

From Viewpoint 1 in the cornfields, return to your car and drive on towards Amfréville, keeping right where the road splits just 100 yards beyond where you parked. On passing that road junction look right into an area of orchards beside the road. Much thicker in 1944, it was into this area that General Roberts moved HQ 11th Armoured Division on the night of 16/17 July, before launching his attack south. Drive on into Amfréville. Go right and immediately left at the separated crossroads in Amfréville, following the D37B, signed Bréville and 'Overlord L'Assaut'. On the afternoon of D-Day Amfréville was taken by No 6 Commando of Lord Lovat's 1st Special Service Brigade which had come ashore at Ouistreham, crossed Pegasus Bridge at around midday and then secured the high ground at the north-east of the 6th Airborne Division's bridgehead.

Drive on into Bréville, passing the church on the left. The view from the roadside, at the main cross-roads, gives an adequate, if rather less good, alternative view of the Goodwood Concentration Area for those who do not want to walk the track to Viewpoint 1, above. The red barn at Viewpoint 2 can be clearly seen, with, left of it the Cagny factory area and right, on the distant skyline, the Bourguébus ridge.

Continue straight over the Bréville cross-roads, the D37B still, signed to Troarn. The road passes the Bréville water tower on the right and threads its way for about a mile, through the woods, to a main cross-roads. Turn right, onto the D113, passing the Bavant ceramics factory on the left and downhill towards the village of Hérouvillette. Follow the new bypass round Hérouvillette until you reach the roundabout at the west end. Turn right, back into the village, and take the first right turn, opposite the Mairie, signed Escoville. In Escoville pass the church with its onion-shaped tower and turn right, beside the Mairie, onto the D227, signed Touffréville and Sannerville. The southern edge of the village marks the front of the British bridgehead in 1944. You are passing through the minefield area; 29th Armoured Brigade's start line is in the fields on your right. The road runs straight for about half a mile and then splits. Keep right, on the D228 signed Cuverville and Cagny, and drive for another half-mile to the red-topped barn, previously identified from Viewpoint 1. Pull in at the far end of it and walk west along the track for about 100 yards, to the far end of the wire fence.

From here you can look back to the ridgeline of Bréville and Amfréville. You are standing about three-quarters of a mile south of the start line. Looking north-west you can see the wooded feature around Ste Honorine La Chardonnerette and the start line for 159th Infantry Brigade's attack on Cuverville (chapter 8). The road you are on runs straight towards Cuverville, about a mile ahead of you, its church and water clearly cutting the skyline. It was the first objective of 3rd Battalion The Monmouthshire Regiment. Just left (east) of the village there is a line of pylons running due south, leading towards the obvious silos of Cagny about four miles further on. Between Cuverville and the line of pylons you can, if you look carefully, make out the church tower of Démouville, in summer almost hidden in the trees where the slope runs downhill. The road running east from Cuverville can be clearly identified by rows of poplars, and about half a mile beyond it is a wooded area. The road and the wooden area, orchards in 1944, were the objectives of 1st Battalion The Herefordshire Regiment on 18 July.

The barn at Viewpoint 2 has been built on the line of 29th Armoured Brigade's advance from their start line just south-west of Escoville towards Cagny, passing east of Cuverville and Démouville. The advance, led by 3rd Royal Tanks (chapter 7) ran parallel to the line of pylons pointed out above, but about 500 yards left of them. It was in the area of the Viewpoint 2 red barn that General Roberts and his small tactical HQ played Grandmother's footsteps with the German artillery (page 70).

To Viewpoint 3.

It is impossible to follow accurately the course of 159th Infantry Brigade's attacks on Cuverville and Démouville (chapter 8). Both villages were almost completely destroyed in the bombing and artillery barrage which preceded the GOODWOOD advance. They have been largely rebuilt and vastly expanded. From Viewpoint 2 drive on into Cuverville. At the road junction turn left onto the D226 and almost immediately right onto the D228 towards Démouville and Cagny. In 1944 there was just one large farm north of the D226 in Cuverville, opposite the turning to Démouville. All the other buildings north of this road are post-war. The village itself was little more than houses astride the Démouville road and the parallel road west of it, as far as the church (photo page 65). Past the church was open country, sloping downhill for approximately three quarters of a mile to Démouville.

As you leave Cuverville heading south, look left (east) to the wooded area about half a mile away - in 1944 orchards which were the objective of 1st Hereford's attack. The Démouville of 1944 started where you can see an obvious old wall on the right of the road, about fifty yards before the second set of traffic lights. The main part of the village stretched about 300 yards west, and, as in Cuverville, the church (photo page 67) was the most southerly building on the road heading south.

Drive south out of Démouville and you will shortly come to a junction with the main N175. About 100 yards before it is a thick double hedge on the left, opposite a single house. This was the line of the first railway. A little imagination is required to envisage it running east between the hedges. 29th Armoured Brigade crossed it about a mile east of this point.

Crossing the N175 is a somewhat dangerous operation. With cars travelling at speed in both directions along the main road it is perhaps as near as one can get to the danger of a German 88mm anti-tank round striking one in the flank! (About two miles east along the N175 is the Commonwealth War Graves Cemetery of Banneville, one of the most serene of the many cemeteries in Normandy. Many of those who died in Operation GOODWOOD lie here). Having negotiated the N175 crossroads continue south towards Cagny. Crossing the Autoroute de Normandie (a post-war invention) by the safer means of a fly-over, watch out for a small cross-roads about three quarters of a

The Commonwealth War Graves Cemetery at Banneville – last resting place of many of those who fell at Goodwood. No-one should visit the battlefields without paying their respects at one of these moving cemeteries.

mile further on. Turn right there and pull in beside the small road to Le Mesnil Frémentel. This is the area of Viewpoint 3.

Looking back from Viewpoint 3 you can clearly identify Démouville church, and to the right of it, on the far skyline, the Bréville water-tower. The parallel N175 and Autoroute are obvious. East, across the Cagny road, is a narrow road to Le Prieuré. The buildings can be clearly seen now, though in 1944 the area was surrounded by thick hedges and orchards. It was from here that Major Becker's 5 Battery engaged 23rd Hussars shortly after they had crossed the first railway (chapter 9), and it was from Le Prieuré that 2nd Armoured Grenadier Guards launched their successful assault on Cagny (chapter 14). Beyond Le Prieuré and slightly right the tops of the woods of the Chateau de Manneville, location of Lieutenant von Rosen and his Tiger tanks, can be clearly seen. Following clockwise Cagny lies just half a mile ahead. The field between you and the village is the area in which C Squadron 2nd Fife and Forfar Yeomanry fell victim to von Luck's and Becker's guns (chapter 9). The peaceful rural scene of today is far removed from that of 1944, with the sight and smell of burning tanks and the horror of burnt and wounded crews. Watch, if convenient, a vehicle driving south towards Cagny. Note, in particular, where, as it enters the village, it seems to turn half left and disappear from view down a gentle slope, beside an old wall. That is the spot at which von Luck deployed the four 88mm anti-aircraft guns with such devastating effect.

The road running from Cagny to Caen can be clearly seen to the right of the village. Beyond it is the second railway line, only visible if an obliging train passes. About three quarters of a mile away, almost due south, there is a fly-over over the railway. This will become Viewpoint 5. About 300 yards further along the small road on which you are standing is the hamlet of Le Mesnil Frémentel, which was captured by Colonel Hunter's 8th Rifle Brigade (chapter 10). The woods and orchards round the hamlet have changed little in the last nearly sixty years. Just to the left of the Le Mesnil Frémentel the village of Bourguébus can be seen on the ridge about three miles ahead. It was in the area of Viewpoint 3 that 11th Armoured Division swung half-right towards Bourguébus and the other ridge villages of Hubert-Folie and Bras further right, hidden behind Le Mesnil Frémentel.

To Viewpoint 4.

Drive on into Cagny. The village is very different from its 1944 parent. At the time of the battle it stretched along the lateral road, about a quarter of a mile both sides of the church, with extensive orchards in the area of the chateau north-east of the church. Cagny has now merged with Frénouville and the road between them has been completely repositioned. In 1944 there was almost a half mile yards gap between the two villages.

At the traffic lights in Cagny, turn left, past the church (photo page 163) and after about 300 yards take the D225 left towards Emiéville. About half a mile after leaving the village you will reach, on the top of a slight spur, the Guards Armoured Division memorial (photo page 125) sited at the scene of Lieutenant John Gorman's unconventional destruction of the King Tiger tank (chapter 14).

This is Viewpoint 4 - a good place from which to see the ground over which the Guards Division had to advance, outflanking Cagny to the east.

To Viewpoint 5
Drive back into Cagny, passing the church on your right and heading north-west along the N13 towards Caen. The village extends somewhat further than it did in 1944. As you leave the village there is a turning to the right, 'Rue de L'Etoile'. Immediately opposite is a farm track which runs about 400 yards south-west to the fly-over over the second railway. Turn left off the main road, down this track. Although it looks like, and indeed is, just a farm track, it is quite adequate for cars, and even buses, except in wet and muddy weather. There is a parking space just before the fly-over. The fly-over is perhaps the best viewpoint of the entire GOODWOOD battlefield, all of which is laid out and clearly identifiable using a good map. [If you consider the route unreasonably demanding for your car or your nerve, park beside the N13 and walk to the fly-over. On returning to your car drive west along the N13 and turn left (south) at the next crossroads, towards Grentheville. Go through Grentheville and on to Soliers (had you turned right at the roundabout in Grentheville you would have come to Major Close's 'drainpipe' (photo page 88). At the T-Junction in Soliers turn right and pick up the directions at * in the third paragraph below.]

Assuming that your courage did not fail you and you have made it to the fly-over, look due north. Three-quarters of a mile away are the obvious woods of Le Mesnil Frémentel. 2nd Fife and Forfar Yeomanry, and later 23rd Hussars, passed between them and Cagny and crossed the ground immediately in front of you, reaching the railway line about half a mile left (west) of where you are standing. East of Le Mesnil Frémentel, on the far skyline, the Bréville water-tower, near Viewpoint 1, can be seen on a clear day. Further right is the obvious line of the Bois de Bavant ridge. Right again and Cagny now appears as a vast, sprawling industrial area, but in the middle, framed by a small and dense patch of trees, it is possible to see the top of the church tower, round which the 1944 village was grouped. Now turn to look south of the railway and the villages of Le Poirier (on your left near the railway), Four (directly down the track ahead), Soliers (half right) and Grentheville (in the trees on your right beside the railway) are all within a half mile radius. The area in front of you is the battleground of 2nd Fife and Forfar Yeomanry and 23rd Hussars (chapters 12 and 13). On the ridge beyond Soliers are, from left to right, the two church spires of Bourguébus, Hubert-Folie with its church tower at the east end of a thick wood, and Bras with a blue-sided barn at the east end. Look right towards Grentheville and running left of it, towards Soliers, you can see the railway embankment which 3rd Royal Tanks had to cross (chapter 11), before it advanced towards the ridge villages.

To Viewpoint 6.
If your nerve fails you about driving on, turn the car round and drive back to the N13, following the directions in brackets [] above. Otherwise, continue south from the fly-over for about 200 yards, turn left at the cross-tracks and go on to the village of Le Poirier. It was from here that the Panther tank caused

Captain Hutchison such trouble (Chapter 12). Breathe a sigh of relief as you rejoin the tarmac road, turning right towards Four. The gap between the two villages was the scene of C Squadron 23rd Hussars abortive attempt to outflank Four. To reach the exact site of Captain Walter's action (chapter 13) stop at the east end of Four, where a new barn has been built on the south side of the road. Then walk east along the track in the cornfields for about 200 yards.

Drive straight on through Four, to Soliers. At the T-junction turn right and shortly left onto * 'Rue de Caen', and take care over the humps in the road. About 300 yards after leaving the village there is a bridge over a disused railway embankment. Park at the bottom on the right and walk up the narrow track onto the top of the embankment. This is the railway embankment mentioned frequently in the narrative.

Stand on the old platform, near the small hut. Look north along the embankment. Just right of it, about half a mile away, you will see some new houses with a wooded area on their right. The wooded area shows the extent of Grentheville as it was in 1944; the new houses have been built on the open ground where 3rd Tanks had its short battle with German defenders (Chapter 11) before crossing west of the railway line. The 'drainpipe' through which Major Close led the regiment is at the left end of the new houses. On the far horizon above Grentheville you may be able to see the Bréville water-tower (near Viewpoint 1). Look right, passing what looks like a vast golf-ball on a tee, and you come to Cagny, and in front of it the fly-over of Viewpoint 5. Continuing clockwise and Soliers, and then Bourguébus are tucked in east of the railway line.

Looking west of the railway line, Hubert-Folie is about a mile away, its church tower obvious at the left end of some dense trees. Right of Hubert-Folie and, with a gap of about 500 yards between them, is Bras.

The industrial area between you and these two villages is, of course, an unwelcome post-war addition, as are most of the factory buildings further right in the direction of Caen. Indeed the whole area, in about a half-mile radius west of the embankment, was a sea of golden corn in July 1944. This is the area of 3rd Royal Tanks many attempts to take the ridge villages (chapters 11 and 17).

To Viewpoint 7.
Drive back into Soliers. Keep right at the roundabout, and go on for a few hundred yards to a second roundabout. Turn half-right, along 'Rue de la Resistance', towards Hubert-Folie. After passing under a bridge the road goes uphill towards the village. You are following the route taken by Lieutenant Stileman and his two carriers on 18 July (chapter 11) and 4th KSLI on 19 July (chapter 17). All the houses east of the church are new. Turn right by the church, as Stileman did (photo page 93), and drive straight on through the village, which looks almost exactly the same as it did when he undertook his mad charge through it on 18 July 1944. There are some obviously new houses in the area, but the chateau and its surrounding woods on the left are almost unchanged. Leaving Hubert-Folie, the road runs for 500 yards to Bras, and it was on this stretch of road that Lieutenant Langdon was knocked out twice (chapters 11 and 17). Don't be put off by the fact that Bras has now inconveniently been

renamed Ifs! Park at the first convenient place on the right - just where the road bends slightly left. Walk up a track on the right, between a rather broken wall with trees on the left and a small works yard on the right. After about 100 yards you come out into the open, with a view north, along the whole length of the GOODWOOD advance, right back to the Bréville water-tower.

From here you will understand the significance of 'ground'. In military parlance this is the 'vital ground' of Operation GOODWOOD. From here the Germans could observe everything that moved north of them. They will have seen the dust thrown up by the advancing artillery barrage and tanks, and their more powerful anti-tank weapons, well concealed among the woods and walls of these small villages, will have been able to pick off the advancing tanks with considerable ease. Just a glance north from here and it is easy to understand why Rommel and other German commanders were so sensitive about this area, and why, in consequence, the German defences stretched some ten miles deep, not the shallow four miles estimated by British Intelligence.

Try to envisage the scene of the evening of 19 July 1944. Yesterday 3rd Tanks attacked up the slope towards you; many of their tanks lie smouldering in the corn in front. The area is pock-marked with bombing and artillery craters and many houses are just broken rubble. Dust, smoke and filth hang in the air. There are dead and wounded of both sides lying around; casualty evacuation and burial of the dead, not possible in open country which has been so hotly disputed over the last thirty-six hours, is just beginning. The corn is criss-crossed by a mass of tank tracks, and in many places the burning tanks have set light to it. 8th Rifle Brigade finally took the village just a few hours ago, F and H Companies approaching behind the tanks of 3rd Royal Tanks up the slope in front and half-left of you. The barn near where you are standing was the start line for G Company's recent attack on Hubert-Folie, with the few remaining tanks of 2nd Fife and Forfar Yeomanry. The tank crews and riflemen of 29th Armoured Brigade are still in the area, catching their breaths after their successful attacks, but ever alert to possible German counter-attacks. Now the three battalions of 159th Lorried Infantry Brigade are moving into the area, to secure it once and for all.

At long last, six weeks after D-Day, the vital Bourguébus ridge has been secured.

* * * *

For those seeking accommodation in the area, there are plenty of hotels in Caen. Many seem to cater for bus parties, which means that they tend to be a bit soulless but are efficiently run. For those seeking something different Chateau d'Audrieu is a seriously comfortable hotel, with excellent service and food about six miles west of Caen, just south of the N13 Caen to Bayeux road. At the other end, so to speak, Chez Marion, at Merville-Franceville Plage, about four miles east of Pegasus Bridge and just north of the GOODWOOD concentration area, is a small, family-run hotel with an excellent fish restaurant. This was where the GOODWOOD Team used to stay for the annual Staff College Battlefield Tours.

SOURCES AND BIBLIOGRAPHY

Personal Accounts given to the author by:
Mr J Addison, Lt Col G Bandomir, Herr A Becker, Mr GN Bell, Gen Sir Cecil Blacker, Lt Col WS Brownlie, Mr JL Caswell, Mr RP Clark, Maj J Clayton, Maj WH Close, Lt Col K Crockford, Dr R Cox, Mr DF Cunliffe, Maj Gen Sir Francis de Guingand, Maj Gen Sir Charles Dunphie, Mr P Elstob, Mr WT Farmer, A Cdre JW Frost, Maj P Gaunt, Col Sir John Gilmour, Mr E Harte, Maj JJ How, Brig JA Hunter, Col JD Hutchison, Mr DW Jones, Mr W Kendall, Sir Anthony Kershaw, Mr FW Kite, Maj J Langdon, Maj RF Lemon, Mr G Mitchell, Mr PR Noakes, Mr EA Powdrill, Maj Gen GPB Roberts, Col MR Robinson, Lord Saye and Sele, Mr DN Smith, Brig DM Stileman, Maj N Thornburn, Mr PC Walter, Mr E Whittaker, Mr T Wilmott, Mr WT Wright and many others whose accounts, while not appearing in the narrative, provided invaluable background information.

Personal Accounts from Staff College Records:
Gen Sir Miles Dempsey, Brig Sir Henry Floyd, Sir John Gorman, Brig Sir Norman Gwatkin, Brig AG Haywood, Gen Sir Richard O'Connor, Col J Vandeleur, Maj Gen R von Rosen and Maj P Wigan.

Staff College Records:
Many maps, books, folders and in particular the Battlefield Tour Files of 1956, 57, 73-75.

Military Documents:
British Army of the Rhine, Battlefield Tour, Operation GOODWOOD, 1947.
German Army Documents Jun-Oct 1944.
Military Operational Research Unit, Report 23, Oct 44.
War Office Post Operational Report, Operation GOODWOOD/ATLANTIC, 18-22 July 1944.

Bibliography.
A Fine Night for Tanks - Ken Tout (Sutton)
A Genius for War - Carlo d'Este (Harper Collins)
Alanbrooke - David Fraser (Collins)
Armoured Guardsmen - Robert Boscawen (Pen & Sword)
A Soldier's Story - Omar Bradley (Eyre & Spottiswoode)
A View from the Turret - Maj Bill Close (Dell & Bredon)
Caen, Anvil of Victory - Alexander McKee (Souvenir)
Churchill as Warlord - Ronald Lewin (Batsford)
Churchill's Generals - ed John Keegan (Warner)
Crusade into Europe - Dwight D Eisenhower (Heinemann)
Decision in Normandy - Carlo d'Este (Collins)

From the Desert to the Baltic - Maj Gen GPB Roberts (Kimber)
Gold Beach - Christopher Dunphie & Garry Johnson (Pen & Sword)
Iron Division - Robin McNish (3 Armd Div)
Knight's Cross, The Life of FM Erwin Rommel - David Fraser (Harper Collins)
Maj & Mrs Holt's BattlefieldTour, Normandy (Pen & Sword)
Monkey Business - Gen Sir Cecil Blacker (Quiller)
Montgomery in Europe 1943-45 - Richard Lamb (Buchan & Enright)
Montgomery of Alamein - Alun Chalfont (Weidenfeld & Nicholson)
Monty - Master of the Battlefield 1942-44 - Nigel Hamilton (Hamish Hamilton)
Normandy 1944 - Stephen Badsey (Osprey)
Normandy to the Baltic - FM Viscount Montgomery (BAOR)
Nothing Less than Victory - Russel Miller (Penguin)
Operation Victory - Maj Gen Sir Francis de Guingand (Hodder & Stoughton)
Overlord - Max Hastings (Michael Joseph)
Panzer Bait - William Moore (Leo Cooper)
Panzer Commander - Hans von Luck (Praeger)
Panzers in Normandy - Eric Lefevre (After the Battle)
Six Armies in Normandy - John Keegan (Penguin)
Sixty-four Days of a Normandy Summer - Keith Jones (Hale)
Soldier in the Saddle - Monkey Blacker (Burke)
Steel Inferno - Michael Reynolds (Spellmount)
Taurus Pursuant - EWIP (BAOR)
The Battle for Normandy - Eversley Belfield & H Essame (Pan)
The Black Bull - Patrick Delaforce (Sutton)
The Bloody Battle for Tilly - Ken Tout (Sutton)
The Charge of the Bull - Jean Brisset (Bates)
The Desert Rats at War - George Forty (Ian Allan)
The Fife and Forfar Yeomanry - RJB Sellar (Blackwood)
The Forgotten Victor - John Baynes (Brassey's)
The History of the 23rd Hussars (Private)
The Lonely Leader, Monty 1944-45 - Alistair Horne & David Montgomery (Macmillan)
The Other Side of the Hill - BH Liddell Hart (Cassell)
The Rifle Brigade 1939-45 - Robin Hastings (Gale & Polden)
The Second World War - Winston Churchill (Cassell)
The Struggle for Europe - Chester Wilmot (Fontana)
The Tanks - BH Liddell Hart (Cassell)
Triumph in the West - Arthur Bryant (Collins)
Ultra Goes to War - Ronald Lewin (Hutchinson)
War Diaries 1939-45, FM Lord Alanbrooke - ed Alex Duncan & Daniel Todman (Weidenfeld & Nicholson)
Warriors for the Working Day - Peter Elstob (Companion)
War Report, D Day to VE Day - Desmond Hawkins (Aeriel)
Wars and Shadows - David Fraser (Allen Lane)
War Walks - Richard Holmes (BBC)

INDEX

People.